A New Short Guide to the
Accentuation of
Ancient Greek

BCP Advanced Language Series

A NEW SHORT GUIDE TO THE ACCENTUATION OF ANCIENT GREEK

Philomen Probert

Bristol Classical Press

This impression 2007
First published in 2003 by
Bristol Classical Press
an imprint of
Gerald Duckworth & Co. Ltd.
90-93 Cowcross Street, London EC1M 6BF
Tel: 020 7490 7300
Fax: 020 7490 0080
inquiries@duckworth-publishers.co.uk
www.ducknet.co.uk

A catalogue record for this book is available
from the British Library

ISBN 978 1 85399 599 6

Printed and bound in Great Britain by
CPI Antony Rowe, Eastbourne

Contents

Contents

Preface

Demosthenes, when asking the citizens of Athens whether they considered Aeschines a hired servant, a μισθωτός, of the Macedonians, is said to have deliberately mispronounced the word as μίσθωτος (Sch. Dem. 18. 104a, b, c). His audience reacted instantly by correcting him with a great cry of 'μισθωτός!' Demosthenes, of course, treated the response as a positive reply to his question. An accent, even an incorrect one if it is carefully planted, can be an effective weapon.

I am often asked whether there is a book one can use — in English — to introduce accents to one's accentless Greek. What is wanted is a handbook modest enough in its compass to assist in gaining rapidly a basic competence in Greek accentuation, but substantial enough to leave readers equipped to progress to higher levels of expertise (not to mention deviousness) on their own.

Happily, J.P. POSTGATE's *A Short Guide to the Accentuation of Ancient Greek* provides an introduction to ancient Greek accentuation in exactly the compass that is wanted. Unhappily, the book has been out of print for a long time. It was therefore a very pleasant surprise when John Betts of Bristol Classical Press asked me whether I would be willing to revise Postgate's book for re-publication. A revised edition would provide the opportunity to bring some of the linguistic information up to date — for in certain respects scholarship on the Greek accent has recently moved rather rapidly — and to make some minor corrections.

ix

A New Short Guide to the Accentuation of Ancient Greek

As work on the revision of Postgate progressed I came to realise that my conception of what is needed in an introductory book on Greek accentuation is subtly different from Postgate's. Postgate's preface begins with the professed aims of bringing 'before the classical scholars, teachers and students of this country the realities of the accentuation of Ancient Greek considered as a whole, its theory and practice, its linguistic, historical and educational aspects'. While finding all these aims eminently worthwhile, I have found myself wanting at every turn to give precedence to the practicalities of where the accents actually go, desiring the book to be as serviceable as possible to those who wish to learn where to place a Greek accent.

The book that has eventually resulted is thus a rather different work, with a different emphasis, from Postgate's, to the extent that it no longer seems appropriate to call it a 'revision'. It owes, however, a very great deal to its model, reflections of which may be found in it almost everywhere. Two other excellent works of similar compass have also helped to provide inspiration for this one, VENDRYES' *Traité d'accentuation grecque*, and BALLY's *Manuel d'accentuation grecque*.

There are a number of things that this book is not. It is not a reference work or compendium of information on ancient Greek accentuation; for that one needs to look to CHANDLER's unsurpassed *A Practical Introduction to Greek Accentuation*. Nor is it a work of theoretical linguistics about the Greek accent; for an introduction to current theoretical discussions one might begin with the recent article by NOYER (reference on p. xvi), through which earlier bibliography may be traced. This book is also not an introduction to the principles of Greek accentuation for those embarking on the learning of Greek who are in the happy position of learning the accents of individual words while learning the

Preface

words for the first time. This method is really the best way to learn Greek accents, and for the purpose there are several grammar books with good sections devoted to accents; one might also use KOSTER's *A Practical Guide for the Writing of the Greek Accents.*

The present book is for those who already have some knowledge of Greek, but either no knowledge or shaky knowledge of the accents. I do not at all believe that it is best to learn Greek first and then learn accents. But it can happen (especially in Britain's fair isles) that one is not encouraged at an early stage to learn the accents, that one regrets this neglect sooner or later, and that one conceives the excellent idea of doing something serious about it. This book is intended to facilitate the project. It is designed not to be read, nor to be kept on a shelf for reference, but to be worked through; exercises appear at frequent intervals and should be done. They are there to assist in *committing the rules and the accents of individual words to memory.*

The result will be a good basic knowledge of the principles of ancient Greek accentuation and the ability to accent correctly a good core vocabulary of Greek words. The accentuation of more words can then be added on a word-by-word basis, as in reading one comes across words whose accents one has not yet learned.

An introductory chapter discusses what is known about the ancient Greek accent and where that knowledge comes from. This chapter, unlike the others, is not there to be worked through but simply to be read. There is no especial need to commit information in chapter 1 to memory; all information given there that will be crucial to the correct placement of the Greek accents is repeated in later chapters. Chapter 1 may, indeed, be skipped by those who already know something about the ancient Greek accent marks, their meanings, and how they come down to us.

xi

The remaining chapters are designed to be worked through in the order in which they appear. They are divided into small sections with an exercise at the end of each section or small group of sections. Each chapter from chapter 3 onwards ends with a cumulative exercise. Answers to exercises are provided on pp. 169–99. More advanced readers using the book to fill gaps should, of course, take individual sections and exercises as required.

I have allowed some repetition of information between chapters in order to reinforce interconnected aspects of the subject and to make the book easier to use. For example, the rule for accenting ordinal numerals (πρῶτος, δεύτερος...) is provided both in chapter 5, where the ordinals belong *qua* adjectives, and in chapter 6, where they belong *qua* numerals.

Many decisions have had to be made as to what to include and what to leave out. In certain cases I have thought it a good idea to include some information but not to make it, as it were, compulsory reading. Bibliographical references and discussions of more minute points are given in smaller type.

All translations of passages from Greek authors are my own; glosses of single words are conventional and based on those in LSJ.

It is a τόπος of prefaces to books on Greek accentuation to discuss whether the accents need to be learned at all. (CHANDLER's two famously cynical prefaces are, incidentally, masterpieces of English style.) It is, however, likely that if you have opened this book then, 'need' or no 'need', you rather *desire* to learn something about Greek accents. I do not think that intellectual pursuits should require justification; but for those who are embarking on the learning of the Greek accents and need to explain to their friends what has got into them, here are some excuses:

• To learn the Greek accents if one is studying ancient Greek is a matter of doing a thing properly.

• To appreciate as fully as possible the sound of ancient Greek poetry and prose, one needs to know what can be known about the accentuation of the language, just as one needs to know what can be known about the pronunciation of the consonants and vowels, or poetic metre.

• '(The accents) are essential for the correct writing and pronunciation of modern Greek; and if classical scholars cease to learn them, they will sacrifice a great part of the advantage that a knowledge of the ancient language gives in the learning of the modern.' (H. Lloyd-Jones in P. Maas, *Greek Metre*, tr. H. Lloyd-Jones (Clarendon Press, 1962), p. 58, n. 1.)

• 'Learning the rules of accentuation for the Greek declensions and conjugations, and the accents of individual words, forces one to learn more thoroughly the declensions, the conjugations, and the words themselves.' (Eleanor Dickey, Columbia University.)

• If one intends to pursue ancient Greek papyrology, or palaeography, or textual criticism, a good knowledge of the Greek accents is crucial. For example, where a word on an accented manuscript or papyrus is difficult to read and the surviving traces include traces of accents, one must be equipped to exploit the information provided by those traces. One can never begin too early in mastering the accents for such purposes.

• The study of the structural characteristics of a language has its fascination; the ancient Greek accents form a particularly intriguing system, wonderful in its combination of regularities and irregularities. To learn the Greek accents is an exciting part of the study of language, and of this language in particular.

I owe thanks to many friends, colleagues, and students for help and encouragement in the preparation of this book. I am particularly indebted to Eleanor Dickey and Ryan Fowler, who read the whole work exceedingly thoroughly and did all the exercises; their criticism has made this a better book and saved me from several embarrassing errors. David Patterson, who lent me patiently of his expertise on pitch range phenomena and kindly allowed me to read his so far unpublished work, brought crucial humility to my attempts to understand Dionysius of Halicarnassus on the melody of ancient Greek speech. For my edification and to my pleasant surprise, Richard Hewitt transcribed for me the marginalia in A.E. Housman's copy of POSTGATE in the Wren library of Trinity College, Cambridge. This book would not have come into existence without Stephen Colvin's persuasion and his involvement in its conception and plan. My colleagues in Oxford have been very generous with their encouragement and support, and in their understanding of the need for other projects to be postponed while this one turned into a larger undertaking than originally intended. Several students have alerted me to matters that ought to be discussed, and their interest has been constantly heart-warming. John Betts, Jean Scott, Graham Douglas, Deborah Blake, and Ray Davies of Bristol Classical Press and Duckworth have been immensely tolerant of my slow progress and have given me the constant benefit of their far-reaching expertise, from discussions about the nature of the book to advice on the details of layout and style. At every stage they have offered guidance, never compulsion; it has been a pleasure to work under their humane direction, and it is a pleasure to be able truthfully to take full responsibility for all shortcomings of this book.

Bibliographical Abbreviations

Modern works

AHRENS = H.L. Ahrens, *De graecae linguae dialectis* (Vandenhoeck & Ruprecht, 1839–43).

ALLEN = W.S. Allen, *Accent and Rhythm* (CUP, 1973).

BALLY = C. Bally, *Manuel d'accentuation grecque* (Francke, 1945; repr. Georg Editeur, 1997).

BARRETT, *HIPPOLYTUS* = W.S. Barrett (ed.), *Euripides: Hippolytos* (Clarendon Press, 1964; repr. 1992).

CHADWICK, *THESSALIAN* = J. Chadwick, 'The Thessalian Accent', *Glotta* 70 (1992), pp. 2–14.

CHANDLER = H.W. Chandler, *A Practical Introduction to Greek Accentuation* (2nd edn, Clarendon Press, 1881; repr. Melissa Media, 1983).

DEVINE AND STEPHENS = A.M. Devine and L.D. Stephens, *The Prosody of Greek Speech* (OUP, 1994).

EHRLICH = H. Ehrlich, *Untersuchungen über die Natur der griechischen Betonung* (Weidmann, 1912).

GOETTLING = K. Goettling, *Allgemeine Lehre vom Accent der griechischen Sprache* (Cröker, 1835).

HERMANN = G. Hermann, *De emendanda ratione graecae grammaticae* (Fleischer, 1801).

KOSTER = A.J. Koster, *A Practical Guide for the Writing of the Greek Accents* (Brill, 1962; repr. 1976).

KRETSCHMER = P. Kretschmer, 'Der Übergang von der musikalischen zur exspiratorischen Betonung im Griechischen', *Zeitschrift für vergleichende Sprachforschung* 30 = N.S. 10 (1890), pp. 591–600.

A New Short Guide to the Accentuation of Ancient Greek

LEHRS, *ARISTARCHUS* = K. Lehrs, *De Aristarchi studiis Homericis* (3rd edn, Hirzel, 1882).

LEHRS, *QUAESTIONES* = K. Lehrs, *Quaestiones epicae* (Bornträger, 1837).

LEJEUNE, *REMARQUES* = M. Lejeune, 'Remarques sur l'analogie en matière d'accentuation grecque', *Revue de philologie*, 3rd series, 18 (1944), pp. 57–68.

LSJ = H.G. Liddell, R. Scott, H.S. Jones *et al.*, *A Greek-English Lexicon* (9th edn, Clarendon Press, 1940; revised supplement, 1996).

LUCIDI, *TRISILLABISMO* = M. Lucidi, 'L'origine del trisillabismo in greco', in M. Lucidi, *Saggi linguistici* (Instituto universitario orientale di Napoli, 1966), pp. 77–102. (First published in *Ricerche linguistiche* 1 (1950), pp. 69–92.)

MEISTER = R. Meister, *Die griechischen Dialekte* (Vandenhoeck & Ruprecht, 1882–9).

MISTELI = F. Misteli, 'Über die Accentuation des Griechischen', *Zeitschrift für vergleichende Sprachforschung* 17 (1868), pp. 81–134, 161–94.

NOYER = R. Noyer, 'Attic Greek Accentuation and Intermediate Derivational Representations', in I. Roca (ed.), *Derivations and Constraints in Phonology* (Clarendon Press, 1997), pp. 501–27.

PÖHLMANN AND WEST = E. Pöhlmann and M.L. West, *Documents of Ancient Greek Music* (Clarendon Press, 2001).

POSTGATE = J.P. Postgate, *A Short Guide to the Accentuation of Ancient Greek* (University Press of Liverpool/Hodder and Stoughton, 1924).

SCHMITT = A. Schmitt, *Untersuchungen zur allgemeinen Akzentlehre mit einer Anwendung auf den Akzent des Griechischen und Lateinischen* (Winter, 1924).

VENDRYES = J. Vendryes, *Traité d'accentuation grecque* (Klincksieck, 1904; repr. with updated bibliography 1945).

WACKERNAGEL, *AKZENTSTUDIEN III* = J. Wackernagel, 'Akzentstudien III: Zum homerischen Akzent', *Nachrichten von der Königlichen Gesellschaft der Wissenschaften zu Göttingen: Philologisch-*

historische Klasse (1914), pp. 97–130. (Repr. in WACKERNAGEL, *KS* ii, pp. 1154–87.)

WACKERNAGEL, *BEITRÄGE* = J. Wackernagel, *Beiträge zur Lehre vom griechischen Akzent* (Reinhardt, 1893; repr. in WACKERNAGEL, *KS* ii, pp. 1072–1107.).

WACKERNAGEL, *KS* = J. Wackernagel, *Kleine Schriften* (Vandenhoeck & Ruprecht, 1955–79).

WACKERNAGEL, *REVIEW OF POSTGATE* = J. Wackernagel, review of POSTGATE, in *Indogermanische Forschungen* 43, *Anzeiger* (1926), pp. 48–59. (Repr. in WACKERNAGEL, *KS* ii, pp. 1188–98.)

WACKERNAGEL, *VERBALACCENT* = J. Wackernagel, 'Der griechische Verbalaccent', *Zeitschrift für vergleichende Sprachforschung* 23 = N.S. 3 (1877), pp. 457–70. (Repr. in WACKERNAGEL, *KS* ii, pp. 1058–71.)

WACKERNAGEL, *ZEUGNISS* = J. Wackernagel, 'Das Zeugniss der delphischen Hymnen über den griechischen Accent', *Rheinisches Museum für Philologie* N.S. 51 (1896), pp. 304–5. (Repr. in WACKERNAGEL, *KS* iii, pp. 1822–3.)

WEST, *AESCHYLUS* = M.L. West (ed.), *Aeschyli tragoediae* (Teubner, 1990; repr. 1998).

WEST, *ILIAD* = M.L. West (ed.), *Homeri Ilias* (Teubner, 1998–2000).

WEST, *LESBIAN* = M.L. West, 'On Lesbian Accentuation', *Glotta* 48 (1970), pp. 194–8.

WEST, *MUSIC* = M.L. West, *Ancient Greek Music* (Clarendon Press, 1992).

WEST, *THEOGONY* = M.L. West (ed.), *Hesiod: Theogony* (Clarendon Press, 1966; repr. Sandpiper, 1997).

Ancient authors and works

Where not otherwise indicated, quotations of ancient authors are taken from the most recent Oxford Classical Text edition. The New Testament is quoted from the edition of B. Aland *et al.* (Deutsche Bibelgesellschaft, 1993). In cases where there are different editorial practices on a point of accentuation, examples have been quoted with accents that conform to the practices advocated in this book (regardless of the conventions followed in the editions being used), except where the differing editorial practices are specifically under discussion.

Aesch. = Aeschylus. Except where otherwise stated in the text, quoted from M.L. West's edition (Teubner, 1998).

Ammonius = *Ammonii qui dicitur liber de adfinium vocabulorum differentia*, ed. K. Nickau (Teubner, 1966).

Ap. Dysc. = Apollonius Dyscolus, ed. R. Schneider and G. Uhlig (Grammatici Graeci ii. 1–3; Teubner, 1878–1910; repr. Olms, 1965). Works: *Pron.* = *Pronomina*; *Adv.* = *Adverbia*; *Synt.* = *Syntaxis.*

Ar. = Aristophanes, ed. V. Coulon (Budé, 1946–54).

Arcadius = (Ps.-) Arcadius, Ἐπιτομὴ τῆς καθολικῆς προσῳδίας Ἡρωδιανοῦ, ed. M. Schmidt (Mauk, 1860; repr. Olms, 1983).

Choer., Th. = *Choerobosci scholia in Theodosii Alexandrini canones*, ed. A. Hilgard (Grammatici Graeci iv. 1–2; Teubner, 1889–94; repr. Olms, 1965).

Eur. = Euripides

Eust. = *Eustathii archiepiscopi Thessalonicensis commentarii ad Homeri Iliadem pertinentes*, ed. M. van der Valk (Brill, 1971–87); *Eustathii archiepiscopi Thessalonicensis commentarii ad Homeri Odysseam*, ed. J.G. Stallbaum (Weigel, 1825–6).

Hdn = *Herodiani technici reliquiae*, ed. A. Lentz (Grammatici Graeci iii. 1–2; Teubner, 1867–70; repr. Olms, 1965).

Il. = Homer, *Iliad*. Except where otherwise stated in the text, quoted from M.L. West's edition (Teubner, 1998–2000).

Od. = Homer, *Odyssey*, ed. P. von der Muehll (Teubner, 1962).

P. Oxy. = *The Oxyrhynchus Papyri*, ed. B.P. Grenfell, A.S. Hunt *et al.* (Egypt Exploration Fund, 1898–).

P. Paris = *Les papyrus grecs du musée du Louvre et de la Bibliothèque impériale*, ed. A.J. Letronne, W. Brunet de Presle, and E. Egger (Imprimerie impériale, 1866).

PG = *Patrologiae cursus completus, series graeca*, ed. J.-P. Migne (Migne, 1857–66).

Photius, *Lexicon* = *Photii patriarchae lexicon*, ed. C. Theodoridis (De Gruyter, 1982–).

Sch. Dem. = *Scholia Demosthenica*, ed. M.R. Dilts (Teubner, 1983–6).

Sch. *Il.* = *Scholia graeca in Homeri Iliadem* (*scholia vetera*), ed. H. Erbse (De Gruyter, 1969–88).

Soph. = Sophocles

Trypho = *Tryphonis grammatici alexandrini fragmenta*, ed. A. von Velsen (Nicolai, 1853; repr. Hakkert, 1965).

General Abbreviations

acc. = accusative
act. = active
adv. = adverb
aor. = aorist
dat. = dative
decl. = declension
fem. = feminine
fut. = future
gen. = genitive
imperat. = imperative
imperf. = imperfect
indef. = indefinite
indic. = indicative
inf. = infinitive
interrog. = interrogative
masc. = masculine

mid. = middle
neut. = neuter
nom. = nominative
opt. = optative
part. = participle
pass. = passive
perf. = perfect
pers. pron. = personal pronoun
pl. = plural
poss. pron. = possessive pronoun
pres. = present
rel. pron. = relative pronoun
sg. = singular
subj. = subjunctive
voc. = vocative

An asterisk (*) highlights the fact that a word-form is non-existent or impossible. (E.g. 'κληδο-όχος contracts to κληδοῦχος, not *κληδούχος.')

Chapter 1: Introductory

Meaning of 'accent'

1. The word 'accent' has several meanings. The two that will be relevant in this book are (a) the pre-eminence given in speech to certain syllables over others, and (b) the diacritic marks that are used in writing and printing to indicate this pre-eminence.

2. As regards the pre-eminence of certain syllables in speech, languages typically make some syllables more prominent than others in one or more of the following ways:

(i) Accented syllables differ in pitch from unaccented syllables, typically by being pitched higher.

(ii) Accented syllables differ in loudness from unaccented syllables, typically by being louder.

(iii) Accented syllables differ in duration from unaccented syllables, typically by taking up a longer period of time.

(iv) Accented syllables differ in the quality of their vowels from unaccented syllables (compare the quality of the accented *o* in English *philósophy* with the unaccented *o* in *philosóphical*).

3. A distinction has traditionally been made between 'pitch accent' and 'stress accent' languages. English, for example, is described as a stress accent language, Japanese as a pitch accent language. The linguistic basis of this distinction has been much debated, since pitch changes may feature in all types of accent, but speakers of a 'pitch accent' language tend to perceive the

1

accentuation of their language in terms of pitch whereas speakers of a 'stress accent' language tend to think of accented syllables in their language as having increased force or effort.

For experimental comparison of the English and Japanese accents, see M.E. Beckman, *Stress and Non-Stress Accent* (Foris, 1986). For a more detailed typology of accents, see DEVINE AND STEPHENS, pp. 198–215; D.R. Ladd, *Intonational Phonology* (CUP, 1996), pp. 155–9.

4. In many languages, every word has one syllable that is more prominent than the others. That syllable carries the main or primary word accent and is often referred to simply as the accented syllable. Some languages also have syllables that are intermediate in prominence between the syllable carrying the main accent and the unaccented syllables. Such syllables are said to carry a secondary accent.

5. Languages differ in the ways in which they determine the position of the main word accent. In some languages, the main word accent always falls on the final syllable, as in French, or on the initial syllable, as in Czech. In others, as in Lithuanian, the main accent can fall on any syllable, and one must learn the position of the accent as part of each individual word. In yet other languages, such as Latin, some syllables are light whereas others are heavy, and the position of the main accent depends on the sequence of light and heavy syllables making up the word.

The terms 'light syllable' and 'heavy syllable' are used in this book where works on Greek and Latin often use the terms 'short syllable' and 'long syllable'. The use of the terms 'light syllable' and 'heavy syllable' allows the words 'short' and 'long' to be reserved for the quantity of *vowels* rather than syllables. On light and heavy syllables in ancient Greek, see §§ 47–57.

1. Introductory (§§ 3–7)

The accent of ancient Greek speech

6. For present purposes 'ancient Greek' will cover the period from our first Greek literature down to about the second century AD.

7. The accent of ancient Greek was a pitch accent. The word προσῳδίᾱ, of which *accentus* is a literal Latin translation, is used of what is *sung* to anything, as a song to a lyre.

The word προσῳδίᾱ was also used in a wider sense, as by Aristotle (*Sophistici elenchi* 177b4, but see A. Gudeman (ed.), *Aristoteles: Περὶ ποιητικῆς* (de Gruyter, 1934), p. 343), to include the 'breathings', 'rough' and 'smooth', which were also regarded as accompanying speech, and much later it was still further extended to distinctions of vowel quantity, indications of elision and of the separation or conjunction of words, for all of which special marks were provided by the grammarians.

Plato's word ἁρμονίᾱ 'musical pitch', used of the accent (*Cratylus*, 416b), describes the musical character of the accent. Another name for it is τόνος (also τάσις), 'tension', related to τείνειν, 'to stretch', since the degree of tension in vibrating strings affects the rapidity of their vibration and the pitch of the sounds thus produced. The names of the three varieties of accent in common use, ὀξεῖα προσῳδίᾱ, the 'sharp' or 'shrill' accent (the acute), βαρεῖα προσῳδίᾱ, the 'heavy' or 'low' (the grave), and ὀξυβάρεια (one of the names for the circumflex), a combination of the acute and the grave, also speak for an accent perceived in terms of pitch. The adjectives ὀξύς and βαρύς, when applied to sound, mean 'high' and 'low' respectively. A passage appearing in two manuscripts of Arcadius' epitome of Herodian's Περὶ καθολικῆς προσῳδίᾱς (see § 21) informs us that Aristophanes of Byzantium likened the accent to the pitches of music:

3

καὶ τοὺς μὲν χρόνους τοῖς ῥυθμοῖς ἤκασε, τοὺς δὲ τόνους τοῖς τόνοις τῆς μουσικῆς. (Arcadius 212. 4–6)

'And he likened the lengths to musical rhythms and the pitches to musical pitches.'

8. Dionysius of Halicarnassus, a scholar and literary critic of the first century BC, gives us some interesting information on the musical interval heard in the ancient Greek accent:

μουσικὴ γάρ τις ἦν καὶ ἡ τῶν πολιτικῶν λόγων ἐπιστήμη τῷ ποσῷ διαλλάττουσα τῆς ἐν ᾠδαῖς καὶ ὀργάνοις, οὐχὶ τῷ ποιῷ. Καὶ γὰρ ἐν ταύτῃ καὶ μέλος ἔχουσιν αἱ λέξεις καὶ ῥυθμὸν καὶ μεταβολὴν καὶ πρέπον, ὥστε καὶ ἐπὶ ταύτης ἡ ἀκοὴ τέρπεται μὲν τοῖς μέλεσιν, ἄγεται δὲ τοῖς ῥυθμοῖς, ἀσπάζεται δὲ τὰς μεταβολάς, ποθεῖ δ' ἐπὶ πάντων τὸ οἰκεῖον, ἡ δὲ διαλλαγὴ κατὰ τὸ μᾶλλον καὶ ἧττον.

Διαλέκτου μὲν οὖν μέλος ἑνὶ μετρεῖται διαστήματι τῷ λεγομένῳ διὰ πέντε ὡς ἔγγιστα, καὶ οὔτε ἐπιτείνεται πέρα τῶν τριῶν τόνων καὶ ἡμιτονίου ἐπὶ τὸ ὀξὺ οὔτ' ἀνίεται τοῦ χωρίου τούτου πλεῖον ἐπὶ τὸ βαρύ.

Οὐ μὴν ἅπασά γ' ἡ λέξις ἡ καθ' ἓν μόριον λόγου ταττομένη ἐπὶ τῆς αὐτῆς λέγεται τάσεως, ἀλλ' ἡ μὲν ἐπὶ τῆς ὀξείας, ἡ δ' ἐπὶ τῆς βαρείας, ἡ δ' ἐπ' ἀμφοῖν. Τῶν δὲ ἀμφοτέρας τὰς τάσεις ἐχουσῶν, αἱ μὲν κατὰ μίαν συλλαβὴν συνεφθαρμένον ἔχουσι τῷ ὀξεῖ τὸ βαρύ, ἃς δὴ περισπωμένας καλοῦμεν· αἱ δὲ ἐν ἑτέρᾳ τε καὶ ἑτέρᾳ χωρὶς ἑκάτερον ἐφ' ἑαυτοῦ τὴν οἰκείαν φυλάττον φύσιν. Καὶ ταῖς μὲν δισυλλάβοις οὐδὲν τὸ διὰ μέσου χωρίον βαρύτητός τε καὶ ὀξύτητος. Ταῖς δὲ πολυσυλλάβοις, ἡλίκαι ποτ' ἂν ὦσιν, ἡ τὸν ὀξὺν τόνον ἔχουσα μία ἐν πολλαῖς βαρείαις ἔνεστιν.

Ἡ δὲ ὀργανική τε καὶ ᾠδικὴ μοῦσα διαστήμασί τε χρῆται πλείοσιν... (Dionysius of Halicarnassus, *De compositione verborum* 11. 13–18, ed. G. Aujac and M. Lebel (Budé, 1981))

'For the art of public speaking is also a musical one, differing in degree, not in kind, from the art of singing and playing instruments. For in this art too the words have melody and rhythm and variation and what is appropriate, so that here too the hearing takes pleasure in the melodies, is led by the rhythms, is pleased by the variation, and desires in everything what is appropriate to it. The difference [between this and music] is a matter of more and less.

'The melody of speech is measured by one interval, closest to that called a fifth, and neither extended upwards beyond the interval of three tones and a semitone nor allowed to move downwards more than this interval.

'It is not that the whole utterance of a single word is spoken at the same pitch, but some parts are spoken at a high pitch, some at a low pitch, and some at both. And of those words that have both pitches, some have the low pitch blended in with the high pitch in a single syllable; these we call perispomena. Other words have each pitch in a different syllable, each separately keeping its own character to itself. Now in words of two syllables there is no space between the high pitch and the low pitch. But in polysyllables, however many syllables there are, the one with the high pitch is among many low-pitched ones.

'But music played on instruments and sung uses more intervals....'

9. It is, however, difficult to understand exactly what Dionysius is saying here. He is sometimes taken to mean that the total range of the voice in speaking, from the highest to the lowest pitch, is a fifth. New evidence from a fragment of papyrus may now speak in favour of this interpretation.

The third-century AD papyrus *P. Oxy.* 53. 3705 contains part of a line of Menander's iambic dialogue written out four times, with different musical notation accompanying each instance. Musical notation accompanying words normally indicates a melody to which the words are to be sung (see § 36 below), but lines of iambic dialogue are not otherwise known to have been set to music at this period. PÖHLMANN AND WEST, p. 185, suggest that the papyrus offers different ways in which an actor might *speak* the line. If so, we would have a unique testimony to possible intonations of ancient Greek speech. The melodies given are related to the word accents, with accented syllables generally assigned to higher notes than unaccented syllables, and, as Pöhlmann and West note, with one exception the notes all fall within the compass of a fifth. The intervals between individual notes are nearly all smaller than a fifth. The evidence of the papyrus needs to be treated with some caution, particularly since the surviving part provides musical notation for only six syllables in total, but it certainly increases the likelihood that Dionysius' fifth refers to the total

5

pitch range of an utterance. For further information and bibliography on the papyrus, see PÖHLMANN AND WEST, pp. 184–5.

A.M. Devine and L.D. Stephens ('Dionysius of Halicarnassus, *De compositione verborum* XI: Reconstructing the Phonetics of the Greek Accent', *TAPA* 121 (1991), p. 243; DEVINE AND STEPHENS, p. 172) argue that it is very unlikely that Dionysius refers to the total range of the voice in speaking, on the grounds that in living languages the total pitch range of an utterance is typically much greater than a fifth. Discussion with David Patterson has, however, persuaded me that there are many different ways to measure the pitch range used by a speaker, and that Dionysius' necessarily impressionistic assessment may well have been roughly equivalent to a procedure that could plausibly have resulted in the measure of a fifth. Most crucially, speakers typically use their most extreme high and low pitches relatively infrequently, so that a judgement based on typical and fairly small stretches of utterance is likely to fall short of the maximum pitch range observable by instrumental measurement over a large stretch.

10. Dionysius appears to be drawing on the tradition of a school of musical experts who were primarily interested in the melodies of sung and instrumental music but who also compared these to the melody of speech. One of these experts was Aristoxenus, a pupil of Aristotle. From him we learn that the Greek accent did not involve a sudden leap of the voice from one note to another but a gradual rise or fall. In a treatise on musical scales, Aristoxenus distinguishes the motion of the voice in speaking, which is 'continuous' (συνεχής), from its motion in singing, which is 'by intervals' (διαστηματική):

Πρῶτον μὲν οὖν ἁπάντων αὐτῆς τῆς κατὰ τόπον κινήσεως τὰς διαφορὰς θεωρῆσαι τίνες εἰσὶ περατέον. πάσης δὲ φωνῆς δυναμένης κινεῖσθαι τὸν εἰρημένον αὐτὸν τρόπον δύο τινές εἰσιν ἰδέαι κινήσεως, ἥ τε συνεχὴς καὶ ἡ διαστηματική. κατὰ μὲν οὖν τὴν συνεχῆ τόπον τινὰ διεξιέναι φαίνεται ἡ φωνὴ τῇ αἰσθήσει οὕτως ὡς ἂν μηδαμοῦ ἱσταμένη μηδ' ἐπ' αὐτῶν τῶν περάτων κατά γε τὴν τῆς αἰσθήσεως φαντασίαν, ἀλλὰ φερομένη συνεχῶς μέχρι σιωπῆς, κατὰ δὲ τὴν ἑτέραν ἣν ὀνομάζομεν διαστηματικὴν ἐναντίως φαίνεται κινεῖσθαι·

διαβαίνουσα γὰρ ἴστησιν αὐτὴν ἐπὶ μιᾶς τάσεως εἶτα πάλιν ἐφ᾽
ἑτέρας καὶ τοῦτο ποιοῦσα συνεχῶς — λέγω δὲ συνεχῶς κατὰ τὸν
χρόνον — ὑπερβαίνουσα μὲν τοὺς περιεχομένους ὑπὸ τῶν τάσεων
τόπους, ἱσταμένη δ᾽ ἐπ᾽ αὐτῶν τῶν τάσεων καὶ φθεγγομένη ταύτας
μόνον αὐτὰς μελῳδεῖ· λέγεται καὶ κινεῖσθαι διαστηματικὴν κίνησιν.
... τὴν μὲν οὖν συνεχῆ λογικὴν εἶναί φαμεν, διαλεγομένων γὰρ ἡμῶν
οὕτως ἡ φωνὴ κινεῖται κατὰ τόπον ὥστε μηδαμοῦ δοκεῖν ἵστασθαι.
κατὰ δὲ τὴν ἑτέραν ἣν ὀνομάζομεν διαστηματικὴν ἐναντίως πέφυκε
γίγνεσθαι· ἀλλὰ γὰρ ἵστασθαί τε δοκεῖ καὶ πάντες τὸν τοῦτο
φαινόμενον ποιεῖν οὐκέτι λέγειν φασὶν ἀλλ᾽ ᾄδειν. (Aristoxenus,
Elementa harmonica 1. 8–9, ed. R. Da Rios (Publica Officina
Polygraphica, 1954))

'First of all we must try to understand what are the different kinds of
spatial motion. While every voice is able to move in the aforementioned
manner, there are two types of motion: continuous motion and motion by
intervals. In continuous motion the voice seems to the senses to pass through
some space in such a way that it doesn't rest anywhere, even at its very limits,
according to the perception of the senses, but is carried along continuously
until it is silent. In the other kind of motion, which we call motion by
intervals, the voice appears to move in the opposite manner. For in passing
over a space it sets itself at a single pitch and then again at another and doing
this continuously — and I mean 'continuously' as regards time — it crosses
over the places between the pitches, comes to rest on the pitches themselves,
and uttering those alone is said to sing them and move by intervals....We say
that continuous motion belongs to speech, for the voice moves in this way
while we speak, so as not to seem to rest anywhere. With the other kind of
motion, which we call motion by intervals, it's the opposite way round: the
voice seems to rest and everybody says that one who appears to do this is not
speaking but singing.'

11. A stress accent, unlike a pitch accent, may cause vowel
changes and even vowel loss in unaccented syllables. In English,
for example, the second vowel of *económics*, which is unstressed,
has a different quality from the second vowel of *ecónomist*, which
is stressed. In most dialects of ancient Greek, including Attic and
the Hellenistic *koiné* based on Attic, it is probably not possible to

find the kinds of vowel changes that can be caused by a stress accent, i.e. vowel changes confined to unaccented syllables.

When a stress accent causes vowel changes, the vowels that occur in unaccented syllables are generally more similar to one another than the vowels occurring in stressed syllables. Thus, the second vowel of *económics* is more similar to the second vowel of *ínfinite* than the second vowel of *ecónomist* is to the second vowel of *infínity*. In standard Russian, a contrast between *a* and *o* exists only in stressed syllables; in unstressed syllables *o* has become *a*.

The Thessalian dialect of ancient Greek, unlike the other dialects, underwent considerable vowel loss. For a hypothesis that Thessalian had a stress accent falling on the initial syllable, see CHADWICK, *THESSALIAN*; cf. §§ 312–14. O. Szemerényi, *Syncope in Greek and Indo-European and the Nature of Indo-European Accent* (Instituto universitario orientale di Napoli, 1964), disputed the view that vowel loss in unaccented syllables is not found in most Greek dialects, but most of his examples have also been explained in other ways.

12. A pitch accent may be ignored by poetic metre, but a stress accent tends to be the basis of metre. Ancient Greek metres are 'quantitative': they are based on the distinction between heavy and light syllables, without regard for the pitch accent.

13. The nature of the Greek accent changed, however, over the course of the early centuries AD, with the result that modern Greek has a stress accent, not a pitch accent. As the pitch accent changed to a stress accent, the accent gradually came to be more important for poetic metre than quantity. The fourth-century AD Christian writer Gregory of Nazianzus wrote two hymns in which the penultimate syllable of each line was almost always accented. In these two hymns syllable quantities play no rôle in the metre, which, apart from the penultimate accent, is based purely on syllable count. These hymns represent one of the first manifestations of the appearance of stress-based metres.

See Gregory of Nazianzus, ῎Επη δογματικά 32, ῎Επη ἠθικά 3 (PG xxxvii, cols 511–14, 632–40); W. Meyer, 'Anfang und Ursprung der lateinischen und griechischen rythmischen Dichtung', *Abhandlungen der philosophisch-*

1. Introductory (§§ 11–14)

philologischen Classe der königlich bayerischen Akademie der Wissenschaften
17. 2 (1885), pp. 313–15, 400–9 (repr. in W. Meyer, *Gesammelte Abhandlungen zur mittellateinischen Rythmik* (Weidmann, 1905–36) ii, pp. 48–51, 141–52).

Babrius, who probably lived around the second century AD, wrote scazons or 'limping iambics', iambic verses characterised by a spondaic verse-end, and almost always placed an accented syllable in the penultimate position. The same is true of scazons by various other authors of about the same period and later. It is likely, however, that in these cases the practice results simply from a preference for high pitch in the penultimate syllable rather than being due to the change to stress accent. See WACKERNAGEL, *REVIEW OF POSTGATE*, pp. 49–51. Cf. also ALLEN, pp. 267–8; A.M. Devine and L.D. Stephens, 'Stress in Greek?', *TAPA* 115 (1985), pp. 136–7.

14. It is not easy to say exactly when the change from pitch to stress accent took place. At the beginning of the grammatical tradition relating to accents, in the early second century BC (see § 17), the accent described is one that is perceived in terms of pitch. Later grammarians who describe the accent in terms of pitch may well be following earlier grammarians, but this cannot have been the case at the *beginning* of the tradition. We can, therefore, safely assume that a pitch accent was still heard, at least by some speakers of Greek, at the beginning of the second century BC. Given that the first poetry showing clear signs of being influenced by a stress accent comes from the fourth century AD (§ 13), the change to a stress accent certainly occurred at some time during the period between the second century BC and the fourth century AD.

It has been argued that at least in some classes of society the change to a stress accent occurred much earlier than the second century BC. See KRETSCHMER, p. 594. Cf. also SCHMITT, pp. 172–7; I.R. Alfageme, 'Notas sobre la evolución del sistema vocalico en la *koiné*', *Cuadernos de filología clásica* 9 (1975), pp. 339–79.

15. The ancient Greek distinction between long and short vowels was lost as the accent changed to a stress accent. In modern Greek the ω of ἄνθρωπος is no longer than the *o*. At the same time, vowels in accented syllables came to be pronounced somewhat longer than those in unaccented syllables. The *a* of ἄνθρωπος tends to be pronounced rather longer in modern Greek than the ω or the *o*. The loss of the ancient Greek vowel length distinction was probably connected intimately with the change to a stress accent, but opinion is divided as to whether the stress accent caused the loss of the old length distinction or *vice versa*.

For the view that a change in the type of accent caused the vowel length distinction to break down, see L. Threatte, *The Grammar of Attic Inscriptions* (De Gruyter, 1980–96) i, p. 385; W.S. Allen, 'The Development of the Attic Vowel System: Conspiracy or Catastrophe?', in J.T. Killen, J.L. Melena, and J.-P. Olivier (eds), *Studies in Mycenaean and Classical Greek Presented to John Chadwick* (*Minos* N.S. 20–2; Ediciones Universidad de Salamanca, 1987), p. 28. For the opposite view, S.-T. Teodorsson, *The Phonemic System of the Attic Dialect 400–340 B.C.* (Institute of Classical Studies of the University of Göteborg, 1974), p. 294. For some discussion of both possibilities, DEVINE AND STEPHENS, p. 216.

16. Because the loss of the ancient vowel length distinction is thought to have gone hand in hand with the change to a stress accent, evidence that the vowel length distinction was breaking down may also count as evidence that the stress accent was taking over, although it is unclear which development was the cause of the other (§ 15). Mistakes involving vowel quantity — suggesting that the long and short vowels were falling together — become common on Attic inscriptions from about 100 AD.

See Threatte (cited in § 15) i, pp. 385–7. Teodorsson (cited in § 15), pp. 218–19, has argued that the loss of distinctive vowel quantity was already complete by the beginning of the third century BC, but see C.J. Ruijgh's review of Teodorsson in *Mnemosyne*, 4th series, 31 (1978), p. 84. For early loss of distinctive vowel quantity, see also KRETSCHMER, pp. 594–9; Alfageme (cited in § 14).

The Greek written accent

17. The invention of written signs for the accents of Greek is traditionally ascribed to Aristophanes of Byzantium, a distinguished scholar and critic who was head of the great library at Alexandria at the beginning of the second century BC. It is likely that the written accents were indeed invented around this time, since there are no strong reasons for believing that they existed earlier, and the first written accents that are preserved appear on literary papyri dating from the second century BC.

18. These accent marks were invented in the context of a concern with preserving works of literature such as the *Iliad* and *Odyssey*, establishing their correct text, and understanding their meaning. The writing of accents facilitated the reading of poetic texts that by the second century BC had become difficult. Spaces were not left between words, so the potential for mis-reading was relatively great. This would have been especially true of texts whose language had become unfamiliar. The writing of accents made words more quickly identifiable and helped to prevent incorrect readings.

19. One of our earliest papyri with accent marks is a fragment of a poem by the sixth-century BC lyric poet Ibycus; the copy on the papyrus was made in the second century BC. The papyrus is typical of accented papyri, especially the earliest ones, in being a copy of a poetic text. As on all accented papyri, the accents are marked not on every word but sporadically. Some of the accents were added later than the original writing of the papyrus, but some go back to the original scribe. Part of the fragment reads:

τωιδ[α]ρατρωιλον
ὡϲειχρυϲονὀρὲι
χάλκωιτριϲἄ΄πεφθο[ν]ήδη
τρωεϲδ[α]ναόιτ᾽ερό[ε]ϲϲαν
μορφανμάλεῐϲκογομοιον·

(*P. Oxy.* 15. 1790, fragments 2 + 3, column ii, lines 41–5; transcription after Turner (cited below), p. 48.)

If written out with gaps between words and modern punctuation, the same extract looks as follows:

τῶι δ᾽ [ἄ]ρα Τρωίλον
ὡσεὶ χρυσὸν ὀρει-
χάλκωι τρὶς ἄπεφθο[ν] ἤδη
Τρῶες Δ[α]ναοί τ᾽ ἐρό[ε]σσαν
μορφὰν μάλ᾽ ἐίσκον ὅμοιον.

(M. Davies (ed.), *Poetarum melicorum graecorum fragmenta* (Clarendon Press, 1991–) i, p. 243.)

'As regards his lovely form, the Trojans and Danaans likened Troilos to him, like thrice-refined gold to brass.'

Of the accent marks on the papyrus, the two grave accents on ὀρεὶχάλκωι are particularly noteworthy. A modern text would not print grave accents here, but originally all syllables that had neither an acute nor a circumflex accent were considered to have a grave, which simply indicated lack of accent. A scribe could therefore mark unaccented syllables with a grave if he so desired. In the case of ὀρεὶχάλκωι the grave accents assist reading by indicating that ὀρὲι is to be taken as part of a larger word, ὀρεὶχάλκωι, and not as the word ὄρει 'on the mountain'.

On accents in Greek papyri, see further see B. Laum, *Das alexandrinische Akzentuationssystem* (Schöningh, 1928); J. Moore-Blunt, 'Problems of Accentuation in Greek Papyri', *Quaderni urbinati di cultura classica* 29 (1978), pp. 137–63; C.M. Mazzucchi, 'Sul sistema di accentazione dei testi greci in età romana e bizantina', *Aegyptus* 59 (1979), pp. 145–67; A. Biondi,

1. Introductory (§§ 19–21)

Gli accenti nei papiri greci biblici (Papyrologica Castroctaviana, 1983); E.G. Turner, *Greek Manuscripts of the Ancient World* (2nd edn, edited by P.J. Parsons; University of London, Institute of Classical Studies, 1987), p. 11. Two scholars have recently argued for specific factors governing the choice of words accented in papyri, beyond the desire to assist in the correct identification of the words: G. Nagy, 'Reading Greek Poetry Aloud: Evidence from the Bacchylides Papyri', *Quaderni urbinati di cultura classica* N.S. 64 (2000), pp. 7–28; A. Nodar, 'Ancient Homeric Scholarship and the Medieval Tradition: Evidence from the Diacritics in the Papyri', to appear in the Proceedings of the Twenty-third International Congress of Papyrology (Vienna).

20. Aristophanes' accent marks were put to good use by his successor in the Alexandrian library, Aristarchus of Samothrace, the greatest scholar and best Homeric critic of antiquity, who in his critical editions of Homer and other poets had frequently to deal with questions of accentuation. Neither his editions nor any treatise he may have written on accentuation survive, but his precepts and opinions are frequently transmitted by scholiasts and later grammarians.

21. The greatest work of codification of the ancient Greek accent was carried out by Aelius Herodian, son of the distinguished grammarian Apollonius Dyscolus of Alexandria. Herodian lived and taught at Rome under the emperor Marcus Aurelius in the second century AD. His great work 'On Prosody in General', περὶ καθολικῆς προσῳδίας, had twenty books, nineteen of which were devoted to accentuation. The work is now known to us chiefly from an epitome written around AD 400 and attributed to either Arcadius or a Theodosius. (It is normally referred to as Arcadius', although the attribution to Arcadius is highly questionable.) All later grammarians who wrote about accents depended directly or indirectly on Herodian. Among these later grammarians may be mentioned Georgius Choeroboscus, ninth century AD, and Iohannes Charax, who lived some time between the sixth and ninth centuries AD. The latter wrote a monograph on enclitics that

13

still survives. Much valuable information on details has been preserved to us in marginal notes, or scholia, to manuscripts of classical authors. A tenth-century manuscript of the *Iliad*, Venetus A, is particularly rich in important scholia on accentuation.

22. An attempt to reconstruct the works of Herodian was made by the nineteenth-century scholar August Lentz. His reconstruction is a useful collection of ancient precepts on accentuation, although many of the statements he incorporates cannot be ascribed to Herodian with any certainty.

A. Lentz (ed.), *Herodiani technici reliquiae* (Grammatici Graeci iii. 1–2; Teubner, 1867–70; repr. Olms 1965). On the current state of scholarship on Herodian, see A.R. Dyck, 'Aelius Herodian: Recent Studies and Prospects for Future Research', in W. Haase (ed.), *Aufstieg und Niedergang der Römischen Welt* II, xxxiv. 1 (De Gruyter, 1993), pp. 772–94.

23. The system of ancient Greek accentuation currently employed in printed texts is based on the precepts of ancient grammarians and the evidence of manuscripts. From the end of the ninth century AD the scribes of manuscripts regularly wrote accent marks on every word, following the precepts of earlier treatises.

24. The traditional written accentuation of ancient Greek, while undoubtedly containing uncertainties, on the whole represents a sound tradition of high antiquity. Comparison with the traditional written accentuation of the oldest Sanskrit texts, the Vedic hymns, shows that at least some features of the ancient Greek accentuation system are extremely old indeed. For example, the movement of the accent between root and ending in the Greek paradigm of the word for 'foot', πούς, πόδα, ποδός, ποδί, etc., is almost exactly replicated in the equivalent cases of the Sanskrit paradigm: *păt, pădam, padás, padí,* etc. Such coincidences between the accentuation of Greek and that of Sanskrit are too striking to have arisen by chance, and there is no route by which they could have been borrowed from one language into the other. They were inherited by both Greek and Sanskrit from the ancestor language ('proto-Indo-European') from which both Greek and Sanskrit are descended.

25. The traditional placement of the word accent in ancient Greek is corroborated by the accentuation of modern Greek, since ancient Greek words that survive into the modern language almost always have the modern accent on the same syllable as the traditional ancient Greek accent, despite the change in the pronunciation of the accent (see § 13).

The meaning of the acute, circumflex, and grave

26. From our earliest accented texts onward, three written accent marks are in use: acute (´), circumflex (^), and grave (`). The use of these accent marks allows us to answer the crucial question about the accentuation of a given word: where does the highest pitch fall? This question has two components. Firstly, on which vowel does the highest pitch fall? Secondly, if the vowel is long, does the highest pitch come near the beginning of the vowel or near the end? The second question arises because accented long vowels had the high pitch either on the first part or on the second.

27. The accented syllable is marked with either the acute (´) or the circumflex (^). Whatever the length of the vowel, the acute indicates that the high pitch falls on the last part of the vowel (and therefore on the *only* 'part' of a short vowel). The circumflex indicates that the high pitch falls on the part of the vowel before the last. The circumflex, therefore, cannot fall on a short vowel.

Examples:

ἔχω: high pitch on the (only part of the) short vowel in the first syllable.

βασιλεύς: high pitch on the second part of the diphthong in the final syllable.

βασιλεῦ: high pitch on the first part of the diphthong in the final syllable.

Notice that the accent marks as printed in our modern texts are always placed, when they occur on a diphthong, over the *second* element of the diphthong (βασιλεύς, βασιλεῦ). In the case of the circumflex this is rather misleading: the circumflex indicates a high pitch on the first part of the diphthong, although it is written over the second.

28. The 'parts' of a vowel we have been referring to, of which a short vowel has one and a long vowel two, are called *morae* (singular *mora*). Although the term is taken from Roman grammarians, they did not use it in exactly this sense.

The modern use of the term *mora* goes back to Gottfried Hermann at the beginning of the nineteenth century. See HERMANN, p. 63.

29. All unaccented syllables were originally considered to carry the grave accent, and in the accented papyri a grave can therefore be written on any syllable that does not have either the acute or the circumflex (§ 19). In medieval manuscripts and in our modern printed texts, however, the use of the grave is different.

30. A word such as βασιλεύς, which when written or pronounced in isolation had an acute on the final syllable, is written with a grave instead of the acute when it is followed by another word in the same sentence, as long as punctuation does not intervene and the following word is not an enclitic. (On enclitics, see §§ 77, 278–300): ὁ βασιλεὺς σοφός· σοφὸς ὁ βασιλεύς.

31. The significance of this use of the grave is disputed. In the early twentieth century Bernhard Laum argued that it was a late and purely orthographic phenomenon except (a) in monosyllables, and (b) in disyllabic prepositions followed immediately by an accented syllable. Evidence has since accrued, however, to show that the final syllable of a word such as βασιλεύς, when followed by another non-enclitic word without intervening punctuation, had an accentual status different from that of other accented syllables at least as early as the Hellenistic period. (For some of this evidence, see § 37). It is likely that the grave that replaces the acute on a final syllable indicates that the syllable is to be pronounced on a pitch higher than that of the preceding unaccented syllables but lower than that of other accented syllables.

See Laum (cited in § 19). Evidence against Laum's hypothesis has been assembled by J. Giessler, *Prosodische Zeichen in den antiken Handschriften griechischer Lyriker* (Doctoral dissertation, Giessen, 1923); WACKERNAGEL, *REVIEW OF POSTGATE*, pp 53–4, 59; A. Debrunner in a review of Laum in *Byzantinische Zeitschrift* 29 (1929), pp. 50–5; E. Hermann in a review of Laum in *Philologische Wochenschrift* 50 (1930), cols 228–33; Moore-Blunt (cited in § 19); Mazzucchi (cited in § 19). For various opinions on the exact phonetic significance of the grave accent, see also EHRLICH, pp. 250–62; M. Grammont, *Phonétique du grec ancien* (I.A.C., 1948), p. 390; ALLEN, pp. 245–8; E.H. Sturtevant, *The Pronunciation of Greek and Latin* (Linguistic Society of America, 1940), pp. 100–1; DEVINE AND STEPHENS, pp. 180–3.

32. In medieval manuscripts and in modern printed texts, the writing of the grave accent is reserved exclusively for final syllables of words such as βασιλεύς within the sentence. It is no longer the case that any unaccented syllable may be marked with a grave.

33. There are hints in our ancient grammatical texts that some grammarians operated with or advocated a system of accentuation other than that involving the triple classification of accents into acute, circumflex, and grave. Various grammarians recognised a 'middle' accent or μέση, which a Roman commentator takes to be a transitional pitch between the acute and the grave. There were also grammarians who recognised more than one combination of pitches on the same syllable: as well as the circumflex (high tone plus low tone), a reversed circumflex, or low tone plus high tone, was possible.

See the passage of [Sergius] in H. Keil (ed.), *Grammatici latini* (Teubner, 1855–80; repr. Olms, 1961) iv, pp. 529–31. On the 'middle' accent, the interpretation of which is wildly disputed, see ALLEN, pp. 253–4, with further bibliography. The 'reversed circumflex' is equivalent to the acute of the standard notation when written over a long vowel or diphthong, as in βασιλεύς (see § 27).

34. The ancient grammarians classified words according to the syllable on which the accent fell, counting syllables from the end of the word, and whether the accent was an acute or a circumflex. The terminology they use has been borrowed by modern scholars and is still in use:

ὀξύτονος (oxytone) = having the acute on the final syllable: λιγυρός

περισπώμενος (perispomenon) = having the circumflex on the final syllable: λιγυροῦ

παροξύτονος (paroxytone) = having the acute on the penultimate syllable: πατέρα

προπερισπώμενος (properispomenon) = having the circumflex on the penultimate syllable: σωτῆρα

προπαροξύτονος (proparoxytone) = having the acute on the antepenultimate syllable: λεγόμενος

As we shall note again later (§ 64), the acute can only fall on one of the last three syllables in a word and the circumflex only on one of the last two, so the five combinations of accent type — acute or circumflex — and accented syllable given here exhaust the possibilities.

1. Introductory (§§ 33–5)

Accentuation and the fragments of ancient Greek music

35. When words are sung to a musical melody, there is normally some distortion of the sounds of speech. This can result in loss of clarity, as becomes obvious if one tries to follow the words of an opera without prior preparation. In some types of ancient Greek music the accentual pitch movements are obscured by the melody. Dionysius of Halicarnassus comments on this happening to some lines from a chorus of Euripides' *Orestes* (140–2):

Τάς τε λέξεις τοῖς μέλεσιν ὑποτάττειν ἀξιοῖ καὶ οὐ τὰ μέλη ταῖς λέξεσιν, ὡς ἐξ ἄλλων τε πολλῶν δῆλον καὶ μάλιστα τῶν Εὐριπίδου μελῶν ἃ πεποίηκεν τὴν Ἠλέκτραν λέγουσαν ἐν Ὀρέστῃ πρὸς τὸν χορόν·

σίγα σίγα, λευκὸν ἴχνος ἀρβύλης
τίθετε, μὴ κτυπεῖτ᾽·
ἀποπρόβατ᾽ ἐκεῖσ᾽, ἀποπρό μοι κοίτας.

Ἐν γὰρ δὴ τούτοις τὸ σίγα σίγα λευκὸν ἐφ᾽ ἑνὸς φθόγγου μελῳδεῖται, καίτοι τῶν τριῶν λέξεων ἑκάστη βαρείας τε τάσεις ἔχει καὶ ὀξείας. Καὶ τὸ ἀρβύλης ἐπὶ μέσῃ συλλαβῇ τὴν τρίτην ὁμότονον ἔχει, ἀμηχάνου ὄντος ἐν ὄνομα δύο λαβεῖν ὀξείας. Καὶ τοῦ τίθετε βαρυτέρα μὲν ἡ πρώτη γίνεται, δύο δ᾽ αἱ μετ᾽ αὐτὴν ὀξύτονοί τε καὶ ὁμόφωνοι. Τοῦ τε κτυπεῖτ᾽ ὁ περισπασμὸς ἠφάνισται· μιᾷ γὰρ αἱ δύο συλλαβαὶ λέγονται τάσει. Καὶ τὸ ἀποπρόβατε οὐ λαμβάνει τὴν τῆς μέσης συλλαβῆς προσῳδίαν ὀξεῖαν, ἀλλ᾽ ἐπὶ τὴν τετάρτην συλλαβὴν καταβέβηκεν ἡ τάσις τῆς τρίτης. (Dionysius of Halicarnassus, *De compositione verborum* 11. 19–21, ed. G. Aujac and M. Lebel (Budé, 1981))

'And [music] demands that the words be subordinated to the melody, not the melody to the words. This is clear from, among many other things, the melody that Euripides has made Electra sing to the chorus in the *Orestes*:

σίγα σίγα, λευκὸν ἴχνος ἀρβύλης
τίθετε, μὴ κτυπεῖτ᾽·
ἀποπρόβατ᾽ ἐκεῖσ᾽, ἀποπρό μοι κοίτας.

19

For in these lines σίγα σίγα, λευκὸν is sung on one note, although each of the three words has both low and high pitches. And ἀρβύλης is sung with the third syllable equal in pitch to the second, although it's impossible for one word to take two acutes. And in τίθετε the first syllable is sung on a lower pitch while the two after it are high pitched and equal in pitch to one another. And the circumflex of κτυπεῖτ' has been obliterated, for the two syllables are sung on a single pitch. And ἀποπρόβᾱτε doesn't receive the high pitch that belongs to the middle syllable, but the pitch of the third syllable has moved onto the fourth.'

On this passage see further PÖHLMANN AND WEST, pp. 10–11.

36. It was not, however, always the case that the accent was disregarded in the setting of words to music. Evidence comes from fragments of ancient Greek musical notation, preserved mostly on inscriptions or papyrus. Some of the fragments are transmitted with words for singing, and of these some show a tendency for the melody not to conflict with the relative pitches of vowels as determined by the accentuation.

37. The following points of correspondence between the words as spoken and as sung are especially noteworthy:

(a) The accented syllable of a word is usually sung on a note no lower than that of any other syllable in the word.

(b) On long vowels that take two notes the first note is usually the higher if the syllable has a circumflex, but the second note if the syllable has an acute. Cf. § 27.

(c) A final syllable with a grave accent (as written in our printed texts) is sung on a note no lower than that of any other syllable in its word, but no higher than the accented and pre-accented syllables of the following word.

See WEST, *MUSIC*, p. 199. Notice that tendency (c) demonstrates the special accentual status of the grave appearing within the sentence on the final syllable of an oxytone word such as βασιλεὺς (cf. § 31): see WACKERNAGEL, *ZEUGNISS*; EHRLICH, p. 252.

1. Introductory (§§ 35–9)

38. The earliest surviving fragment of Greek musical notation displaying such correspondences between melody and word accent comes from the third century BC. Our evidence suggests that the melody largely respected the word accent in non-strophic compositions, i.e. in compositions not characterised by the presence of groups of lines or strophes each matching the metrical structure of a following group or antistrophe. In strophic compositions (such as the chorus from Euripides' *Orestes* discussed by Dionysius of Halicarnassus, quoted in § 35), on the other hand, a strophe and the corresponding antistrophe were sung to the same melody. If the melody had respected the word accents in such compositions, the words of the antistrophe would have had to be chosen so as to correspond in accent to those of the strophe. We have no evidence that such an accentually-determined choice of words was ever made.

See E. Pöhlmann, *Griechische Musikfragmente: Ein Weg zur altgriechischen Musik* (Hans Carl 1960), p 23; WEST, *MUSIC*, pp. 198–9.

39. The fragments of ancient Greek music help to confirm the accuracy of what we know from other sources about the syllable on which the accent fell in a given word, and corroborate our impression that the most important phonetic characteristic of the Greek accent was raised pitch.

For an excellent and accessible introduction to all aspects of ancient Greek music, see WEST, *MUSIC*. The extant fragments of ancient Greek music are collected, with commentary and transcription into modern musical notation, by PÖHLMANN AND WEST.

21

Chapter 2: Basic Information

Lengths of vowels and weights of syllables

40. For the correct placement of the Greek accents it is important to know which vowels are long and which are short (especially in final and penultimate syllables). It is also important to distinguish carefully between the length of a vowel and the weight of a syllable. For Greek accentuation the lengths of the vowels in a word always play a rôle. The weights of the syllables in most cases do not. They are, however, discussed in this chapter both because we shall encounter a number of rules that do depend on syllable weight (§§ 158, 170–2, 176–9, 181–2, 184–5, 198, 212, 214, 255–6, 290) and because in order not to confuse syllabic weight with vowel quantity it is useful to have a clear grasp of both.

Lengths of vowels

41. Greek vowels are either long or short. The vowels η and ω are always long, ε and ο always short. The vowels α, ι, and υ are sometimes long and sometimes short. In this book, α, ι, and υ are marked with a macron when long (ᾱ, ῑ, ῡ) and left unmarked when short (α, ι, υ). Because the circumflex accent can fall only on a long vowel or diphthong, a vowel marked with a circumflex may be assumed to be long. A macron is not placed in this book over a vowel that is already marked with a circumflex.

42. Although in this book the macron is used to indicate long ᾱ, ῑ, and ῡ, the lengths of α, ι, and υ in individual words (especially in the last two syllables) should be gradually committed to memory. (It is helpful to adopt the practice of always writing a macron over a long ᾱ, ῑ, and ῡ.) In cases of doubt, the length of the vowel may be looked up in LSJ or, if the vowel is in an ending, in a Greek grammar that indicates vowel lengths. The lengths of α, ι, and υ vowels frequently encountered in endings are as follows:

Long:
  (a) Nominative, vocative, and accusative singular endings of most first-declension nouns keeping alpha throughout the singular: nom. χώρᾱ, voc. χώρᾱ, acc. χώρᾱν. But some, such as μοῖρᾰ and γέφῡρᾰ, have a short ᾰ in these cases.
  (b) Nominative, vocative, and accusative singular endings of the feminines of adjectives (including participles) declining according to the first and second declensions, where these endings have alpha: nom. μακρά, voc. μακρά, acc. μακράν.
  (c) Every first-declension genitive singular ending that has alpha: χώρᾱς, μοίρᾱς.
  (d) First-declension accusative plural ending -ᾱς: τῑμάς, χώρᾱς, νεᾱνίᾱς.
  (e) First-declension nominative/accusative dual ending -ᾱ: τῑμά, χώρᾱ, νεᾱνίᾱ.
  (f) The masculine first-declension nominative singular ending when it has alpha: νεᾱνίᾱς.
  (g) Vocative singular ending -ᾱ and accusative singular ending -ᾱν of masculine first-declension nouns with nominative singular in -ᾱς: νεᾱνίᾱ, νεᾱνίᾱν.
  (h) Accusative singular ending -έᾱ and accusative plural ending -έᾱς of nouns in -εύς: βασιλέᾱ, βασιλέᾱς.
  (i) Accusative singular ending -έᾱ of names in -κλῆς: Περικλέᾱ.

(j) The alpha that begins the endings of participles in -ᾱς, -ᾱσα, -αν, in those forms in which it precedes sigma: λύσᾱς, λύσᾱσι, λύσᾱσα, λύσᾱσαν, etc.

(k) The alpha of the third person plural perfect indicative active or (for μι-verbs) third person plural present indicative active ending -ᾱσι: λελύκᾱσι, ἱστᾶσι, διδόᾱσι.

(l) The upsilon of verbs in -νῡμι in the singular forms of the present and imperfect indicative active, in the second singular present imperative active, and in the forms of the present participle active in which the upsilon precedes sigma: pres. δείκνῡμι, δείκνῡς, δείκνῡσι; imperf. ἐδείκνῡν, ἐδείκνῡς, ἐδείκνῡ; imperat. δείκνῡ; part. δεικνύς, δεικνῦσι, δεικνῦσα, δεικνῦσαν, etc.

(m) All alphas arising from contraction. Note especially the contractions in contract verbs of type τῑμάω: τῑμᾶτε < τῑμάετε, ἐτίμᾱ < ἐτίμαε, etc.

Short:

(n) Nominative, vocative, and accusative singular endings of first-declension nouns with alpha in the nominative, vocative, and accusative singular but η (in Attic) in the genitive and dative singular: nom. μοῦσᾰ, voc. μοῦσᾰ, acc. μοῦσᾰν; cf. gen. μούσης, dat. μούσῃ.

(o) Nominative, vocative, and accusative singular endings of the feminines of adjectives (including participles) declining according to the first and third declensions: nom. μέλαινᾰ, voc. μέλαινᾰ, acc. μέλαινᾰν; nom. γλυκεῖᾰ, voc. γλυκεῖᾰ, acc. γλυκεῖᾰν; nom. λύουσᾰ, voc. λύουσᾰ, acc. λύουσᾰν.

(p) Second- and third-declension nominative/accusative plural neuter ending -ᾰ: σοφᾰ́, σώματᾰ.

(q) Third-declension accusative singular ending -ᾰ (but not the alpha of the -έᾱ endings mentioned under (h) and (i) above), dative singular ending -ῐ, accusative plural ending -ᾰς (but not -ᾱς mentioned under (h) above), and dative plural ending -σῐ: ἐλπίδᾰ, ἐλπίδῐ, ἐλπίδᾰς, ἐλπίσῐ.

(r) The iota or upsilon in the nominative, vocative, and accusative singular endings of nouns in -ις, -υς, or -υ with genitive in -εως: πόλῐς, πόλῐ, πόλῐν; πῆχῠς, πῆχῠ, πῆχῠν; ἄστῠ.

(s) Alpha at the end of a numeral: μίᾰ, τρίᾰ, ἑπτᾰ, ἐννέᾰ, δέκᾰ, τριάκοντᾰ, etc.

(t) Alphas and iotas occurring in the endings of finite verb forms and not belonging to diphthongs (see §§ 43–6), except for the alphas mentioned under (k) and (m) above: ἔλῡσᾰ, ἔλῡσᾰς, ἐλύσᾰμεν, ἐλύσᾰτε, ἔλῡσᾰν, λέλυκᾰ, λέλυκᾰς, λελύκᾰμεν, λελύκᾰτε, ἐλῡσάμεθᾰ, λῡσάσθων, λύουσῐ, δίδωμῐ, στῆθῐ, etc.

(u) The alpha that begins the endings of participles in -ᾱς, -ᾱσα, -αν, in those forms in which it precedes nu: λῡσᾰν, λύσᾰντα, λύσᾰντος, λύσᾰντ᾽, etc.

(v) The upsilon of all forms of verbs in -νῡμι other than those listed under (l) above: δείκνῠμεν, δείκνῠτε, δεικνύᾱσι, ἐδείκνῠμεν, ἐδείκνῠτε, ἐδείκνῠσαν, δεικνύοιμι, δεικνύτω, δείκνῠμαι, δείκνῠσαι, δείκνῠται, δεικνύντα, δεικνύντος, δεικνύναι, etc.

43. The following sequences of vowels normally belong to a single syllable, i.e. they are diphthongs: αι, αυ, ει, ευ, οι, ου, ηυ, υι, ᾳ, ῃ, ῳ. Other sequences of vowels normally belong to different syllables. Thus, the words ἰῶτα, χειμῶνα, βουβῶνα, ἀηδόνα, αἰγιαλοῦ, υἱός, διυφαίζω, ἡνιόχῳ, παιήονα, ἐπιτηδείου, βιαίῳ, and διυγιαίνω may be divided into syllables as follows (a single consonant belonging to the same syllable as the vowel that follows: § 48), with syllable divisions indicated by means of a dot:

ἰ.ῶ.τα, χει.μῶ.να, βου.βῶ.να, ἀ.η.δό.να, αἰ.γι.α.λοῦ, υἱ.ός, δι.υ.φαί.νω, ἠ.νι.ό.χῳ, παι.ή.ο.να, ἐ.πι.τη.δεί.ου, βι.αί.ῳ, δι.υ.γι.αί.νω.

Strictly speaking, ει and ου were not pronounced as diphthongs in the classical period but simply as respectively a long *ē* and a long *ō* vowel each with the tongue placed higher in the mouth than for η and ω. For the purposes of dividing syllables and placing the accent, however, they obey the same rules as the diphthongs proper. In this book, as in many Greek grammars, all sequences written as two vowels and belonging to the same syllable are referred to as 'diphthongs'.

44. Sometimes, however, a sequence of vowels that would normally form a diphthong is instead divided between syllables. In such cases, a diaeresis mark (¨) is written over the second vowel in the sequence. Thus, προΐημι, δυϊκοῦ, προϋφαιρέω = προ.ΐ.η.μι, δυ.ϊ.κοῦ, προ.ϋ.φαι.ρέ.ω.

45. Sequences of identical vowels and of vowels that differ only in length always belong to separate syllables: ἀάσατο = ἀ.ά.σα.το. When two iotas occur in sequence a diaeresis mark is usually written even though the division of syllables is predictable: δίϊημι = δι.ΐ.η.μι.

46. All diphthongs are long in duration, although we shall see further on (§§ 66–8) that certain diphthongs are treated *for the purposes of the accentuation rules* as if they were short.

Weights of syllables

47. Greek syllables are either light or heavy. A syllable is light if it ends in a short vowel: λο, γυ, τε, κι. A syllable is heavy if it contains a long vowel or diphthong, or if it ends with a consonant: ἀν, θρω, που, δηκ.

48. A single consonant always belongs to the same syllable as the following vowel. The words λιγυροῦ, ποικίλῳ, and σωτῆρα may be divided into syllables as follows: λι.γυ.ροῦ, ποι.κί.λῳ, σω.τῆ.ρα.

The letters ζ, ξ, and ψ, however, represent clusters of two consonants, not single consonants: see § 51.

49. The first consonant of a cluster of two consonants occurring in the middle of a word (including the first member of a double consonant, such as λλ) generally belongs to the same syllable as the vowel that precedes, while the second consonant belongs to the same syllable as the following vowel: πίπ.τω, νυκ.τί, ἄλ.λου. If the consonant cluster contains more than two consonants (as in ἀνθρώπου), in most cases the syllable division comes between the first and second consonants: ἀν.θρώ.που. (For an important series of exceptions, see § 52).

50. There are exceptions to the rule given for dividing clusters of more than two consonants, and cases where the syllable division is uncertain. But these will not concern us here, since the important point is that in a cluster of more than two consonants falling in the middle of a word the syllable division always falls somewhere within the cluster.

For discussion of the syllabification of consonant clusters, see DEVINE AND STEPHENS, pp. 33–43.

51. The letters ζ, ξ, and ψ represent consonant clusters (σδ, κσ, πσ). When one of these letters appears by itself in the middle of a word the syllable division will come between the two consonants represented by the letter: ἔζη = ἔσ.δη, ἄξω = ἄκ.σω, ἄψω = ἄπ.σω.

52. If a consonant cluster consists of a stop (π, τ, κ, β, δ, γ, φ, θ, χ) followed by a liquid or nasal (ρ, λ, μ, or ν), the syllable division may fall either before the stop or between the stop and the liquid or nasal: πα.τρί or πατ.ρί, τέ.κνου or τέκ.νου, ὕ.πνῳ or ὕπ.νῳ. But when the stop is voiced — β, δ, or γ — and is followed by a nasal — μ, ν — the syllable division is after the stop and before the nasal: δόγ.μα.

53. The weights of syllables in the examples above are as follows:

λι.γυ.ροῦ = light — light — heavy
ποι.κί.λῳ = heavy — light — heavy
σω.τῆ.ρα = heavy — heavy — light
πίπ.τω = heavy — heavy
νυκ.τί = heavy — light
ἄλ.λου = heavy — heavy
ἀν.θρώ.που = heavy — heavy — heavy
ἔσ.δη (ἔζη) = heavy — heavy
ἄκ.σω (ἄξω) = heavy — heavy
ἄπ.σω (ἄψω) = heavy —heavy
πα.τρί = light — light, but πατ.ρί = heavy — light
τέ.κνου = light — heavy, but τέκ.νου = heavy — heavy
ὔ.πνῳ = light — heavy, but ὔπ.νῳ = heavy — heavy
δόγ.μα = heavy — light

54. The syllabification rules do not take account of word boundaries. Thus, a single consonant at the end of a word belongs to the first syllable of the *following* word if there is a following word beginning with a vowel: ἄν.θρω.πο.ς ἔ.λε.γε. Similarly, if a word ends in a vowel and the following word begins with a consonant cluster, the first consonant in the cluster normally belongs to the syllable of the vowel that precedes: εὐ.ρεῖ.α χ.θών. If the consonant cluster consists of a sequence of stop plus liquid or nasal, the syllable division may come, in the usual way, either before the stop or between the stop and the liquid or nasal: εἶ .θρασύς or εἶ θ.ρασύς. But if a stop and a following liquid or nasal belong to different words or to separate parts of a compound word, the syllable division falls between them: ἐκ.λού.ω, ἐκ. μέ.σου.

28

55. However, for the purposes of the rules of Greek accentuation (but not for the purposes of poetic scansion), the syllabification rules may be taken to apply to individual words as if there were no following word. For these purposes a single consonant at the end of a word should simply be ignored: ἄν.θρω.πο(ς) = heavy — heavy — light.

56. Relatively few Greek words end in a consonant cluster, the only possible word-final clusters being ξ and ψ (cf. νύξ, φλέψ). The final syllable in a word ending in ξ or ψ is always heavy, whether another word follows or not, and needs to be taken as heavy for the purposes of the accentuation rules (see § 64c): νύξ = heavy, κῆ.ρυξ = heavy — heavy.

57. Notice that a syllable may be heavy although it contains a short vowel (as the first syllable of νυκ.τί); a syllable containing a *long* vowel will *always* be heavy.

Readers familiar with the scansion of poetry will recognise that heavy syllables are those that 'scan long' in poetry, light syllables those that 'scan short'.

EXERCISE 1: LENGTHS OF VOWELS AND WEIGHTS OF SYLLABLES

Indicate the syllable divisions in the following words, showing which vowels are short and which are long, and which syllables are light and which are heavy. Ignore single consonants at the ends of words, and classify all diphthongs as long vowels.

Examples: ἄνθρωπος, πικρός

ἄν.θρω.πο(ς):   Vowels: short — long — short.
                       Syllables: heavy — heavy — light
πι.κρό(ς) or πικ.ρό(ς): Vowels: short — short.
                       Syllables: light — light or heavy — light.

29

1. κλοπή	11. μῑμητικός	21. πράσσω	31. λαῖλαψ
2. τέχνη	12. γλαυκός	22. εὑρίσκω	32. μάχη
3. ὀφρύϊ	13. φοῖνιξ	23. μιμνήσκω	33. δείκνῡμι
4. ὄγδοος	14. ἐκλέγω	24. Κύπρις	34. τοιούτῳ
5. ἅπαξ	15. ὀφλισκάνω	25. λῡπρός	35. μῑκροψῡχίᾱ
6. νεβρός	16. ἐστράφην	26. ἵζω	36. πρᾶγμα
7. ἔγνων	17. ναυκρατέω	27. αἰσχρῶν	37. ἐμπλέκω
8. ἐκλύω	18. ὀφθαλμός	28. ἐπιεικής	38. λισσόμεθα
9. πενθερός	19. τάξις	29. καλλίστου	
10. ἀγρός	20. Ἀθηναίου	30. Ἀλέξανδρος	

Writing the accents

58. There are three accent marks: acute (´), circumflex (ˆ), and grave (`).

59. The acute and grave accents may fall either on a short vowel or on a long vowel or diphthong. The circumflex may fall only on a long vowel or diphthong (but not on a diphthong that counts 'short' for accentuation: see § 66–8).

60. An accent falling on a single long or short vowel is simply written over the vowel: σωτήρ, σωτὴρ, ἱστᾶσι.

61. An accent falling on a diphthong is written over the second vowel of the diphthong βασιλεύς, βασιλεὺς, βασιλεῦ.

This convention applies to all accents falling on diphthongs (except for the 'long' diphthongs discussed in § 62) although it is somewhat illogical in the case of a circumflex, since the circumflex indicates a high pitch on the first mora of the diphthong (§ 27).

62. This convention does not apply, however, to an accent falling on one of the 'long' diphthongs ᾳ, ῃ, or ῳ. When the iota of these diphthongs is written subscript, it is obvious that the accent cannot be written over the iota and needs simply to be written over the whole letter: κλῄς, κλῇς, λιγυρῷ. The iota of these diphthongs

30

is, however, written adscript (a) when the diphthong occurs at the beginning of a word whose first letter is capitalised, and (b) in certain editions whose convention is always to write iota adscript. Even in these cases the accent is not written over the iota but before (in the case of a capital letter) or over the first vowel of the combination: ῞Αιδης = ᾅδης, ῞Ηισθετο = ᾔσθετο, ῝Ωι = ᾧ, κλῆις = κλῇς, κλῆις = κλῇς, λιγυοῶι = λιγυρῷ. In this book, iotas are written subscript in the diphthongs ᾳ, ῃ, and ῳ except at the beginning of a word whose first letter is capitalised.

Notice that at the beginning of a word it is not only the accent but also the breathing that is written on the first vowel in these (and only these) cases. Notice also that observance of the placement of accents and breathings can help to distinguish between the diphthongs ᾳ and αι at the beginnings of capitalised words or in texts in which all iotas are written adscript. Cf. ῞Αιδης = ᾅδης but Αἰνείᾱς = αἰνείᾱς; αγοραι = ἀγορᾷ but ἀγοραί = ἀγοραί.

Acute and circumflex accents

63. The acute may only fall on one of the last three syllables of a word, the circumflex only on one of the last two. Further restrictions on the position of the accent are described in §§ 64–5. The traditional terms indicating the position of the accent, which were given in § 34, are repeated here for convenience:

oxytone (ὀξύτονος) = having the acute on the final syllable: λιγυρός

perispomenon (περισπώμενος) = having the circumflex on the final syllable: λιγυροῦ

paroxytone (παροξύτονος) = having the acute on the penultimate syllable: πατέρα

properispomenon (προπερισπώμενος) = having the circumflex on the penultimate syllable: σωτῆρα

proparoxytone (προπαροξύτονος) = having the acute on the antepenultimate syllable: λεγόμενος

The English versions of these terms are used in this book and should be committed to memory.

EXERCISE 2: NAMES FOR THE POSITIONS OF THE ACCENT

For each of the following words, say whether it is oxytone, perispomenon, paroxytone, properispomenon, or proparoxytone.

1. κλοπή	8. πράσσω	15. σοφώτατος	22. ἐμπλέκω
2. ἅπαξ	9. λαῖλαψ	16. καλοῦμαι	23. τέχνη
3. κακοῦργος	10. ἐκλύω	17. ὀφλισκάνω	24. ἕτερος
4. Ζεύς	11. μάχη	18. δείκνυμι	25. ὀφθαλμός
5. λῦπρός	12. πρᾶγμα	19. εὑρίσκω	26. μῑμητικός
6. ἴζω	13. νοῦ	20. πατράσι	27. πανοῦργος
7. ἀληθῶς	14. ἀργυροῦς	21. γλαυκός	28. πενθερός

Write each of the following words with the accent indicated, taking care to write an accent falling on a diphthong over the second vowel of the diphthong unless there is an iota subscript written adscript. (The only iota subscripts written adscript in this exercise occur after a capital letter.)

29. φοινιξ (properispomenon)
30. μιμνησκω (paroxytone)
31. λιπειν (perispomenon)
32. ἀνθρωπος (proparoxytone)
33. Κυπρις (paroxytone)
34. νεβρος (oxytone)
35. ἀρετη (perispomenon)
36. αισχρων (perispomenon)
37. Αἰσχυλος (paroxytone)
38. Ζευ (perispomenon)

39. Ἀιδου (paroxytone)
40. αἰχμαλωτος (proparoxytone)
41. μεταβολη (oxytone)
42. νους (perispomenon)
43. οἰμαι (properispomenon)
44. παντοιος (properispomenon)
45. ἐγνων (paroxytone)
46. ναυκρατεω (paroxytone)
47. Ὠιμωζον (proparoxytone)
48. ἀγρος (oxytone)

49. ἀρεται (oxytone)	53. καλλιστου (paroxytone)
50. λιγυρου (perispomenon)	54. σωτηρα (properispomenon)
51. ἱερευσι (properispomenon)	55. ἐκλεγω (paroxytone)
52. Ἀλεξανδρος (proparoxytone)	

Limits on the position of the accent

64. The Greek accent may not fall further than a certain distance from the end of a word. The rules determining this distance are known collectively as the 'law of limitation', and may be stated as follows (an asterisk will be used to indicate an impossible form):

(a) An acute accent may not fall further from the end of the word than the antepenultimate syllable (λεγόμενος is possible but *λέγομενος is not).

(b) A circumflex may not fall further from the end of a word than the penultimate syllable (σωτῆρα is possible but *σῶτηρα is not).

(c) If the final syllable contains a long vowel or ends with a consonant cluster (i.e. is a heavy syllable for the purposes of accentuation: see §§ 55–6), no accent may fall further from the end of the word than the penultimate syllable (λεγομένου, πομφόλυξ, and πολυπῖδαξ are possible but *λεγόμενου, *πόμφολυξ, and *πολύπιδαξ are not).

(d) If the final syllable contains a long vowel, a circumflex may fall only on the final syllable (λιγυροῦ and ἀνθρώπου are possible but *ἀνθρῶπου is not).

For the way in which the law of limitation applies to words ending in a consonant cluster, see most recently D. Steriade, 'Greek Accent: A Case for Preserving Structure', *Linguistic Inquiry* 19 (1988), pp. 273–5. For two restricted sets of exceptions to the law of limitation, see §§ 113, 123.

65. There is one further rule limiting the position of the accent, known as the σωτῆρα rule or 'final trochee rule':

If the final syllable contains a short vowel and the penultimate syllable contains a long accented vowel, the accent on that vowel *must* be a circumflex (σωτῆρα is possible but *σωτήρα is not).

The term 'final trochee rule' has often been used, but is most inappropriate. The term 'trochee' refers to a sequence of two syllables in which the first is heavy and the second light (as in μοῦσα, νύκτα), but the σωτῆρα rule applies to words in which the penultimate syllable has a *long vowel* and the final syllable a *short vowel*, regardless of the weight of the *syllables* involved. Thus, the σωτῆρα rule does not apply to νύκτα although the word has 'trochaic' form. It does apply to κῆρυξ (assuming that κῆρυξ genuinely had a short υ, but see the note to § 156) although the word does not have 'trochaic' form. But cf. also § 290.

'Lengths' of final diphthongs

66. In general, diphthongs count as long vowels for the purposes of the accent. The diphthongs -αι and -οι, however, count as short for accentuation when they occur at the absolute end of a word in indicatives, subjunctives, imperatives, infinitives, or nominatives plural: βούλομαι, βούλονται, βούλωμαι, βούλωνται, παίδευσαι (imperat.), παιδεῦσαι (aor. inf.), ἄνθρωποι, τράπεζαι, οἶκοι (nom. pl.), βουλόμενοι, βουλόμεναι.

67. But in the optative final -αι and -οι count as long: παιδεύσαι (opt.), παιδεύοι. Final -αι and -οι likewise count as long in adverbs with the meaning 'at (a place)', e.g. οἴκοι 'at home', Μεγαροῖ 'at Megara', and in certain interjections, e.g. αἰαῖ 'alas'.

68. Notice that although some final diphthongs count as 'short' for the purposes of the accent rules, they make a syllable 'scan long' in poetry just like other diphthongs.

Recessive words

69. A Greek word whose accent falls as far from the end of the word as permitted by the law of limitation is known as 'recessive'. Many Greek words, including almost all finite verb forms, are recessive. The rules given so far in this chapter will allow you to place the accent correctly on any recessive word, once you know it is recessive. Notice that a monosyllable containing a long vowel or diphthong is recessive only if it has a circumflex (like Ζεῦ), not if it has an acute (like Ζεύς), because the circumflex represents an accent on the first part, or *mora*, of the long vowel or diphthong, the acute an accent on the second *mora* (see §§ 26–8).

EXERCISE 3: RECESSIVE WORDS

(a) Look again at the words in exercise 2. Which of them are recessive?

(b) The following parts of λύω are all recessive. Write them with their correct accents.

1. λῡω	8. λῡσατω	15. λῡσαιμεθα	22. ἐλῡοντο
2. λῡεις	9. λελυκοι	16. λῡοι	23. λυθησομαι
3. ἐλελυκη	10. λῡονται	17. λελυμαι	
4. λῡσοιντο	11. λῡειν	18. ἐλυθησαν	
5. λῡουσι	12. λῡσοιο	19. λῡσομενοι	
6. λελυνται	13. λῡη	20. λῡσαι (aor. imperat. mid.)	
7. λῡηται	14. λῡε	21. λῡσαι (aor. opt.)	

Rules of contraction

70. When two vowels contract into one, if neither of the contracted vowels was accented in the uncontracted form, the accent remains in the same place as in the uncontracted form: Περίκλεες > Περίκλεις (voc.).

71. If, however, one of the vowels of the uncontracted form was accented, then the contracted vowel will also carry the accent. The accent of the contracted form is a circumflex if the accent of the uncontracted form fell on the first of the two original vowels, or if

the accent of the uncontracted form was a circumflex: Περικλέης >
Περικλῆς, φιλέετε > φιλεῖτε, ἱππῆες > ἱππῆς, σῡκεῶν > σῡκῶν.

72. If the uncontracted form had an acute on the second of the
two vowels, the accent of the contracted form is an acute: κληΐς >
κλῄς.

73. However, the σωτῆρα rule (§ 65) takes precedence over the
rule in § 72. Thus, κληδο-όχος contracts to κληδοῦχος, not to
*κληδούχος, which would violate the σωτῆρα rule.

74. Certain contracted forms violate the normal rules of
contraction; these will be discussed under the rules for accenting
particular categories of word. (See §§ 96, 112, 121–2, 127.)

EXERCISE 4: CONTRACTED WORDS
Write the following contracted words with their correct accents
(uncontracted forms are given in parentheses):

1. ῥους (ῥόος)
2. αἰδω (αἰδόα)
3. φιλητε (φιλέητε)
4. φιλει (imperat.) (φίλεε)
5. φιλει (indic.) (φιλέει)
6. Ἑρμης (Ἑρμέᾱς)
7. Ἑρμων (Ἑρμεῶν)
8. ἐτῑμᾱ (ἐτίμαε)
9. φιλουμεθα (φιλεόμεθα)
10. ἑστιουχος (ἑστιο-όχος)
11. ζως (ζωός)

The grave accent

75. An 'oxytone' word such as ἀγαθός, which when written in
isolation has an acute on the final syllable, normally changes its
acute to a grave when it is followed by another word in the same
sentence, as long as punctuation or verse-end does not intervene:

ὁ ἀνὴρ ἀγαθός.
but
ἀγαθὸς ὁ ἀνήρ.

36

2. Basic Information (§§ 71–7)

Cf. (with an oxytone word at verse-end):

γήραϊ δὴ πολέμοιο πεπαυμένοι, ἀλλ᾽ ἀγορηταί
ἐσθλοί, τεττίγεσσιν ἐοικότες,... (*Il.* 3. 150–1)

Notice that it is only the acute on a genuine oxytone word that changes to a grave in this way. A word whose final vowel is lost, or *elided*, before another vowel does not change an acute on the preceding vowel to a grave: ἔνθ᾽ ἄλλοι = ἔνθα ἄλλοι.

Not all editors retain an acute on a final syllable at verse-end. Thus, D.B. Monro and T.W. Allen (OCT) print ἀλλ᾽ ἀγορηταὶ / ἐσθλοί,... at *Il.* 3. 150–1, but see WACKERNAGEL, *BEITRÄGE*, p. 8; WEST, *AESCHYLUS*, p. xxxi (suggesting, however, that a *proclitic* at verse-end should *not* be written with a final acute; on proclitics see §§ 267–77, 296).

76. There are two exceptions to the rule given in § 75. The first is that the interrogative form τίς 'who?', and its neuter τί 'what?', never change their acute to a grave: τίς ἔνδον; 'Who is inside?'

77. The second exception is that an acute on a final syllable remains before certain words called *enclitics*. The most commonly encountered enclitics are the following (for a fuller list, a definition of enclitics, and further details of their effects on accentuation, see §§ 278–300):

(a) All forms of the indefinite pronoun τις 'someone, a certain', τι 'something'.

(b) The indefinite adverbs πω 'up to this time', πη 'somehow', που 'somewhere', ποι 'to somewhere', πως 'somehow', ποτέ 'at some time', ποθέν 'from somewhere', ποθί 'somewhere'.

(c) The non-emphasised pronoun forms με, μου, μοι, σε, σου, σοι, ἑ, οὑ, οἱ.

(d) Present indicative forms of εἰμί 'I am' and φημί 'I say', except for (i) the second person singular forms εἶ, φής, and (ii) the third person singular form when it is paroxytone ἔστι. (But see § 283.)

(e) The particles γε, τε, νυν (but not νῦν 'now'), νυ, κε(ν), τοι, ῥα, περ.

Thus, αὐτός μοι, γυνή τις, ἀνήρ φησι.

We postpone discussion of the rules for writing the enclitics themselves to §§ 278–300, where we shall see that after a word with an acute on the final syllable an enclitic is normally written without accent: see § 285 but compare § 297.

EXERCISE 5: THE GRAVE ACCENT

The underlined words in the following passage all have an acute on the final syllable when written in isolation. They have been written here without accents for the sake of practice. Write them with the correct accents for their contexts in the sentences.

οὗτος ἐμος τε ἑταῖρος ἦν ἐκ νέου καὶ ὑμῶν τῷ πλήθει ἑταῖρός τε καὶ συνέφυγε τὴν φυγὴν ταύτην καὶ μεθ' ὑμῶν κατῆλθε. καὶ ἴστε δὴ οἷος ἦν Χαιρεφῶν, ὡς σφοδρος ἐφ' ὅτι ὁρμήσειεν. καὶ δὴ ποτε[1] καὶ εἰς Δελφους ἐλθὼν ἐτόλμησε τοῦτο μαντεύσασθαι — καὶ, ὅπερ λέγω, μη θορυβεῖτε, ὦ ἄνδρες — ἤρετο γαρ δη εἴ τις ἐμοῦ εἴη σοφώτερος. ἀνεῖλεν οὖν ἡ Πυθίᾱ μηδένα σοφώτερον εἶναι. καὶ τούτων πέρι ὁ ἀδελφος ὑμῖν αὐτοῦ οὑτοσι μαρτυρήσει, ἐπειδη ἐκεῖνος τετελεύτηκεν.

Σκέψασθε δη ὧν ἕνεκα ταῦτα λέγω· μέλλω γαρ ὑμᾶς διδάξειν ὅθεν μοι ἡ διαβολη γέγονεν. ταῦτα γαρ ἐγω ἀκούσᾱς ἐνεθῡμούμην οὑτωσι· "Τι[2] ποτε[3] λέγει ὁ θεος, καὶ τι[4] ποτε[5] αἰνίττεται; ἐγω γαρ δη οὔτε μέγα οὔτε σμῑκρον σύνοιδα ἐμαυτῷ σοφος ὤν· τι[6] οὖν ποτε λέγει φάσκων ἐμε σοφώτατον εἶναι; οὐ γαρ δήπου ψεύδεταί γε· οὐ γαρ θέμις αὐτῷ." καὶ πολυν μεν χρόνον ἠπόρουν τι[7] ποτε[8] λέγει· (Plato, *Apology of Socrates* 21a–b)

[1]Indef. [2]Interrog. [3]Indef. [4]Interrog. [5]Indef. [6]Interrog. [7]Interrog. [8]Indef.

Elided words

78. The loss, or *elision*, of the final vowel of a word before another vowel affects the accent of the word only when the lost vowel would normally carry the accent. In such a case the elided word has instead an acute (never a circumflex) on the penultimate syllable: πόλλ᾽ ἐπέτελλον (unelided form πολλά), εἴπ᾽ ἐμοί (unelided form εἰπέ), δεῖν᾽ ἔδρᾱσας (unelided form δεινά). If, however, the elided word is a preposition (e.g. ἐπί, παρά), or one of the conjunctions οὐδέ, μηδέ, ἀλλά, ἠδέ ('and'), ἰδέ ('and'), or one of the indefinites τινά 'someone, a certain' (acc. sg. masc./fem. or nom./acc. pl. neut.) or ποτέ 'at some time', the elided form has *no accent*: παρ᾽ ἐμοῦ, ἀλλ᾽ οὖν, ἀλλ᾽ οὐδ᾽ ὡς, οὐδέν ποτ᾽ ἄλλο.

The words that fail to acquire an accent on the penultimate syllable when elided are proclitic or (in the case of τινά and ποτέ) enclitic (but see further the notes to §§ 274, 275, 294). Proclitics and enclitics are defined and discussed in chapter 7; cf. also § 77.

Ancient grammarians debated whether the accent on an elided word such as δεῖν᾽, with long vowel or diphthong in the syllable before the elision, should be an acute or a circumflex: see the passages cited by CHANDLER, pp. 255–6; cf. EHRLICH, pp. 262–5. Modern editorial practice follows the rule as given above (with acute).

79. If a monosyllabic word is elided, it simply loses its accent: μέσσῳ δ᾽ ἀμφοτέρων (unelided form δέ). (Cf. § 295.)

EXERCISE 6: ELIDED WORDS

Write the underlined elided words in the following phrases with their correct accents, given the unelided forms shown in parentheses. (Oxytone words are given in parentheses in the form with final acute even if they would, if not elided, have had a grave in the sentence.)

1. πολλὰ <u>κακ᾿</u> ἀνθρώπους ἐεόργει· (κακά) (*Od.* 14. 289)
2. πατρῷον <u>δ᾿</u> ἐκτίνεις <u>τιν᾿</u> ἆθλον. (δέ, indef. τινά) (Soph., *Antigone* 856)
3. <u>ἀγλα᾿</u> ἄποινα / οὐκ ἔθελον δέξασθαι. (ἀγλαά) (*Il.* 1. 111–12)
4. ἆ <u>δειλ᾿</u>, ἦ μάλα δή σε κιχάνεται αἰπὺς ὄλεθρος. (δειλέ) (*Il.* 11. 441)
5. οὐκ ἄν τις <u>αὐτ᾿</u> ἔμαρψεν ἄλλος <u>ἀντ᾿</u> ἐμοῦ. (αὐτά, ἀντί) (Soph., *Ajax* 444)
6. <u>ἀλλ᾿</u> εἴ τι χρήζεις ἱστορεῖν, <u>παρειμ᾿</u> ἐγώ. (ἀλλά, πάρειμι) (Soph., *Trachiniae* 397)
7. ἤδη <u>ποτ᾿</u> εἶδον <u>ἀνδρ᾿</u> ἐγὼ γλώσσῃ θρασύν. (indefinite ποτέ, ἄνδρα) (Soph., *Ajax* 1142)
8. ἔκλαγξαν <u>δ᾿</u> <u>ἀρ᾿</u> ὀϊστοὶ <u>ἐπ᾿</u> ὤμων χωομένοιο. (δέ, ἄρα, ἐπί) (*Il.* 1. 46)
9. ὣς <u>ἔφατ᾿</u>, <u>οὐδ᾿</u> ἀπίθησε ποδήνεμος ὠκέα Ἶρις. (ἔφατο, οὐδέ) (*Il.* 11. 195)
10. οἳ <u>δ᾿</u> Ἀσπληδόνα ναῖον <u>ἰδ᾿</u> Ὀρχομενὸν Μινύειον, / τῶν <u>ἦρχ᾿</u> Ἀσκάλαφος καὶ Ἰάλμενος. (δέ, ἰδέ 'and', ἦρχε) (*Il.* 2. 511–12)

Prodelision and crasis

80. In poetry, a short vowel beginning a word is sometimes lost after a word ending in a long vowel or diphthong ('prodelision', or 'aphaeresis'): μὴ 'μοί = μὴ ἐμοί, μὴ 'γώ = μὴ ἐγώ, ποῦ 'στιν = ποῦ ἐστιν. No modification of the accent results unless the lost vowel would have been accented and the preceding word is oxytone. In

40

such a case the oxytone word retains its acute accent rather than changing it to a grave. Thus ἃ μή 'θιγες = ἃ μὴ ἔθιγες (Soph., *Antigone* 546).

This rule rests solely on the evidence of manuscripts and is not followed by all editors. Thus, at Soph., *Antigone* 546, Lloyd-Jones and Wilson (OCT) print ἃ μὴ 'θιγες.

81. When the final vowel of a word contracts with the initial vowel of the following word ('crasis'), the original accent of the first word is lost while that of the second word is kept: κἀγαθός = καὶ ἀγαθός, ὦνθρωπε = ὦ ἄνθρωπε, τοὐρανοῦ = τοῦ οὐρανοῦ, τἀν = τὰ ἐν. However, the sequence resulting from crasis must obey the σωτῆρα rule (§ 65), and an acute is replaced by a circumflex if the σωτῆρα rule requires it: τοὖργον = τὸ ἔργον.

There is, however, uncertainty in our evidence on the last point: see CHANDLER, pp. 261–3; VENDRYES, p. 250. Not all modern editors make the combined words obey the σωτῆρα rule. Thus, at Soph., *Antigone* 542, Lloyd-Jones and Wilson (OCT) print τοὔργον, not τοὖργον.

EXERCISE 7: PRODELISION AND CRASIS

Write the following phrases with their correct accents, given the full forms shown in parentheses:

1. ἁνηρ (ὁ ἀνήρ)
2. κἀκει (καὶ ἐκεῖ)
3. τοὖπος (τὸ ἔπος)
4. οὑνεκα (οὗ ἕνεκα)
5. θἠμερᾳ (τῇ ἡμέρᾳ)
6. προὗργου (πρὸ ἔργου)

7. εἰ μη 'σθιε (εἰ μὴ ἔσθιε)
   (Ar., *Knights* 1106)
8. ἡ 'ξομη (ἡ ἐξομῇ) (Soph., *Antigone* 535)
9. τοὐψον (τὸ ὄψον) (Ar., *Knights* 1106)
10. τρεπεται δη 'πειτα (τρέπεται δὴ ἔπειτα)
    (Ar., *Wasps* 665)

41

Chapter 3: Accentuation of Verbs

Accents of finite verbs: non-contracted

82. Finite verbs (i.e. verbs in the indicative, subjunctive, optative, and imperative) are generally recessive: ἔβη, μένε, μένεις, μένῃς, μεῖναι (opt.), μεῖνον (imperat.), ἔβαινον, ἤθελον, παίδευσαι (imperat.), παιδεῦσαι (opt.), λεγόμεθα, λεγώμεθα, λέγωνται.

83. But second person singular imperatives of the second (or 'strong') aorist middle are perispomenon: λαβοῦ, λιποῦ. Herodian, however, tells us that ἰδου 'look!' is recessive (though manuscripts and modern texts sometimes have ἰδοῦ).

Ionic forms in -εο such as πύθεο are recessive. On the interjection ἰδού 'behold', see §§ 265, 267b, 277.

84. Five imperatives of the second (or 'strong') aorist active are oxytone in the second person singular: εἰπέ, ἐλθέ, εὑρέ, and, in Attic, ἰδέ, λαβέ. The μι-verb imperative φαθί is also oxytone.

85. The word χρή 'it is necessary', which was originally a noun, is oxytone.

86. Most of the present indicative forms of εἰμί 'I am' and φημί 'I say' are *enclitic*; these will be discussed in chapter 7 (see §§ 278–97 and esp. §§ 279d, 282–3).

EXERCISE 8: FINITE VERBS

Write the following finite verbs with their correct accents:

1. μαχομαι
2. λυσαιμι
3. ἐζευξατε
4. λαθου
5. πυθου
6. λαθε
7. βουλευοι
8. φαθι
9. λελοιπα
10. λυσοι
11. διδοιην
12. θου
13. χρη
14. ἐλαθον
15. λιπωμεν

16. διδωμι
17. ἐλθε
18. φευγε
19. λυσαις
20. παυσον
21. λιπου
22. φυγε
23. γενου
24. φευγε
25. ἐθου
26. τιθεμεν
27. εἰπον
28. ἐθελει
29. πυνθανη
30. ἐζευξας

31. δεικνυμαι
32. ἐφυλαξα
33. γεγραμμαι
34. βουλευσον
35. πυθωμεθα
36. βασιλευοι
37. λελυκητε
38. βουλευοιτε
39. πυνθανομαι
40. λιπωνται
41. βουλευσαι (aor. imperat. mid.)
42. ἰδου 'look!' (Herodian's accent)
43. λυσαι (aor. imperat. mid.)
44. εἰπε (3rd sg. aor. indic.)
45. παυσαι (aor. imperat. mid.)

46. πυνθανωμαι
47. ἰδε (Attic accent)
48. λυσαι (aor. opt.)
49. εἰπε (aor. imperat.)
50. παυσαι (aor. opt.)
51. λαβε (Attic accent)
52. βασιλευσον
53. εὑρε (aor. imperat.)
54. βασιλευοιμι
55. λελοιπαμεν

Accents of finite verbs: contracted

87. In contracted verbs, the *uncontracted* form has a recessive accent and the accent of the contracted form is derived by the rules of contraction (§§ 70–4): ἐφίλεε > ἐφίλει, φίλεε (imperat.) > φίλει, φιλέει (indic.) > φιλεῖ, φιλέω > φιλῶ, φιλέομεν > φιλοῦμεν.

88. Contracted verbs include the following:

(a) Present and imperfect tenses of verbs in -άω, -έω, -όω: τῑμάω > τῑμῶ, φιλέη > φιλῇ, δηλόοιμεν > δηλοῖμεν, τῑμάετε > τῑμᾶτε, ἐφιλέομεν > ἐφιλοῦμεν, τῑμάομαι > τῑμῶμαι, φιλέησθε > φιλῆσθε, δηλόοιο > δηλοῖο, τῑμάεσθε > τῑμᾶσθε, ἐτῑμάου > ἐτῑμῶ, ἐτῑμαόμεθα > ἐτῑμώμεθα.

(b) 'Attic' futures in -ῶ or -οῦμαι are accented (in all their moods) as if they were contracted (and historically some of them were): φανῶ, φανεῖς, φανεῖ, φανοῦμεν, φανεῖτε, φανοῦσι (as if from φανέ-ω, -εις, -ει, -ομεν, -ετε, -ουσι); φανοῦμαι, φανεῖ or φανῇ, φανεῖται, φανούμεθα, φανεῖσθε, φανοῦνται (as if from φαν-έ-ομαι, -έ-ει or -έ-η, -έ-εται, -ε-όμεθα, -έ-εσθε, -έ-ονται); opt. φανοίην or φανοῖμι (as if from φανε-οίην, φανέ-οιμι); φανοίμην, φανοῖο (as if from φανε-οίμην, φανέ-οιο). Similarly e.g. ἀγγελῶ, φθερῶ, τεμῶ, κτενῶ, κομιῶ, ἀρῶ, σκεδῶ.

(c) The third person plural present indicatives ἱστᾶσι and ἱᾶσι, and the third person plural perfect indicatives ἑστᾶσι, τεθνᾶσι.

(d) Aorists subjunctive passive, and subjunctives of -μι verbs, but not of -νῡμι verbs or of εἶμι 'I shall go', and not perfect subjunctives with -κ- or subjunctives of *first aorists*, such as στήσω. Thus, the following forms are contracted: λυθῶ (from λυθή-ω), λυθῆς (as if from λυθή-ης), λυθῶμεν (as if from λυθή-ωμεν), ἱστῶ (from ἱστά-ω), τιθῶ (from τιθή-ω), διδῶ (from διδώ-ω), ἱστῶμαι (as if from ἱστά-ωμαι), ἱστῇ (as if from ἱστά-η), θῆς (as if from θή-ης), δώμεθα (as if from δω-ώμεθα). The following forms (subjunctives of -νῡμι verbs, of εἶμι 'I shall go', perfect subjunctives with -κ-, and subjunctives of *first aorists*) are not contracted but simply recessive: δεικνύω, δεικνύῃς, δεικνύωμεν, ἴω, ἴῃ, ἴωσι, ἑστήκω, ἑστήκητε, ἑστήκωσι, στήσω, στήσῃς, στήσωμεν. The subjunctives of three μι-type middle verbs with no actives corresponding, δύναμαι, ἐπίσταμαι, and κρέμαμαι 'I hang', are also treated as not contracted, i.e. they are simply recessive: δύνωμαι, ἐπίστωμαι, κρέμωμαι.

For the proper historical development of the contracted forms, see A.L. Sihler, *New Comparative Grammar of Greek and Latin* (OUP, 1995), pp. 593-4.

(e) Aorists optative passive, and optatives of -μι verbs (but not of -νῡμι verbs or of εἶμι 'I shall go', and not perfect optatives with -κ- or optatives of *first aorists*, such as στήσαιμι), are accented as if they were contracted from recessive forms in which the -ι- formed a separate syllable: λυθείην (as if from λυθε-ί-ην), λυθεῖμεν (as if from λυθέ-ί-μεν), ἱσταίην (as if from ἱστα-ί-ην), ἱσταίημεν (as if from ἱστα-ί-ημεν), ἱσταῖμεν (as if from ἱστά-ί-μεν), ἱσταῖεν (as if from ἱστά-ί-εν), ἱσταίμην (as if from ἱστα-ί-μην), ἱσταῖο (as if from ἱστά-ί-ο), ἱσταίμεθα (as if from ἱστα-ί-μεθα), ἱσταῖσθε (as if from ἱστά-ί-σθε), σταίην (as if from στα-ί-ην), σταῖμεν (as if from στά-ί-μεν). The following forms (optatives of -νῡμι verbs, of εἶμι 'I shall go', perfect optatives with -κ-, and optatives of *first aorists*) are not contracted but simply recessive: δεικνύοιμι, δεικνύοις, δεικνύοιτε, ἴοιμι, ἴοιμεν, ἴοιεν, ἑστήκοιμι, ἑστήκοι, ἑστήκοιτε, στήσαιμεν, στήσαιο, στήσαιτο. The optatives of the three μι-type middle verbs mentioned under (d) above, δύναμαι, ἐπίσταμαι, and κρέμαμαι 'I hang', are also simply recessive: δυναίμην, δύναιο, δύναιτο.

The correct historical explanation for the accentuation of the 'contracted' optatives is unclear. For discussion, see LEJEUNE, *REMARQUES*, pp. 64–5.

(f) A few verbs with perfect stem ending in a vowel, such as κτάομαι and μιμνήσκω, form a perfect subjunctive middle and perfect optative middle by adding subjunctive or optative endings to the vowel stem, instead of using periphrastic forms of the type λελυμένος ὦ, λελυμένος εἴην, etc. When this happens, the forms are contracted and accented accordingly: subj. κεκτῶμαι (< κεκτή-ωμαι), opt. κεκτήμην (< κεκτη-ί-μην), κεκτῆο (< κεκτή-ί-ο) or κεκτῴμην (< κεκτη-οίμην), κεκτῷο (< κεκτή-οιο); subj. μεμνῶμαι (< μεμνή-ωμαι), opt. μεμνήμην (< μεμνη-ί-μην) or μεμνῴμην (< μεμνη-οίμην).

EXERCISE 9: CONTRACTED VERBS

The following finite verb forms obey the rules given in §§ 87–8. Write them with their correct accents:

1. δηλουσι	22. τεμει	43. λειφθωσι	64. φανουμαι
2. δωτε	23. κτενεις	44. ἐτῑμᾱσθε	65. φιλει (indic.)
3. τῑμᾱς	24. θω	45. ἱσταιμεθα	66. τιθωμεθα
4. φιλωσι	25. φανοιεν	46. κομιουμεν	67. φανουμεθα
5. στωμεν	26. ἱη	47. στησαιτε	68. φανειητε
6. τιθω	27. λειφθης	48. ἱστωμαι	69. φανη (fut.)
7. τιθειεν	28. τιθωμεν	49. φανειμεν	70. φανεισθε
8. διδως	29. φιλου	50. δεδωκοιμι	71. τῑμωμαι (indic.)
9. ἱησθε	30. διδοιη	51. ἀρουμεν	72. τῑμωμαι (subj.)
10. ἱειτε	31. στησαιτο	52. λειφθωμεν	73. φανουνται
11. ἱσταιο	32. διδωνται	53. λυθειτε	74. γελωμεν (subj.)
12. τεμεις	33. τιθειτε	54. ἱσταιης	75. φιλει (imperat.)
13. δωσι	34. ἀρω (fut.)	55. δυναιντο	76. φιλω (indic.)
14. εἰεν	35. τῑμῳο	56. φθερειτε	77. φιλω (subj.)
15. λειφθω	36. ἱσταιμεν	57. λυθειης	78. κεκτῳτο (opt.)
16. φανοισθε	37. στησαιο	58. φανειην	79. γελωμαι (indic.)
17. ἰοιτε	38. δηλωμεν	59. κομιουσι	80. κεκτηται (subj.)
18. λυθωμεν	39. λυθη	60. κομιουμεθα	81. τεμω (fut.)
19. ἐδηλουτε	40. δεικνυοιντο	61. λυθειμεν	
20. κομιεισθε	41. διδοιεν	62. δεδωκη	
21. ἐφιλουν	42. ἱστᾱσι	63. θειεν	

Accents of finite verbs in composition

89. Finite verb forms compounded with prepositions are generally recessive, even when the non-compound form is an oxytone second person singular second (or 'strong') aorist imperative active of type εἰπέ (see § 84). Thus κάτοιδα, κατάκειμαι, κάτειπε (imperat.). Notice that the present indicative forms of εἰμί 'I am' and φημί 'I say' are recessive, in accordance with this general rule, when compounded with prepositions: ἔξεστι, σύμφημι. (On the accentuation of the non-compound forms, see §§ 278–97 and esp. §§ 279d, 282–3.) Compounds of χρή are likewise recessive: ἀπόχρη.

Manuscripts tend to accent the 2nd sg. φής on the final syllable in composition: either συμφής or συμφῆς. But such an accentuation is not prescribed by ancient grammarians, and modern texts often follow the general rule (σύμφης). See WACKERNAGEL, *VERBALACCENT*, p. 466; VENDRYES, p. 129.

90. But if the preposition is followed by the augment or by reduplication, the accent cannot fall further from the end of the word than the augment or reduplication: ἀπῆγον 'I was leading away', παρέσχον 'I provided', ἀφῖγμαι 'I have arrived', ἐφῆπται 'has been fixed onto'.

91. The third person singular future indicative of the verb 'to be', ἔσται, oddly retains its acute on the penultimate syllable in compounds: παρέσται, ἐξέσται.

The reason for this accent is not clear; the influence of the (Homeric) form παρέσσεται may be involved. For discussion, see LEJEUNE, *REMARQUES*, p. 65.

92. Compounds of the monosyllabic aorist imperatives θές, δός, ἔς, and σχές accent the last syllable of the preposition (or of the last preposition, if there is more than one preposition): κατάθες 'lay down', ἀπόδος 'give back', συναπόδος 'join in repaying', πάρες 'let go', ἐπίσχες 'hold out, hold back'.

93. Compounds of monosyllabic second person singular μι-verb aorist middle imperatives in -ου accent the last syllable of a disyllabic preposition: κατάθου lay down', περίδου 'place a bet for'. But they are perispomenon, like the non-compound forms, if the preposition is monosyllabic: προσθοῦ 'take to yourself', ἀφοῦ 'let go of' (aor. imperat. mid. of ἀφίημι).

47

94. Compounds of non-monosyllabic second person singular second (or 'strong') aorist imperatives middle in -ου are accented like the non-compound forms (see § 83): ἐπιβαλοῦ, ἀπολιποῦ.

95. In all 'contracted' forms (except for those mentioned in § 96) the accent follows the rules of contraction as in the non-compound form: ἀπολειφθῶ, ἀποτῑμᾷς, ἐκδημεῖ.

96. However, μι-verb second aorists middle subjunctive and optative are generally recessive in composition, regardless of 'contraction' (but variation is found in manuscripts, in modern texts, and in textbooks): ἀπόθωμαι, ἀπόδοιτο.

EXERCISE 10: FINITE VERBS IN COMPOSITION

Write the following compounded finite verbs with their correct accents:

1. κατηλθε
2. παρεισι
3. ἀφιξαι
4. ἀναδος
5. ἀποθου
6. ἀφηκα
7. παρεσται
8. ἀποχρη
9. καταθου
10. ἀποδοιο
11. παρενθες
12. ἀνες
13. ἀφιᾶσι
14. προφερε
15. ἐκθου
16. περιθες
17. ἐνθου
18. ἀπολιποιεν
19. προου
20. ἀπολιπε
21. ἀποδωται
22. ἐξηυρον
23. ἀποθεσθε
24. ἀντιτενεις
25. ἀποδιδω
26. ἀπολυθητε
27. ἀφιστᾶσι
28. συμφημι
29. ἀποκτενει
30. συνεξαγε
31. κατεδησε
32. προσηγε
33. ἀνασχου
34. ἀπειργεν
35. ἀναστησον
36. καταλεγε
37. συνεξηγον
38. προλεγονται
39. προυλαβε
40. ἀποθειντο
41. ἀπολιποιο
42. ἐντιθωμαι
43. συνεγραψε
44. ἀπολιπου
45. παραβαλου
46. ἀντισχες
47. ἀπολυθειτε
48. ἐπιτῑμωμεν (indic.)
49. ἀποφανω (aor. subj. pass.)
50. ἐξειπε (aor. imperat.)
51. ἀμφιβαλω (aor. subj.)
52. ἀποφανω (fut.)
53. ἀποφανοιμεν
54. ἐξαγγελλουσι
55. ἀποκτεινω (subj.)
56. ἀποφηνωμαι
57. ἀφειτε (aor. indic.)
58. ἀφειτε (aor. opt.)
59. ἀμφιβαλω (fut.)
60. ἐξειπε (aor. indic.)
61. ἐξαγγελουσι
62. συνετῑμηθη
63. ἀποφανουμαι
64. περιποιουμεν

48

3. Verbs (§§ 94–8)

Accents of infinitives and participles

97. Infinitives and participles are not finite verbs, though they belong to the verbal system, but verbal nouns and verbal adjectives respectively.

98. The following conspectus shows the accentuation of the infinitives and nominative singular masculine forms of participles:

	INFINITIVE	PARTICIPLE (nom. sg. masc.)
2nd ('strong') aor. inf. in -ειν and corresponding participles	Perispomenon: βαλεῖν	Oxytone: βαλών
All infs in -ναι and corresponding participles	Accent the penultimate: βεβληκέναι, διδόναι, βληθῆναι, εἶναι, ἰέναι	Oxytone βεβληκώς, διδούς, βληθείς, ὤν, ἰών
Perf. mid./ pass.	Accent the penultimate: βεβλῆσθαι, λελύσθαι	Paroxytone: βεβλημένος, λελυμένος
1st aor. act.	Accent the penultimate: ἁρμόσαι, βουλεῦσαι	Recessive: ἁρμόσᾱς, βουλεύσᾱς
2nd aor. mid. inf. in -εσθαι and corresponding participles	Paroxytone: βαλέσθαι	Recessive: βαλόμενος
Homeric infs in -μεναι and -μεν	Accent the vowel before -μεναι or -μεν: εἰπέμεναι, εἰπέμεν, ζευγνύμεναι, ζευγνῦμεν	

49

All other infs and corresponding participles	Recessive:	Recessive:
	βουλεύειν,	βουλεύων,
	βουλεύσειν,	βουλεύσων,
	βουλεύεσθαι,	βουλευόμενος
	βουλεύσεσθαι,	βουλευσόμενος,
	βουλεύσασθαι,	βουλευσάμενος,
	βουλευθήσεσθαι,	βουλευθησόμενος,
	τίθεσθαι, πρίασθαι	τιθέμενος, πριάμενος

99. For forms of participles other than the nominative singular masculine, with the partial exception of the genitive plural feminine (see § 101), the accent remains as near as possible to the syllable on which the accent falls in the nominative singular masculine, counting syllables from the beginning of the word. In other words, where the accent can fall on the same syllable as the accent of the nominative singular masculine, it does so. Thus, on the basis of the nominative singular masculine βουλεύων the nominative singular feminine is βουλεύουσα and the nominative/accusative singular neuter is βουλεῦον, the accent in both forms remaining on the second syllable from the beginning of the word. The form βουλεῦον illustrates the important point that the accent remains, where possible, on the same syllable as in the nominative singular masculine even if it has to change from an acute to a circumflex to comply with the σωτῆρα rule. Where the law of limitation prevents the accent from falling on the same syllable as that of the nominative singular masculine, the accent changes syllable in order to comply with the law of limitation, but it moves no further than necessary. Thus, the dative singular feminine of βουλεύων is βουλευούσῃ: the law of limitation does not allow an accent on the syllable λευ but does allow an acute on the immediately following syllable ου. The accent has thus changed syllable to comply with the law of limitation, but it has not moved further than necessary. The following examples provide further

50

3. Verbs (§§ 98–101)

illustration of the accentuation of participle forms: τιθείς, τιθεῖσα, τιθέν; λυόμενος, λυομένη, λυόμενον; λελυκώς, λελυκυῖα, λελυκός.

100. An accent that adheres as far as possible to the position of the accent in a basic form (or 'base form'), as the accents of participles adhere to that in the nominative singular masculine, is called a *persistent accent*. Persistent accentuation is a general feature of most nouns and adjectives and will be explored in more detail in the next chapter. As far as participles are concerned, however, the application of persistent accentuation is very straightforward and the only real complication is the one described in § 101. Notice that once the accent of the nominative singular masculine of a participle is known (by § 98) then with the exception of the rule given in § 101 there is no need to learn special rules as to which of the other forms in the paradigm have a circumflex and which have an acute. Once the syllable on which the accent falls has been determined the type of accent is provided by attention to the following three rules: (i) the rule that a short vowel never has a circumflex (§ 59); (ii) the law of limitation (§ 64), and (iii) the σωτῆρα rule (§ 65). Thus, once we know the accentuation of the nominative singular masculine form τιθείς we may accent correctly τιθεῖσα by reasoning (a) that since the accent can fall on the second syllable from the beginning, as in τιθείς, the principle of persistent accentuation requires it to do so; and (b) that the σωτῆρα rule requires an accent on the relevant syllable to be a circumflex. Likewise, we may accent correctly τιθέν by reasoning (a) that since the accent can again fall on the same syllable as in τιθείς it must do so; and (b) that since the vowel in the relevant syllable is short the accent must be an acute.

101. Genitive plural feminine forms of participles, however, are perispomenon unless the nominative singular masculine is in -ος, in which case the genitive plural feminine is identical in form, including accent, to the genitive plural masculine: λῡουσῶν, λῡσᾱσῶν, δεικνῡσῶν, λελυκυιῶν but λῡομένων, λῡσαμένων, λῡσομένων, λελυμένων, τιθεμένων.

102. In verbs with contracted presents or futures the *uncontracted* forms of present or future infinitives and participles are accented in accordance with the rules given above, and the accent of the contracted form is derived by the rules of contraction (§§ 70–4): φιλεῖν (< φιλέειν), φιλῶν (< φιλέων), φιλοῦσα (< φιλέουσα), φιλοῦν (< φιλέον), φιλοῦντος (< φιλέοντος), φιλούσης (< φιλεούσης), φιλεῖσθαι (< φιλέεσθαι), φιλούμενος (< φιλεόμενος), φιλουμένη (< φιλεομένη), φανεῖν (< φανέειν), φανῶν (< φανέων).

103. Infinitives and participles always retain their accent in composition with prepositions: κεῖσθαι, κατακεῖσθαι; ἑλών, καθελών.

EXERCISE 11: INFINITIVES AND PARTICIPLES
Write the following infinitives and participles with their correct accents:

1. πεισθεις	14. λελυκοτα	27. τιθεισα
2. λελυσθαι	15. δοσθαι	28. λῡσεσθαι
3. λαβοντος	16. φιλεισθαι	29. τιθεισων
4. δεικνῡς	17. τῑμωσαι	30. λελυμενη
5. μαθουσα	18. φιλουντος	31. τιθεναι
6. πεισθηναι	19. ἀποδουναι	32. ἐκτιθεισα
7. ἀπολιπον	20. δεικνυναι	33. κεκηρῡγμενος
8. λαβον	21. λελυκεναι	34. παυσαμενων (gen. pl. fem.)
9. δομενος	22. λιπομενον	35. λυθησομενῳ
10. μαθειν	23. λιπεσθαι	36. βουλευσᾱσαν
11. λῡσαμεναι	24. ἀγγελων	37. φυλασσεμεναι (Homeric)
12. ἀπολειπειν	25. λαβειν	38. λειφθησομενοι
13. λῡσομενην	26. δεικνῡσαν	39. ἀκουεμεν (Homeric)

3. Verbs (§§ 101–3)

40. δεικνυμενος   44. δηλουμενον   48. παυσαμενων (gen. pl. masc.)
41. δεικνυσθαι   45. φανουμενη   49. λιπομενων (gen. pl. masc.)
42. λειπομενος   46. βολευσαν   50. βουλευσαι (inf.)
43. παυσασθαι   47. λελυκυια

EXERCISE 12: CUMULATIVE EXERCISE

Write the following phrases with their correct accents, remembering that an acute on a final syllable changes to a grave before another word that is not an enclitic, as long as punctuation does not intervene. (There are no enclitics in this exercise.)

1. λαθε βιωσας.
2. απεθανε καθευδων.
3. φερ' ειπε, ηκουσας;
4. ακουσαντες απιτε.
5. ελπιζω ιεναι.
6. σπευδωμεν μαχεσθαι.
7. παθων γελας;
8. οιμωξας επεσεν.
9. ανασταντες απηλθον.
10. μαχομενος απωλετο.
11. νικαν αξιουσιν.
12. χρη μαθειν.
13. εξον αποφυγειν προειλοντο πολεμησαι.
14. ελειφθησαν τεθνηκοτες.
15. χρη αναβηναι.
16. σπευδων θανειν εσῳζετο.
17. ισταιντο παυσαμεναι.

53

Chapter 4: Accentuation of Nouns and Adjectives: General Rules

Base accent and case accent

104. In nouns and adjectives the accent remains, with some exceptions, as far as possible on the same syllable throughout the paradigm, counting syllables from the beginning of the word: the accent is *persistent* (§ 100). We may distinguish between the *base accent,* the accent of one case-form (the *base form*) from which that of the others can be predicted, and the *case accent* or accent of an individual case-form.

105. In nouns it is usually the nominative singular that provides the base accent. Thus, the accent of the nominative singular ἄνθρωπος sets the pattern for that of the other forms ἄνθρωπον, ἀνθρώπου, ἀνθρώπῳ, ἀνθρώπω, ἀνθρώποιν, ἄνθρωποι, ἀνθρώπους, ἀνθρώπων, ἀνθρώποις. Where the accent can fall on the first syllable of the word, as in the 'model' form ἄνθρωπος, it does so. Where the law of limitation prevents the accent from falling in the position of the base accent, as in ἀνθρώπου, the accent falls as near as possible to the position of the base accent. Note that (with the exceptions detailed in the paragraphs below) a case accent falls, if possible, on the same syllable as the base accent, even if it needs to change either from acute to circumflex or *vice versa* in order to comply with the law of limitation and the σωτῆρα rule: nom. sg. δῶρον, gen. sg. δώρου; nom. sg. σωτήρ, gen. sg. σωτῆρος.

Beginners sometimes make the mistake of trying to retain the same type of accent (acute or circumflex) as that of the base form by changing the syllable on which the accent falls (e.g. incorrect *δωροῦ as gen. sg. of δῶρον, instead of correct δώρου). This error can be avoided if one remembers that *a persistent accent changes shape rather than changing syllable.*

106. In adjectives it is usually the nominative singular masculine that provides the base accent. Thus, the accent of the nominative singular masculine μέλᾱς provides the model for that of all the other forms except the genitive plural feminine (see § 116): μέλαινα, μέλαν, μέλανα, μέλαιναν, μέλανος, μελαίνης, etc.

In addition to the fairly systematic exceptions and complications detailed in the remainder of this chapter, according to Herodian two old feminines of adjectives are exceptions: ἐλάχεια despite nom. sg. masc. ἐλαχύς 'small', and λίγεια despite nom. sg. masc. λιγύς 'shrill'. But modern texts often print ἐλαχεῖα and λιγεῖα.

107. The following endings containing a long vowel, or a diphthong that counts 'long' for accentuation (see §§ 66–8), receive a circumflex, not an acute, when they are accented at all: all first- and second-declension genitive and dative endings (gen. sg. -ῆς, -ᾱς, -οῦ; dat. sg. -ῃ, -ᾳ, -ῳ; gen./dat. dual -αῖν, -οῖν; gen. pl. -ῶν; dat. pl. -αῖς, -οῖς), and the third-declension genitive/dative dual ending -οῖν and genitive plural ending -ῶν. The endings of the 'Attic second declension' (or 'Attic declension') are exceptional: see § 113.

108. All first- and second-declension nominative, vocative, and accusative endings containing a long vowel, or a diphthong that counts 'long' for accentuation, receive an acute, not a circumflex, when they are accented: nom. sg. -ή, -ά, -ής; voc. sg. -ή, -ά; acc. sg. -ήν, -άν; nom./acc. dual -ά, -ώ; acc. pl. -άς, -ούς.

109. An ending containing a short vowel, or a diphthong that counts 'short' for accentuation, *necessarily* receives an acute, not a circumflex, if it is accented at all (§ 59). Thus 1st-decl. nom. pl.

-αί; 2nd-decl. nom. sg. -ός, voc. sg. -έ, acc. sg. or nom./acc. sg. neut. -όν, nom. pl. -οί, nom./acc. pl. neut. -ά; 3rd-decl. gen. sg. -ός, dat. sg. -ί, dat. pl. -σί.

110. The principles outlined in §§ 104–9 may be illustrated by the paradigms of σοφός and κριτής, whose paradigms in addition have a persistent accent, and θήρ, whose paradigm does not (§ 133a):

	Masc.	Fem.	Neut.
	Sg.	Sg.	Sg.
Nom.	σοφός	σοφή	σοφόν
Voc.	σοφέ	σοφή	σοφόν
Acc.	σοφόν	σοφήν	σοφόν
Gen.	σοφοῦ	σοφῆς	σοφοῦ
Dat.	σοφῷ	σοφῇ	σοφῷ
	Dual	Dual	Dual
Nom./Voc./Acc.	σοφώ	σοφά	σοφώ
Gen./Dat.	σοφοῖν	σοφαῖν	σοφοῖν
	Pl.	Pl.	Pl.
Nom./Voc.	σοφοί	σοφαί	σοφά
Acc.	σοφούς	σοφάς	σοφά
Gen.	σοφῶν	σοφῶν	σοφῶν
Dat.	σοφοῖς	σοφαῖς	σοφοῖς

	Sg.	Dual	Pl.
Nom.	κριτής	κριτά	κριταί
Voc.	κριτά	" "	" "
Acc.	κριτήν	" "	κριτάς
Gen.	κριτοῦ	κριταῖν	κριτῶν
Dat.	κριτῇ	" "	κριταῖς

56

	Sg.	Dual	Pl.
Nom.	θήρ	θῆρε	θῆρες
Voc.	θήρ	" "	" "
Acc.	θῆρα	" "	θῆρας
Gen.	θηρός	θηροῖν	θηρῶν
Dat.	θηρί	" "	θηρσί

111. If an ending is contracted with a stem-final vowel and one or the other vowel was accented before contraction, the normal rules for the accentuation of contracted forms generally apply (but see § 112), and this can lead to an ending that would normally take the acute appearing with a circumflex: σῡκέα > σῡκῆ, Ἑρμέᾱν > Ἑρμῆν. The word γῆ 'earth' is accented as if contracted from a form *γέᾱ (which is indeed attested in the plural γέαι, etc.), although the actual origins of the form γῆ are uncertain.

112. However, a nominative/accusative dual ending in -ω always has an acute, never a circumflex, if accented on the final syllable, regardless of contraction: νόω > νώ (not *νῶ); ὀστέω > ὀστώ (not *ὀστῶ).

For further exceptions to the normal rules for contracted forms, see §§ 121–2, 127.

113. In the 'Attic second declension' (or 'Attic declension'), all cases have exactly the same accent as the base form. Thus, if the base form is oxytone all the forms are oxytone, regardless of endings: sg. νεώς 'temple', νεών, νεώ, νεῴ; dual νεώ, νεῴν; pl. νεῴ, νεώς, νεών, νεώς. Some nouns and adjectives of the Attic declension violate the law of limitation in the base form and throughout almost the whole paradigm: sg. ἵλεως 'propitious', ἵλεων, ἵλεω, ἵλεῳ, nom./acc. neut. ἵλεων; dual ἵλεω, ἵλεων; pl. ἵλεῳ, ἵλεως, ἵλεων, ἵλεως, nom./acc. neut. ἵλεα.

Historically, some words of the Attic second declension, such as ἵλεως, originally had a short vowel in the final syllable of the base form: ἵλᾱος > ἵληος > ἵλεως. The accent of the original base form obeyed the law of limitation and has remained in place although changes in the form of the word have caused it subsequently to violate the law of limitation. But some forms in the paradigm, such as the gen. pl. ἵλεων, never had a short vowel in the final syllable and yet have acquired an anomalous accent under the influence of the base form.

The accentuation of λαγῶς/λαγώς 'hare' was disputed in antiquity and there is considerable variation in modern texts. According to Herodian, the nom. was λαγῶς (see Arcadius 107. 18), but according to Trypho (quoted by Athenaeus 9. 400a–d = Trypho fr. 19 Velsen) it was λαγώς. If Herodian's accentuation is accepted then following our rule, but allowing § 112 to take precedence for the nom./acc. dual, gives sg. λαγῶς, λαγῶν, λαγῶ, λαγῷ; dual λαγώ, λαγῷν; pl. λαγῷ, λαγῶς, λαγῶν, λαγῶς. Trypho implies (but not entirely clearly) that the paradigm was sg. λαγώς, λαγών, λαγῶ, λαγῷ; dual λαγώ, λαγῷν; pl. λαγῷ, λαγώς, λαγῶν, λαγῶς (i.e. an acute on all the nom., voc., and acc. forms, a circumflex on all the gen. and dat. forms): see CHANDLER, pp. 155–8; VENDRYES, p. 215. The fragment of Trypho implies, however, that not everybody followed his rule in pronunciation, and it is likely that at least in the Hellenistic period there was variation in actual practice.

114. The genitive plural of a first-declension *noun* (whether feminine or masculine) is perispomenon, regardless of the base accent. Thus, gen. pl. γεφυρῶν to nom. sg. γέφῡρα; gen. pl. χωρῶν to nom. sg. χώρᾱ; gen. pl. ταμιῶν to nom. sg. ταμίᾱς 'treasurer'; gen. pl. βουλῶν to nom. sg. βουλή.

Historically, the reason for this rule is that the 1st-decl. gen. pl. ending -ῶν is contracted from -άων; uncontracted -άων is found in Homer.

The gen. pl. forms of ἀφύη (small fry of various fish), χρήστης 'lender', χλούνης 'wild boar', and ἐτησίαι 'Etesian winds' are exceptional: ἀφύων, χρήστων, χλούνων, ἐτησίων. The words χλούνης and ἐτησίαι are properly adjectives, though also used as nouns; the accentuation of the genitives plural is that to be expected in adjectives (§ 115).

115. In first-declension feminines of *adjectives*, however, the genitive plural has the same accent as the genitive plural masculine if it is otherwise identical in form to the genitive plural masculine (and neuter). Thus, the gen. pl. fem. of ξύλινος 'of wood' is ξυλίνων, like the gen. pl. masc./neut.; the gen. pl. masc., fem., and neut. of ποικίλος 'many-coloured' is ποικίλων; the gen. pl. masc., fem., and neut. of λιγυρός 'shrill' is λιγυρῶν.

Historically the gen. pl. of 1st-decl. feminines of adjectives is contracted from -άων, like the gen. pl. of 1st-decl. nouns (see the first note to § 114). However, in those adjectives where the gen. pl. fem. is identical in other respects to the gen. pl. masc./neut., the influence of the gen. pl. masc./neut. has caused the gen. pl. fem. no longer to be accented as a contracted form.

116. First-declension feminines of adjectives in which the genitive plural differs in form from the genitive plural masculine/neuter accent the genitive plural feminine with a circumflex on the final syllable, regardless of the base accent or the accent of the genitive plural masculine/neuter. Thus, μέλας, gen. pl. masc./neut. μελάνων but gen. pl. fem. μελαινῶν; γλυκύς, gen. pl. masc./neut. γλυκέων but gen. pl. fem. γλυκειῶν.

117. Note that §§ 115–16 apply also to participles (cf. § 101): gen. pl. masc./neut. λυόντων, gen. pl. fem. λυουσῶν; gen. pl. masc./neut. λύσάντων, gen. pl. fem. λυσᾱσῶν; gen. pl. masc./neut. δεικνύντων, gen. pl. fem. δεικνῡσῶν; gen. pl. masc./neut. λελυκότων, gen. pl. fem. λελυκυιῶν; but gen. pl. masc., fem., and neut. λυομένων; gen. pl. masc., fem., and neut. λῡσαμένων; gen. pl. masc., fem., and neut. λῡσομένων; gen. pl. masc., fem., and neut. λελυμένων; gen. pl. masc., fem., and neut. τιθεμένων.

EXERCISE 13: BASE ACCENT AND CASE ACCENT (i)

All the forms of nouns and adjectives given below obey the rules given in §§ 104–17. Write them with the correct case accents, given the accents of the base forms shown in parentheses:

1. σοφου, σοφαιν, σοφων (gen. pl. masc.), σοφων (gen. pl. fem.), σοφαις (σοφός)
2. δωρου, δωρα, δωροις, δωρων (δῶρον)
3. πλουν, πλους (acc. pl.), πλω, πλοι (πλοῦς < πλόος)
4. χωρᾶν, χωραι, χωρᾱς (acc. pl.), χωρων, χωραις (χώρᾱ)
5. λεῳ (dat. sg.), λεως (acc. pl.), λεων (gen. pl.), λεως (λεώς)
6. ταλαν (nom./acc. sg. neut.), ταλανος, ταλαινη, ταλανας (acc. pl. masc.), ταλαινᾱς (acc. pl. fem.), ταλανων, ταλαινων (τάλᾱς)
7. σκιᾶν, σκιᾱς (gen. sg.), σκιᾳ, σκιαι, σκιᾱς (acc. pl.), σκιων, σκιαις (σκιά)
8. ρητορ, ρητορα, ρητορε, ρητοροιν, ρητορες, ρητορας, ρητορων, ρητορσι (ῥήτωρ)
9. ἱλεων (gen. pl.), ἱλεων (acc. sg.), ἱλεῳ (nom. pl. masc./fem.), ἱλεως, ἱλεα (ἵλεως)
10. σατραπου, σατραπην, σατραπαι, σατραπων, σατραπαις (σατράπης)
11. ἑκουσα, ἑκουσης, ἑκουσων, ἑκοντα, ἑκοντων, ἑκουσι, ἑκουσαις, ἑκουσαι (ἑκών)
12. σῡκην, σῡκης, σῡκαι, σῡκων, σῡκη, σῡκαις (σῡκῆ < σῡκέᾱ)
13. δεκαδος, δεκαδι, δεκαδων, δεκαδες, δεκασι (δεκάς)
14. σωτηρα, σωτηρι, σωτηρες, σωτηρων, σωτηρσι (σωτήρ)
15. μναν, μνᾱς (gen. sg.), μνᾳ, μνᾱ (nom./voc./acc. dual), μναι, μνων, μναις (μνᾶ < μνάᾱ)

4. Nouns and Adjectives: General (§§ 118–20)

Properly recessive adjectives and proper names

118. Some adjectives with recessive nominatives singular masculine are properly recessive in all their forms, even though this means that in the nominative/accusative singular neuter the accent falls further from the end of the word than in the nominative singular masculine. These are the comparative adjectives in ΄-ων and most compound adjectives in ΄-ων (genitive ΄-ονος): καλλίων but κάλλιον; πολυπράγμων but πολύπραγμον. Compound adjectives in -φρων, however, keep the accent of the base form (always on the syllable preceding the element -φρων), subject to the σωτῆρα rule and law of limitation: nom. sg. masc. ταλαίφρων 'wretched', nom./acc. sg. neut. ταλαῖφρον (cf. § 210h).

119. Most compound adjectives or proper names in ΄-ων (genitive ΄-ονος) with vocatives singular in -ον likewise accent them recessively: nom. sg. masc. εὐδαίμων but voc. εὔδαιμον. But the vocatives singular of compound adjectives and proper names in -φρων again keep the accent of the base form (on the syllable preceding the element -φρων/-φρον), subject to the σωτῆρα rule: nom. sg. masc. ταλαίφρων and voc. sg. ταλαῖφρον; nom. Λυκόφρων and voc. Λυκόφρον (cf. § 210h).

120. Some compound adjectives and proper names in -ης, genitive -ους, have a recessive base form (nominative ΄-ης, genitive ΄-ους). These are properly recessive in their non-contracted forms. (On the accentuation of the contracted forms, see § 124.) It follows that in the nominative/accusative singular neuter and in the vocative singular the accent falls further from the end of the word than in the nominative singular masculine: nom. sg. αὐθάδης 'self-willed', dat. pl. αὐθάδεσι, voc. sg. and nom./acc. sg. neut. αὔθαδες; nom. sg. Σωκράτης, voc. sg. Σώκρατες. However, compound adjectives in -ήρης, -ώλης, and -ώδης keep the accent of the base form in all their non-contracted forms, subject to the

61

σωτῆρα rule: nom. sg. masc. φρενήρης 'sound of mind', ἐξώλης 'utterly destroyed', εὐώδης 'sweet-smelling'; voc. sg. and nom./acc. sg. neut. φρενῆρες, ἔξωλες, εὖωδες.

For further exceptions to the general rule above, see CHANDLER, pp. 200–1.

It is likely that -φρων, -ήρης, -ώλης, and -ώδης, although originally the second members of compounds, had come to be regarded simply as suffixes; hence adjectives with these terminations do not follow the normal rule for compound adjectives in ʹ-ων and ʹ-ης, gen. ʹ-ους, but are accented as if they were non-compound forms.

EXERCISE 14: BASE ACCENT AND CASE ACCENT (ii)

All the forms of nouns and adjectives given below obey the rules given in §§ 118–20. Write them with the correct case accents, given the accents of the base forms shown in parentheses:

1. δυσωδες (nom. sg. neut.), δυσωδεσι (δυσώδης, gen. -ους, 'foul-smelling')

2. κακοδαιμονες, κακοδαιμονων (gen. pl. masc.), κακοδαιμον (nom. sg. neut.), κακοδαιμοσι, κακοδαιμον (voc. sg.), κακοδαιμονων (gen. pl. fem.) (κακοδαίμων)

3. τειχηρες (acc. sg. neut.), τειχηρεσι (τειχήρης, gen. -ους, 'enclosed by walls')

4. φιλοφρονος, φιλοφρον (nom. sg. neut.), φιλοφρον (voc. sg.), φιλοφρονι, φιλοφρονα (nom. pl. neut.), φιλοφρονες, φιλοφρονων, φιλοφροσι (φιλόφρων 'kindly-minded')

5. ἡδιονα (acc. sg. masc.), ἡδιω (acc. sg. masc.), ἡδιονος, ἡδιον, ἡδιονων (gen. pl. fem.), ἡδιονων (gen. pl. neut.) (ἡδίων)

6. Δημοσθενες (Δημοσθένης, gen. -ους)

7. πανωλες (nom. sg. neut.), πανωλεσι (πανώλης, gen. -ους, 'utterly destroyed')

8. περιμηκες (nom. sg. neut.), περιμηκεσι (περιμήκης, gen. -ους, 'very long')

9. αὐταρκεσι, αὐταρκες (nom. sg. neut.), αὐταρκες (voc. sg.)
(αὐτάρκης, gen. -ους, 'self-sufficient')

10. αἰσχῖω (nom. pl. neut.), αἰσχῖονα (nom. pl. neut.), αἰσχῖονοιν,
αἰσχῖον, αἰσχῖονες (αἰσχῖων)

11. δαΐφρονα (acc. sg. fem.), δαΐφρον (voc. sg.), δαΐφρον (acc. sg.
neut.), δαΐφρονων (gen. pl. masc.), δαΐφρονων (gen. pl. fem.)
(δαΐφρων)

12. καταντεσι, καταντες (acc. sg. neut.) (κατάντης, gen. -ους,
'downhill')

13. ἐλᾱττον, ἐλᾱττσι, ἐλᾱττονι, ἐλᾱττονας, ἐλᾱττους (acc. pl.
masc.), ἐλᾱττονων (gen. pl. neut.) (ἐλᾱττων)

14. εὐδαιμον (voc. sg.), εὐδαιμον (nom. sg. neut.), εὐδαιμονος,
εὐδαιμονι, εὐδαιμονων, εὐδαιμοσι (εὐδαίμων)

15. ποδηρες (acc. sg. neut.), ποδηρεσι (ποδήρης, gen. -ους,
'reaching to the feet')

Contracted nouns and adjectives in -ους from -οος

121. In contracted nouns and adjectives ending in -ους from -οος,
such as εὔνους (from εὔνοος), the rules of contraction are
disregarded in all cases except the nominative singular and the
accent of the contracted nominative is carried throughout (subject
to the σωτῆρα rule), except that the nominative/accusative dual in
-ω is oxytone (compare § 112): εὔνους (nom. sg. masc./fem.),
εὔνουν (acc. sg. masc./fem.), εὔνουν (nom./acc. sg. neut.), εὔνου,
εὔνῳ; εὐνώ, εὔνοιν; εὖνοι, εὔνους (acc. pl. masc./fem.), εὔνοα
(nom./acc. pl. neut.), εὔνων, εὔνοις; ἁπλοῦς (nom. sg. masc., <
ἁπλόος), ἁπλοῦν (acc. sg. masc.), ἁπλοῦ, ἁπλῷ, ἁπλῆ, ἁπλῆν, ἁπλῆς,
ἁπλῆ, ἁπλώ, ἁπλοῖν, ἁπλᾶ (nom./acc. dual fem.), ἁπλαῖν, ἁπλοῖ,
ἁπλοῦς, ἁπλῶν, ἁπλοῖς, etc.

Adjectives of material in -οῦς from -εος

122. Adjectives in -οῦς (< -εος) that indicate the material something is made out of, such as ἀργυροῦς 'made of silver', are accented as if the uncontracted base form were paroxytone (*ἀργύρεος), although the actual uncontracted forms found e.g. in Homer are recessive (ἀργύρεος). The result is that every form in the contracted paradigm, except for the nominative/accusative dual masculine/neuter (see § 112), is perispomenon: ἀργυροῦς, ἀργυροῦν, ἀργυροῦ, ἀργυρῷ, ἀργυρώ, ἀργυροῖν, ἀργυροῖ, etc.

The corresponding material suffix of Vedic Sanskrit, -áya- (as in hiraṇyáya- 'made of gold'), is accented like the uncontracted form -éo- implied by the Attic paradigm, rather than like the Homeric -εο-. This makes it likely that, historically, the uncontracted forms such as *ἀργυρέος implied by the Attic paradigm preserve the original accentuation for adjectives of material with the suffix -εο-, the recessive accent found in the Homeric forms being an innovation.

EXERCISE 15: BASE ACCENT AND CASE ACCENT (iii)

All the forms of nouns and adjectives given below obey the rules given in §§ 121–2. Write them with the correct case accents, given the accents of the base forms shown in parentheses:

1. χρυσου, χρυσης, χρυσω, χρυσαις, χρυσαι, χρυσας (χρυσοῦς < *χρύσεος)

2. διπλουν, διπλου, διπλω, διπλην, διπλη, διπλω, διπλα (nom./acc. dual fem.), διπλοιν, διπλα (nom. pl. neut.), διπλαιν, διπλοι, διπλαις (διπλοῦς < διπλόος)

3. εκπλοις, εκπλου, εκπλω, εκπλοι, εκπλω, εκπλους (acc. pl.), εκπλουν, εκπλων (ἔκπλους < ἔκπλοος)

4. χαλκη, χαλκαις, χαλκω, χαλκουν (nom. sg. neut.), χαλκας, χαλκα (acc. pl. neut.), χαλκα (nom./acc. dual fem.), χαλκου, χαλκην, χαλκοι, χαλκαι (χαλκοῦς < *χαλκέος)

4. Nouns and Adjectives: General (§§ 122–3)

5. δύσνουν (acc. sg. masc.), δύσνου, δύσνῳ, δύσνω, δύσνοιν, δύσνοι, δύσνων, δύσοις, δύσνους (acc. pl. masc.) (δύσνους < δύσνοος)

6. περίπλουν, περίπλου (gen. sg.), περίπλῳ, περίπλοι, περίπλων (περίπλους 'circumnavigation' < περίπλοος)

7. εἴσπλων, εἴσπλοι, εἴσπλῳ, εἴσπλω, εἴσπλους (acc. pl.), εἴσπλουν, εἴσπλοιν, εἴσπλου, εἴσπλοις (εἴσπλους 'sailing in' < εἴσπλοος)

8. νου (voc. sg.), νοι, νῳ, νων, νω, νουν, νους (acc. pl.), νου (gen. sg.), νοις (νοῦς < νόος)

9. ἄργυροι, ἀργυρω, ἀργυρᾶ (nom. pl. neut.), ἀργυρᾶ (nom. sg. fem.), ἀργυρᾶ (nom./acc. dual fem.), ἀργυρᾷ, ἀργυρουν (acc. sg. masc.), ἀργυρων (gen. pl. fem.), ἀργυρων (gen. pl. neut.) (ἀργυροῦς < *ἀργυρέος)

10. Πειρίθουν, Πειρίθου, Πειρίθῳ (Πειρίθους < Πειρίθοος)

Nouns in -ις, -εως and -υς/-υ, -εως

123. The nouns that end in -ις, genitive -εως (e.g. πόλις, πόλεως), together with four in -υς, πῆχυς 'forearm', πρέσβυς 'old man', πέλεκυς 'axe', ἔγχελυς 'eel', and one in -υ, ἄστυ, are recessive throughout the paradigm, except that in the genitive singular in -εως and genitive plural in -εων the accent falls one syllable further from the end of the word than the law of limitation would normally allow: sg. πόλις, πόλι, πόλιν, πόλεως, πόλει; dual πόλει (from πόλεε), πολέοιν; pl. πόλεις, πόλεις, πόλεων, πόλεσι; sg. ὑπόσχεσις 'promise', ὑπόσχεσιν, ὑποσχέσεως, ὑποσχέσει; pl. ὑποσχέσεις, ὑποσχέσεις, ὑποσχέσεων, ὑποσχέσεσι; sg. πέλεκυς, πέλεκυν, πελέκεως, πελέκει; dual πελέκει (from πελέκεε), πελεκέοιν; pl. πελέκεις, πελέκεις, πελέκεων, πελέκεσι.

Greek also has a small group of i-stem neuter nouns in -ι (all loan words). When these are declined with gen. sg. in -εως they follow the same pattern of accentuation as the nouns discussed above. Thus sg. κίκι 'castor oil', κίκι,

65

A New Short Guide to the Accentuation of Ancient Greek

κίκεως, κίκει; sg. σίναπι 'mustard', σίναπι, σινάπεως, σινάπει; sg. πέπερι 'pepper', πέπερι, πεπέρεως, πεπέρει.

For ἔγχελυς, the accentuation ἐγχέλυς is sometimes found in manuscripts.

EXERCISE 16: BASE ACCENT AND CASE ACCENT (iv)

All the forms of nouns and adjectives given below obey the rule given in § 123. Write them with the correct case accents, given the accents of the base forms shown in parentheses:

1. παιδευσιν, παιδευσεως, παιδευσει (dat. sg.) (παίδευσις 'education')

2. ἐγχελεσι, ἐγχελυν, ἐγχελεων, ἐγχελει (dat. sg.), ἐγχελεις (nom. pl.), ἐγχελεως (ἔγχελυς)

3. ἀκροπολεις (nom. pl.), ἀκροπολεων, ἀκροπολεσι, ἀκροπολεως, ἀκροπολιν (ἀκρόπολις)

4. πρεσβυ, πρεσβεως, πρεσβεσι, πρεσβεων, πρεσβεις (acc. pl.) (πρέσβυς)

5. ἀστεων, ἀστεως, ἀστη, ἀστει (dat. sg.), ἀστεσι (ἄστυ)

6. δυναμει (dat. sg.), δυναμιν, δυναμεως, δυναμεσι, δυναμεις (acc. pl.), δυναμεων (δύναμις)

7. κτισει (dat. sg.), κτισεις (nom. pl.), κτισεως, κτισεσι, κτισεων (κτίσις 'founding')

8. πελεκεως, πελεκεις (acc. pl.), πελεκυν, πελεκεων, πελεκεσι, πελεκει (dat. sg.) (πέλεκυς)

9. μητροπολεως, μητροπολεις (nom. pl.), μητροπολεων, μητροπολει (dat. sg.), μητροπολεσι, μητροπολιν (μητρόπολις)

10. μεταθεσιν, μεταθεσεως, μεταθεσει (dat. sg.), μεταθεσεις (acc. pl.), μεταθεσεων, μεταθεσεσι (μετάθεσις 'transposition')

11. πηχεων, πηχει (dat. sg.), πηχεις (nom. pl.), πηχει (nom./acc. dual), πηχυν, πηχεις (acc. pl.), πηχεσι, πηχεοιν, πηχεως (πῆχυς)

66

4. Nouns and Adjectives: General (§§ 123–4)

S-stem nouns and adjectives

124. S-stem nouns and adjectives (the types of γένος, genitive -ους, and αὐθάδης, genitive -ους; εὐγενής, genitive -οῦς) are contracted in most of their forms; these obey the rules of contraction (§§ 70–4): sg. γένος (not contracted), γένους (from γένε-ος), γένει (from γένε-ι); dual γένει (from γένε-ε), γενοῖν (from γενέ-οιν); pl. γένη (from γένε-α), γενῶν (from γενέ-ων), γένεσι (not contracted); sg. αὐθάδης (not contracted), voc. and nom./acc. neut. αὔθαδες (properly recessive and not contracted: see § 120), αὐθάδη (from αὐθάδε-α), αὐθάδους (from αὐθάδε-ος), αὐθάδει (from αὐθάδε-ι); dual αὐθάδει (from αὐθάδε-ε), αὐθαδοῖν (from αὐθαδέ-οιν); pl. nom./acc. masc./fem. αὐθάδεις (from αὐθάδε-ες), nom./acc. neut. αὐθάδη (from αὐθάδε-α), αὐθαδῶν (from αὐθαδέων), αὐθάδεσι (not contracted); sg. εὐγενής (not contracted), voc. and nom./acc. neut. εὐγενές (not contracted), εὐγενῆ (from εὐγενέ-α), εὐγενοῦς (from εὐγενέ-ος), εὐγενεῖ (from εὐγενέ-ι); dual εὐγενεῖ (from εὐγενέ-ε), εὐγενοῖν (from εὐγενέ-οιν); pl. nom./acc. masc./fem. εὐγενεῖς (from εὐγενέ-ες), nom./acc. neut. εὐγενῆ (from εὐγενέ-α), εὐγενῶν (from εὐγενέ-ων), εὐγενέσι (not contracted).

The accentuation of the contracted genitives plural of some s-stems in '-ης was disputed in antiquity. Aristarchus accented the genitives plural of forms in -ώδης with a simple recessive accent, disregarding the rules of contraction: δυσώδων, εὐώδων, νοσώδων (gen. pl. forms of δυσώδης 'ill-smelling', εὐώδης 'sweet-smelling', νοσώδης 'diseased'). Herodian, however, thought that such forms should be perispomenon following our general rule: δυσωδῶν, εὐωδῶν, νοσωδῶν. Some speakers appear to have given simple recessive accents also to τριήρων, αὐτάρκων, αὐθάδων, συνήθων, and κακοήθων. See Hdn i. 428. 11–22 together with Lentz' note; CHANDLER, pp. 192, 201; VENDRYES, pp. 222–3. Manuscripts vary, as do modern texts and textbooks. In this book we apply the normal rules for contracted words to all contracted forms of s-stems (hence δυσωδῶν from δυσωδέων, τριηρῶν from τριηρέων, etc.).

67

αἰδώς, ἠώς

125. The Attic noun αἰδώς 'shame', and Ionic ἠώς 'dawn', follow another type of *s*-stem declension in which most forms are contracted and built on a stem in *-o-*, e.g. αἰδό- (originally αἰδόσ-). They follow the normal rules of contraction (§§ 70–4): αἰδώς (not contracted), αἰδῶ (from αἰδό-α), αἰδοῦς (from αἰδό-ος), αἰδοῖ (from αἰδό-ι). Similarly ἠώς, ἠῶ, ἠοῦς, ἠοῖ.

The Attic form ἕως 'dawn' follows a variant (with acc. sg. in -ω) of the Attic 2nd decl., and is recessive in all its forms: nom. ἕως, acc. ἕω, gen. ἕω, dat. ἕῳ (cf. §§ 113, 195).

EXERCISE 17: BASE ACCENT AND CASE ACCENT (v)
All the forms of nouns and adjectives given below obey the rules given in §§ 124–5. Write them with the correct case accents, given the accents of the base forms shown in parentheses:

1. αμαθους, αμαθη (acc. sg. fem.), αμαθεις (acc. pl. masc.), αμαθεσι, αμαθες (nom. sg. neut.) (ἀμαθής, gen. -οῦς)

2. αιδους, αιδω, αιδοι (αἰδώς)

3. Δημοσθενους, Δημοσθενη, Δημοσθενες, Δημοσθενει (Δημοσθένης, gen. -ους)

4. περιμηκη (acc. pl. neut.), περιμηκει (dat. sg.), περιμηκες (nom. sg. neut.), περιμηκεσι, περιμηκη (acc. sg. fem.) (περιμήκης, gen. -ους, 'very long')

5. αυταρκεις (nom. pl. masc.), αυταρκων (gen. pl. masc.), αυταρκες (nom. sg. neut.), αυταρκεσι, αυταρκη (acc. sg. masc.) (αὐτάρκης, gen. -ους, 'self-sufficient')

6. ευωδη (acc. sg. masc.), ευωδες (nom. sg. neut.), ευωδους, ευωδει (dat. sg.), ευωδεσι, ευωδη (acc. pl. neut.), ευωδεις (nom. pl. fem.), ευωδων (gen. pl. masc.) (εὐώδης, gen. -ους)

7. τειχη, τειχους, τειχει (dat. sg.), τειχων, τειχεσι (τεῖχος, gen. -ους)

8. καταντων (gen. pl. fem.), καταντεσι, καταντεις (nom. pl. fem.), καταντη (nom. pl. neut.), καταντες (acc. sg. neut.), καταντους (κατάντης, gen. -ους, 'downhill')

9. ἀληθους, ἀληθεσι, ἀληθων (gen. pl. fem.), ἀληθες (acc. sg. neut.), ἀληθει (dat. sg.) (ἀληθής)

10. ποδηρη (acc. pl. neut.), ποδηρη (acc. sg. fem.), ποδηρων (gen. pl. neut.), ποδηρες (acc. sg. neut.), ποδηρεσι (ποδήρης, gen. -ους, 'reaching to the feet')

11. παθους, παθη, παθων, παθει (dat. sg.), παθεσι (πάθος, gen. -ους)

12. ἠους, ἠω, ἠοι (ἠώς)

13. θεοειδες (voc. sg. masc.), θεοειδες (acc. sg. neut.), θεοειδει (dat. sg.), θεοειδεις (acc. pl. masc.), θεοειδεσι, θεοειδων (gen. pl. masc.) (θεοειδής, gen. -οῦς, 'divine in form')

14. ξιφος (acc. sg.), ξιφει (nom./acc. dual), ξιφη, ξιφους, ξιφει (dat. sg.), ξιφων, ξιφοιν, ξιφεσι (ξίφος, gen. -ους)

15. τειχηρη (acc. sg. fem.), τειχηρει (dat. sg.), τειχηροιν, τειχηρεις (acc. pl. fem.), τειχηρους, τειχηρες (acc. sg. neut.), τειχηρεσι, τειχηρων (gen. pl. fem.) (τειχήρης, gen. -ους, 'enclosed by walls')

16. εὐσεβη (acc. pl. neut.), εὐσεβεσι, εὐσεβεις (nom. pl. masc.), εὐσεβει (dat. sg.), εὐσεβους, εὐσεβων (gen. pl. fem.) (εὐσεβής, gen. -οῦς)

17. πανωλους, πανωλεις (nom. pl. masc.), πανωλων (gen. pl. masc.), πανωλες (nom. sg. neut.), πανωλεσι (πανώλης, gen. -ους, 'utterly destroyed')

-εύς nouns of more than one syllable (βασιλεύς type)

126. Nouns of more than one syllable in -ευς (e.g. βασιλεύς, γονεύς 'parent', 'Οδυσσεύς) are accented on the same syllable as the nominative singular, counting syllables from the beginning of the word. Thus, in βασιλεύς the accent falls throughout on the third

syllable from the beginning, in γονεύς on the second syllable from
the beginning. The accent is an acute in the nominative singular.
In all the other cases the accent is a circumflex when it falls on a
long vowel or diphthong but (by necessity) an acute when it falls
on a short vowel: βασιλεύς, βασιλεῦ, βασιλέᾱ, βασιλέως, βασιλεῖ,
βασιλέε, βασιλέοιν, βασιλῆς/βασιλεῖς, βασιλέᾱς, βασιλέων,
βασιλεῦσι.

Feminine nouns in -ώ

127. Feminine nouns in -ώ, such as πειθώ 'persuasion', Σαπφώ,
have an accusative singular in -ώ (πειθώ) under the influence of
the nominative, although the accusative singular was originally
contracted from a form in -ό-α. The genitive and dative singular
obey the rules of contraction (§§ 70–4): πειθοῦς (from πειθό-ος),
πειθοῖ (from πειθό-ι). The vocative singular, although not
contracted, is perispomenon: πειθοῖ (see § 131).

EXERCISE 18: BASE ACCENT AND CASE ACCENT (vi)

All the forms of nouns and adjectives given below obey the rules
given in §§ 126–7. Write them with the correct case accents,
given the accents of the base forms shown in parentheses:

1. ἱερεᾱς, ἱερευσι, ἱερεᾱ, ἱερεως, ἱερευ, ἱερεων, ἱερει, ἱερεις (ἱερεύς)
2. Καλυψω (acc. sg.), Καλυψους, Καλυψοι (dat. sg.), Καλυψοι (voc. sg.) (Καλυψώ)
3. ηχοι (voc. sg.), ηχω (acc. sg.), ηχους (gen. sg.), ηχοι (dat. sg.) (ἠχώ 'echo')
4. ἱππει, ἱππευ, ἱππεᾱ, ἱππεων, ἱππεᾱς, ἱππης, ἱππεως, ἱππευσι (ἱππεύς)
5. Ἀργω (acc. sg.), Ἀργους, Ἀργοι (dat. sg.), Ἀργοι (voc. sg.) (Ἀργώ)

6. γραμματευ, γραμματεως, γραμματευσι, γραμματεᾱ, γραμματεᾱς, γραμματεων (γραμματεύς)
7. Λητους (gen. sg.), Λητοι (dat. sg.), Λητοι (voc. sg.), Λητω (acc. sg.) (Λητώ)
8. φειδους, φειδοι (dat. sg.), φειδω (acc. sg.) (φειδώ)
9. γονευσι, γονεᾱ, γονεις, γονεων, γονει, γονευ, γονεᾱς, γονεως (γονεύς)
10. πειθω (acc. sg.), πειθοι (voc. sg.), πειθοι (dat. sg.), πειθους (πειθώ)
11. Ἀχιλλεως, Ἀχιλλει, Ἀχιλλευ, Ἀχιλλεᾱ (Ἀχιλλεύς)
12. Ἐρατοι (voc. sg.), Ἐρατω (acc. sg.), Ἐρατοι (dat. sg.), Ἐρατους (Ἐρατώ)
13. χαλκευ, χαλκεις, χαλκει, χαλκεᾱς, χαλκεως, χαλκευσι, χαλκεων, χαλκεᾱ (χαλκεύς 'bronzesmith')
14. Σαπφοι (dat. sg.), Σαπφω (acc. sg.), Σαπφους, Σαπφοι (voc. sg.) (Σαπφώ)
15. φονεις, φονεᾱ, φονευσι, φονεων, φονευ, φονεᾱς, φονει, φονεως, φονευσι (φονεύς 'murderer')

Accent of the vocative singular

128. Where the vocative singular has the same form as the nominative singular it also has the same accent: ἀδελφή 'sister', ἀνδράποδον 'slave'.

129. Where the vocative singular differs in form from the nominative, it most often keeps the base accent (subject to the σωτῆρα rule): nom. υἱός, voc. υἱέ; nom. τλήμων 'suffering', voc. τλῆμον.

130. In the following words, however, the vocative singular has a recessive accent, regardless of the base accent:

(a) In the first declension, nominative δεσπότης but vocative δέσποτα.

(b) In the second declension, nominative ἀδελφός but, in Attic, vocative ἄδελφε.

For the voc. of ἀδελφός (ἄδελφε in Attic, ἀδελφέ in the *koiné*), see Ammonius 405 Nickau (citing Trypho = Trypho fr. 17 Velsen).

(c) In the third declension, the following kinship terms: nominatives πατήρ, ἀνήρ, γυνή, θυγάτηρ, μήτηρ, δāήρ 'brother-in-law', εἰνάτηρ 'sister-in-law'; vocatives singular πάτερ, ἄνερ, γύναι, θύγατερ, μῆτερ, δᾶερ, εἴνατερ.

(d) Names of certain gods: nominatives Ἀπόλλων, Ποσειδῶν, Δημήτηρ but vocatives Ἄπολλον, Πόσειδον, Δήμητερ. Note also nominative σωτήρ, vocative σῶτερ.

The nom. Ποσειδῶν is contracted from Ποσειδάων, but the voc. Πόσειδον has a non-contracted variant of the stem (cf. § 206).

(e) Most compound adjectives and proper names in ʹ-ων, genitive ʹ-ονος, or ʹ-ης, genitive ʹ-ους (see § 119–20). Thus, nominatives εὐδαίμων, Ἀριστοτέλης, Σωκράτης, αὐτάρκης 'self-sufficient', κακοήθης 'ill-disposed', but vocatives εὔδαιμον, Ἀριστότελες, Σώκρατες, αὔταρκες, κακόηθες. Contracted names in -κλῆς, such as Ἡρακλῆς (from Ἡρακλέης), are also recessive in the vocative: thus Ἡράκλεις, from Ἡράκλεες. However, the vocatives of compound adjectives and proper names in ʹ-φρων, -ήρης, -ώλης, and -ώδης keep the accent of the nominative singular masculine (subject to the σωτῆρα rule): nominatives Λυκόφρων, ταλαίφρων 'wretched', φρενήρης 'sound of mind', ἐξώλης 'utterly destroyed', εὐώδης 'sweet-smelling', and vocatives Λυκόφρον, ταλαίφρον, φρενῆρες, ἐξῶλες, εὐῶδες. The vocative of Λακεδαίμων is Λακεδαῖμον.

131. Nouns in -εύς and -ώ are perispomenon rather than oxytone in the vocative singular (see §§ 126–7): nominatives βασιλεύς, ἠχώ, Σαπφώ but vocatives βασιλεῦ, ἠχοῖ, Σαπφοῖ.

EXERCISE 19: THE VOCATIVE

All the vocatives singular given below obey the rules given in §§ 128–31. Write them with their correct accents, given the accents of the base forms shown in parentheses:

1. σωτερ (σωτήρ)
2. μιαρε (μιαρός)
3. βουλη (βουλή)
4. υἱε (υἱός)
5. καλε (καλός)
6. ἀνερ (ἀνήρ)
7. ἱερευ (ἱερεύς)
8. Λητοι (Λητώ)
9. φιλε (φίλος)
10. πατερ (πατήρ)
11. μητερ (μήτηρ)
12. αἰδως (αἰδώς)
13. ἠχοι (ἠχώ)
14. Πηλευ (Πηλεύς)
15. αὐταρκες (αὐτάρκης)
16. παρθενε (παρθένος)
17. δαιμον (δαίμων)
18. βουκολε (βουκόλος)
19. δαϊφρον (δαΐφρων)
20. παιδιον (παιδίον)
21. δᾱερ (δᾱήρ)
22. Ἐρατοι (Ἐρατώ)
23. Δημοσθενες (Δημοσθένης)
24. Ἀστυαγες (Ἀστυάγης)
25. Ποσειδον (Ποσειδῶν)
26. βασιλευ (βασιλεύς)
27. Ἀπολλον (Ἀπόλλων)
28. θυγατερ (θυγάτηρ)
29. στρατιωτα (στρατιώτης)
30. εὐδαιμον (εὐδαίμων)
31. κακοδαιμον (κακοδαίμων)
32. Δημητερ (Δημήτηρ)
33. νεᾱνισκε (νεᾱνίσκος)
34. Διογενες (Διογένης)
35. φρενηρες (φρενήρης)
36. εἰνατερ (εἰνάτηρ)
37. πρεσβυ (πρέσβυς)
38. ἀδελφε (Attic accent; nom. ἀδελφός)
39. αὐτοκρατορ (αὐτοκράτωρ)
40. δεσποτα (δεσπότης)
41. Σωκρατες (Σωκράτης)
42. Λυκοφρον (Λυκόφρων)
43. Ἡρακλεις (Ἡρακλῆς)
44. Λακεδαιμον (Λακεδαίμων)

45. γονευ (γονεύς)   47. ταλαιφρον (ταλαίφρων)
46. γυναι (γυνή)   48. γραμματευ (γραμματεύς)

Third-declension nouns and adjectives with mobile accent

132. A number of third-declension nouns, and a few adjectives, as described in the following paragraphs, sometimes accent the stem and sometimes the case ending. Thus, χεῖρα (acc.) but χειρός (gen.).

This variation is a relic from Indo-European times (cf. § 24).

133. The following nouns and adjectives accent the case ending in the genitive and dative (of all numbers, unless otherwise specified), accenting the stem in the nominative, vocative, and accusative (of all numbers):

(a) With the partial exceptions listed under (b) below, third-declension nouns whose nominative singular is monosyllabic. Thus, χείρ, χεῖρα, χειρός, χειρί, χεῖρε, χεροῖν, χεῖρες, χεῖρας, χειρῶν (poetic χερῶν), χερσί; πούς, πόδα, ποδός, ποδί, πόδε, ποδοῖν, πόδες, πόδας, ποδῶν, ποσί.

(b) But παῖς, δάς 'torch', οὖς 'ear', δμώς 'slave', θώς 'jackal', φῶς 'light', and Τρώς 'Trojan' only accent the ending in the genitive and dative singular and dative plural; the genitive/dative dual and genitive plural accent the stem: thus παῖς, παῖ, παῖδα, <u>παιδός</u>, <u>παιδί</u>, παῖδε, παίδοιν, παῖδες, παῖδας, παίδων, <u>παισί</u>. The same pattern is followed by the oblique cases of γόνυ and δόρυ when they decline without -α(τ)-: δόρυ, <u>δουρός</u>, <u>δουρί</u> (Attic poetry <u>δορός</u>, <u>δορί</u>), but gen. pl. δούρων. Forms with -α(τ)- are accented recessively: δούρατος, δούρατι (Attic δόρατος, δόρατι), δούρασι.

(c) The numerals δύο, τρεῖς, all forms of εἷς (including the feminine forms, although they follow the first declension), and

74

the masculine and neuter singular of πᾶς: δύο, δυοῖν; τρεῖς, τρία, τριῶν, τρισί; εἷς, ἕνα, ἕν, ἑνός, ἑνί, μία, μίαν, μιᾶς, μιᾷ; πᾶς, πάντα, πᾶν, παντός, παντί (but plural forms πάντες, πάντας, πάντα, πάντων, πᾶσι; the feminine forms of πᾶς, which follow the first declension, follow the accent of the base form except in the genitive plural, as expected: πᾶσα, πᾶσαν, πάσης, πάσῃ, πᾶσαι, πάσᾱς, πασῶν, πάσαις).

The long vowel of πᾶν is irregular. In compounds, the -a- of the nom./acc. sg. neut. is regularly short in Attic: ἅπᾰν, πρόπᾰν, σύμπᾰν.

(d) All singular forms of οὐδείς and μηδείς (again including the feminine forms, which follow the first declension): οὐδείς, οὐδένα, οὐδέν, οὐδενός, οὐδενί, οὐδεμία, οὐδεμίαν, οὐδεμιᾶς, οὐδεμιᾷ, and similarly μηδείς, μηδένα, etc. The accentuation of these compounds of εἷς is exactly the same in the singular as that of the simplex εἷς, except that the nominative singular masculine is perispomenon in εἷς but oxytone in οὐδείς and μηδείς. Masculine and neuter plural forms of οὐδείς and μηδείς sometimes occur, and these follow the accent of the base form: οὐδένες, οὐδένας, οὐδένων, οὐδέσι; μηδένες, μηδένας, μηδένων, μηδέσι.

Fem. pl. forms are virtually never used. The accentuation for the nom., acc., and gen. would be οὐδεμίαι, οὐδεμίας, οὐδεμιῶν (and similarly μηδεμίαι, etc.). The dat. pl. fem. is not attested, and it is impossible to know how it would have been accented.

(e) The following nouns in -ηρ, with disyllabic nominatives: ἀνήρ, πατήρ, μήτηρ, θυγάτηρ, and γαστήρ, in the forms of the stem with -δρ- or -τρ-.

Thus

ἀνδρ-
πατρ-
μητρ-   }   -ός, -ί, -οῖν, -ῶν, -άσι
μητρ-
θυγατρ-
γαστρ-

(though not all the possible combinations of stem plus ending implied here are actually attested).

If the stem has the longer form in -ερ-, this -ερ- takes the accent (except in the vocatives ἄνερ, πάτερ, μῆτερ, θύγατερ: see § 130c): πατέρων, μητέρων, θυγατέροιν, ἀνέρος (poetic). Thus, the normal Attic paradigm of θυγάτηρ: θυγάτηρ, θύγατερ, θυγατέρα, θυγατρός, θυγατρί; θυγατέρε, θυγατέροιν; θυγατέρες, θυγατέρας, θυγατέρων, θυγατράσι. The accusative singular ἄνδρα, nominative/accusative dual ἄνδρε, nominative plural ἄνδρες, and accusative plural ἄνδρας accent the first syllable.

(f) ἀρήν 'lamb' follows the same pattern as ἀνήρ: ἀρήν, ἄρνα, ἀρνός, ἀρνί; pl. ἄρνες, ἄρνας, ἀρνῶν, ἀρνάσι. Ἀστήρ 'star' has the stem in -ερ- throughout (so ἀστέρος, ἀστέρων), except for the dative plural ἀστράσι.

The accent of ἀστράσι was, however, disputed in antiquity. Aristarchus prescribed ἀστράσι, but other grammarians thought ἄστρασι better on the (rather doubtful) grounds that ἄστρασι was a variant form of ἄστροις (dat. pl. of ἄστρον) and should be accented in the same way: see Sch. *Il.* 22. 28a (A).

(g) Two irregular nouns with disyllabic nominatives, κύων 'dog' (stem κυν-) and γυνή 'woman' (stem γυναικ-), are accented like the monosyllables under (a) above. Thus κύων, κύον, κύνα, κυνός, κυνί; pl. κύνες, κύνας, κυνῶν, κυσί; γυνή, γύναι, γυναῖκα, γυναικός, γυναικί; pl. γυναῖκες, γυναῖκας, γυναικῶν, γυναιξί.

134. Epic datives plural in *-εσσι* are always proparoxytone: ἄνδρεσσι, δούρεσσι, κύνεσσι.

EXERCISE 20: NOUNS AND ADJECTIVES WITH MOBILE ACCENT

Write the following nouns and adjectives with their correct case accent, given the accent of the base form shown in parentheses:

1. παισι, παιδων, παιδος, παιδα, παιδι, παιδε, παιδας, παιδες, παι, παιδοιν (παῖς)

2. ἑνα, ἑν, ἑνος, ἑνι, μια, μιαν, μιᾱς, μιᾳ (εἷς)

3. ἀνερ, ἀνδρα, ἀνδρος, ἀνδρι, ἀνδρε, ἀνδροιν, ἀνδρες, ἀνδρας, ἀνδρων, ἀνδρασι, ἀνδρεσσι (ἀνήρ)

4. φρενα, φρενος, φρενες, φρενων, φρεσι (φρήν)

5. μητερ, μητερα, μητρος, μητρι, μητεροιν, μητερας, μητερων, μητρασι (μήτηρ)

6. παντα (acc. sg. masc.), πᾱν, παντος, πᾱσαν, πᾱσης, παντι, πᾱσῃ, παντες, παντας, παντων, πᾱσι, παντα (nom./acc. pl. neut.), πᾱσαι, πᾱσᾱς, πᾱσων, πᾱσαις (πᾱς)

7. γυναι, γυναικα, γυναικος, γυναικι, γυναικες, γυναικας, γυναικων, γυναιξι (γυνή)

8. Τρωος, Τρωα, Τρωι, Τρωες, Τρωας, Τρωσι, Τρωων (Τρώς)

9. θυγατερ, θυγατερα, θυγατρος, θυγατρι, θυγατερε, θυγατερες, θυγατερων, θυγατρασι (θυγάτηρ)

10. ὠτος, ὠτε, ὠτι, ὠτα, ὠτων, ὠτοιν, ὠσι (οὖς)

11. τρια, τριων, τρισι (τρεῖς)

12. μηδενα, μηδεμιαν, μηδενος, μηδενων, μηδεν, μηδενι, μηδεμιᾳ, μηδεμιᾱς, μηδεμια, μηδενας, μηδενες, μηδεσι (μηδείς)

13. πατερ, πατερα, πατρος, πατρι, πατερες, πατερας, πατερων, πατρασι (πατήρ)

14. γονατος, γουνατος, γουνος, γουνατα, γουνα, γουνατων, γουνων, γουνασι, γουνεσσι (γόνυ)

Irregular nouns with monosyllabic nominative singular:
ναῦς, γραῦς, βοῦς, οἶς, Ζεύς

135. The nouns ναῦς, γραῦς, βοῦς, οἶς 'sheep', and Ζεύς accent the first or only syllable in the nominative, vocative, and accusative of all numbers and the last syllable (the ending) in the genitive and dative of all numbers. The accent on the nominative, vocative, and accusative of all numbers is a circumflex except in the nominative singular Ζεύς, and except where it falls on a short vowel (βόε, βόες, Δία). The accent on the ending of the genitive and dative of all numbers is acute or circumflex in accordance with the rules given in §§ 107–9, but note that the irregular genitive singular νεώς is oxytone: βοῦς, βοῦ, βοῦν, βοός, βοΐ, βόε, βοοῖν, βόες, βοῦς, βοῶν, βουσί; γραῦς, γραῦ, γραῦν, γραός, γραΐ, γρᾶε, γρᾱοῖν, γρᾶες, γραῦς, γρᾱῶν, γραυσί; ναῦς, ναῦ, ναῦν, νεώς, νηΐ, νῆε, νεοῖν, νῆες, ναῦς, νεῶν, ναυσί; οἶς, οἶ, οἶν, οἰός, οἰΐ, οἶε, οἰοῖν, οἶες, οἶς, οἰῶν, οἰσί; Ζεύς, Ζεῦ, Δία, Διός, Διΐ.

EXERCISE 21: ναῦς, γραῦς, βοῦς, οἶς, Ζεύς
Write the following forms with their correct accents:

1. Ζευ	11. γραυν	21. νεως	31. οιε	41. οις (nom. sg.)
2. νεοιν	12. Δια	22. γρᾱϊ	32. γραυσι	42. γραυς (acc. pl.)
3. βοοιν	13. νηϊ	23. νηες	33. βοε	43. ναυς (acc. pl.)
4. νηε	14. ναυσι	24. οιν	34. γρᾱος	44. οις (acc. pl.)
5. βοων	15. γραυ	25. οιϊ	35. Ζευς	45. βους (nom. sg.)
6. Διϊ	16. οιων	26. Διος	36. βοες	46. γρᾱοιν
7. οιες	17. οισι	27. γρᾱε	37. ναυ	47. βους (acc. pl.)
8. βοος	18. γρᾱων	28. νεων	38. βουσι	48. βοϊ
9. οι	19. ναυν	29. οιοιν	39. γρᾱες	49. γραυς (nom. sg.)
10. βουν	20. οιος	30. βου	40. ναυς (nom. sg.)	

EXERCISE 22: CUMULATIVE EXERCISE

Write the following phrases with their correct accents, remembering that an acute on a final syllable changes to a grave before another word that is not an enclitic, as long as punctuation does not intervene. (There are no enclitics in this exercise.) The base forms of nouns and adjectives (except participles) are indicated in parentheses.

1. σῑγᾱν κελευω.

2. αἰδους μετεχειν δυναιο. (αἰδώς)

3. πληρης εἰην δυναμεις. (πλήρης, δύναμις)

4. παθηματα μαθηματα. (πάθημα, μάθημα)

5. βους ἐχουσι καλλιστους. (βοῦς, κάλλιστος)

6. κελευομεν αὐτους διδοναι δικην. (αὐτός, δίκη)

7. αὐτοι πεπεισμενοι ἀλλους ἐπειθον. (αὐτός, ἄλλος)

8. διαβολη χρωμενοι ἀνδρας ἀνεπειθον. (διαβολή, ἀνήρ)

9. ἡττους λογους κρειττους ποιουσιν. (ἥττων, λόγος, κρείττων)

10. βουλη ἀκουσαι Γοργιου; (Γοργίας)

11. θυγατερ, θεους χρη δεσποτᾱς καλειν. (θυγάτηρ, θεός, δεσπότης)

12. ἀπολογου, Καλυψοι, βασιλεως κατηγορουντος. (Καλυψώ, βασιλεύς)

13. ταυτα δρᾱσᾱσ᾽ ἡλιον προσβλεπεις, ἐργα τλᾱσα δυσσεβη; (οὗτος, ἥλιος, ἔργον, δυσσεβής)

14. οὐδεν βελτῑον, Ἡρακλεις, ἀγαθων πολῑτων. (οὐδείς, βελτίων, Ἡρακλῆς, ἀγαθός, πολίτης)

15. διεκπλοι νεων ἀμεινον πλεουσων ἐργα ἠσαν. (διέκπλους < διέκπλοος, ναῦς, ἀμείνων, ἔργον)

16. τῑμαις ἡρωικαις ἐτιμησαν αὐτον τετελευτηκοτα, νεων οἰκοδομουντες. (τῑμή, ἡρωικός, αὐτός, νεώς)

17. φιλη δεσποινα, χρῡσης κομης ἀναδημα δεξαι. (φίλος, δέσποινα, χρῡσοῦς, κόμη, ἀνάδημα) (≈ Eur., *Hippolytus* 82–3)

18. παντων τουτων διδασκαλους είναι δει κοινους, ἀρνυμενους μισθον.
(πᾶς, οὗτος, διδάσκαλος, κοινός, μισθός) (≈ Plato, *Laws* 813e)

19. κακων γυναικων ἐργα ποιει Λῡσιστρατην ἀθῡμον περιπατειν.
(κακός, γυνή, ἔργον, Λῡσιστράτη, ἄθῡμος. Note that περιπατέω is
a contracted verb.)

20. γυναι γεραιᾱ, βασιλιδος πιστη τροφε, Φαιδρᾱς ὁρωμεν πολλᾱς
δυστηνους τυχᾱς. (γυνή, γεραιός, βασιλίς, πιστός, τροφός, Φαίδρᾱ,
πολύς, δύστηνος, τύχη) (≈ Eur., *Hippolytus* 267–8)

Chapter 5: Simplex Nouns and Adjectives: Accenting the Base Forms

136. In order to place an accent correctly on a noun or adjective, one needs to know on the one hand the rules given in chapters 2 and 4, and on the other the accent of the base form. Thus, once the accent of the nominative singular φωνή 'voice' is known, the accents of the other forms will follow given the rules already encountered: φωνήν, φωνῆς, φωνῇ; plural φωναί, φωνάς, φωνῶν, φωναῖς. In general, no firm rules can be given for the accents of the base forms and one needs to learn these individually. However, some kinds of nouns and adjectives are accented more regularly than others. For the most regularly accented categories in particular, some hints can be given.

137. It is a matter of taste how far to learn the accents of base forms individually and how far to rely on rules. The value of learning those rules that apply almost without exception (for example, adjectives in -ικος are accented -ικός) is self-evident, but one can reasonably disagree about the value of some rules that apply much less regularly (for example, nouns in -ρος are mostly recessive). If one makes use of such rules, one needs to learn large numbers of exceptions. Some will find these rules, with their lists of exceptions, helpful; others will prefer to learn more base forms individually than to learn large numbers of partial regularities.

138. The rules given in this chapter are arranged in three sections, proceeding from the most regular to the least. It is

81

recommended that the rules in the first two sections be committed to memory, together with (in the second section) the exceptions given. In the third section it is recommended that at least the words mentioned be committed to memory with their accents; the rules given may (or may not) be found helpful as an aid to the memory.

139. This chapter concerns primarily the accentuation of simplex (non-compound) nouns and adjectives, the accentuation of compounds being reserved for the following chapter. However, some of the rules given in this chapter apply as well to compounds as to simplicia. Such is the case wherever a restriction to simplicia is not indicated in the statement of a rule.

140. Within each section of rules that follows, subdivisions are made according to whether a word belongs to the first, second, or third declension. This arrangement is for convenience of reference only. 'Second declension' here includes adjectives whose feminines are of the first declension but whose masculines and neuters belong to the second declension (since the base form in such adjectives belongs to the second declension). 'Third declension' similarly includes adjectives whose feminines are of the first declension but whose masculine and neuter forms belong to the third declension.

I. Rules applying without exception

(a) First declension

141. Nouns in short -α are recessive: πότνια, γαῖα, ἀλήθεια, θάλαττα, τόλμα 'courage', γέφῦρα, βασίλεια 'queen' (contrast βασιλείᾱ 'kingdom', with long ᾱ).

142. Nouns in -συνη are paroxytone: δικαιοσύνη, ἀφροσύνη 'folly', δεσποσύνη 'power of a master'.

5. Nouns and Adjectives: Base Forms (§§ 138–50)

143. Masculine ā-stem nouns (with Attic genitive singular -ου) not ending in -της are paroxytone: νεᾱνίᾱς, σατράπης, Αἰνείᾱς, Θουκυδίδης.

(b) Second declension

144. Verbal adjectives in -τεος (or impersonal -τεον) are paroxytone: συλλογιστέος, αἱρετέον, προσδιανοητέον.

145. Ordinal numerals are recessive except for those in -στος, which are oxytone: πρῶτος, δεύτερος, τρίτος, τέταρτος...εἰκοστός, τριᾱκοστός, τεσσαρακοστός... (but πόστος 'which in numerical order?' and ὁπόστος 'in which place in numerical order').

146. Adjectives with the superlative suffixes -τατο- and -ιστο- are recessive: σοφώτατος, πικρότατος, ἀληθέστατος, ἥδιστος, αἴσχιστος, ἄριστος, λῷστος 'best', as are those adjectives in -ατος with superlative meaning: ἔσχατος 'furthest', ὕπατος 'highest', πύματος 'last', etc.

147. Simplex nouns in -θμος are oxytone: ἀριθμός, σταθμός 'farmstead', πορθμός 'strait', ῥυθμός 'rhythm'.

148. Nouns in -ιον (with the vowel of the penultimate syllable consisting simply of short -ι-), if they have more than three syllables, are recessive: μειράκιον, ἀργύριον, τὰ 'Ολύμπια 'the Olympic games' (but ἡ 'Ολυμπίᾱ 'Olympia'), χρηστήριον 'oracle', παγκράτιον 'boxing/wrestling contest', δεσμωτήριον 'prison'.

149. Nouns in -ισκος are paroxytone: ἀνθρωπίσκος, παιδίσκος, δεσποτίσκος.

150. Contracted adjectives of material in -ους (< -εος) are perispomenon: χρῡσοῦς, ἀργυροῦς, etc. (See § 122.)

(c) Third declension

151. Neuter nouns of the third declension are recessive: πῦρ, μένος, ὄνειδος, γῆρας, ὄνομα. (On the case accent of monosyllables such as πῦρ, see § 133.)

152. Nouns and adjectives in -ας, genitive -αδος, are oxytone: Ἀρκάς, φυγάς, Ἑλλάς, ὁλκάς 'trading vessel'.

153. Adjectives in -εις, genitive -εντος, are paroxytone: χαρίεις 'graceful', πτερόεις 'winged', φωνήεις 'endowed with speech'.

154. Nouns in -ευς are oxytone: βασιλεύς, φονεύς 'murderer', ἱππεύς, ἱερεύς, Ἀχιλλεύς. (On the case accent of these nouns, see § 126; on the monosyllable Ζεύς, see § 135.)

155. Nouns of more than one syllable in -ις, genitive -ιτος, are recessive: χάρις 'grace', θέμις 'right' (also declining with gen. θέμιστος or θέμιδος).

156. Simplex nouns and adjectives in -ξ and -ψ, if they have more than one syllable, take an accent on the penultimate syllable. If the penultimate syllable contains a long vowel or diphthong, the accent is acute or circumflex in accordance with the σωτῆρα rule: ἄναξ, θώραξ, κῆρυξ, ἄνθραξ 'charcoal', ἀλώπηξ 'fox', φοῖνιξ 'Phoenician; purple; date palm'.

According to Herodian, the υ in the nom. sg. of κῆρυξ, and the last ι in that of φοῖνιξ, was short, and the accent of the penultimate syllable was accordingly a circumflex. It is not clear why the υ and ι of the nom. sg. forms should be short, however, since the oblique cases have long vowels: κήρῡκος, φοίνῑκος, etc. WEST, *AESCHYLUS*, p. xlviii, argues for a long vowel in the final syllable of the nom. sg. forms, and paroxytone accentuation: κήρῡξ, φοίνῑξ. The argument involves, however, attributing to Herodian the rather elementary error of thinking that an α, ι, or υ that was 'long by position' (i.e. in a closed syllable) could not also be 'long by nature' (i.e. a long vowel); the possibility that Herodian made this error seems contradicted by his assertion that ἴξ 'grub' and Φίξ (Boeotian for Σφίγξ) had a (naturally) long -ῑ- (Hdn ii. 9. 5).

5. *Nouns and Adjectives: Base Forms* (§§ 151–7)

Aristarchus thought that πτερύγος (gen. sg. as if from *πτερύξ) rather than πτέρυγος (gen. sg. of πτέριξ) should be read at *Il.* 2. 316 and *Il.* 23. 875, where ancient commentators took the meaning to be 'part of the bird including the wings' rather than simply 'wing'. See Sch. *Il.* 2. 316b (AT), with the other sources cited by Erbse *ad loc.*

157. Feminine nouns in -ω are oxytone: ἠχώ 'echo', πειθώ 'persuasion', Γοργώ. (On the case accent of these nouns, see § 127.)

EXERCISE 23: RULES APPLYING WITHOUT EXCEPTION

Write the base forms given below with their correct accents:

1. βασιλευς	19. σταθμος	37. λαμπας (-αδος)
2. μελι	20. γειος	38. ἁβροσυνη 'luxury'
3. σωμα	21. ἐσχατος	39. τριας (-αδος) 'triad'
4. νεανισκος	22. φοινιξ	40. πεντηκοστος
5. ἀλωπηξ	23. νοητεον	41. δικαιοσυνη
6. χαριεις	24. ποιητεος	42. φειδω 'sparing'
7. ταχιστος	25. σιδηρους	43. παλλαδιον 'statue of Pallas'
8. χαλκους	26. χαρις	44. σατραπης
9. φιλτατος	27. ἀργυριον	45. σαλπιγξ 'trumpet'
10. ὀγδοος	28. ἀληθεια	46. δεκας (-αδος) 'company of ten'
11. θεμις	29. ἰχθυοεις	47. ὀβελισκος 'small spit'
12. μελιττα	30. Βορεας	48. κλεπτοσυνη 'thievishness'
13. χαλκευς	31. κεραμευς	49. Ὀλυμπια 'Olympic games'
14. ῥυθμος	32. πεμπτος	50. βασιλεια 'queen'
15. θαλαττα	33. νεανιας	51. τριακοσιοστος
16. πρωτος	34. ἀργυρους	52. Ἑλλας (-αδος)
17. ἀριθμος	35. ὑδωρ	53. σοφωτατος
18. ἡδιστος	36. παιδισκος	54. πειθω 'persuasion'

55. Ὀλυμπιας (-αδος) 'Olympic games'
56. μεταπυργιον 'space between towers'

II. Rules applying almost without exception

(a) First declension

158. Masculine *ā*-stem nouns in -της (with Attic genitive singular -ου) with light penultimate syllable are paroxytone: δεσπότης, ἐρέτης, ἱκέτης, τοξότης. EXCEPT κριτής, εὑρετής, ἐφευρετής 'contriver', ὑποκριτής 'answerer, actor'.

(b) Second declension

159. Comparative adjectives are recessive: σοφώτερος, πικρότερος, ἀληθέστερος, ἡδίων, αἰσχίων, ἀμείνων. Also recessive are 'contrastives' in -τερο-, words that are not genuinely comparative in meaning but refer to one member of a contrasting pair: ἕτερος (and ἅτερος, θάτερον = ὁ ἕτερος, τὸ ἕτερον), οὐδέτερος, μηδέτερος, ὕστερος, πρότερος. EXCEPT ἀριστερός, δεξιτερός.

ἅτερος and θάτερον were created by crasis of the article with ἅτερος, which was an old form of ἕτερος. Cf. § 81.

160. Simplex adjectives in -ικος (with the vowel of the penultimate syllable consisting simply of short -ι-) are oxytone: Μακεδονικός, μανικός 'mad', ξενικός 'foreign'; the same is true of -ικός adjectives that have come to be used as nouns, e.g. ναυτικόν 'fleet', Ἀττική (sc. γῆ) 'Attica', μουσική (sc. τέχνη) 'music'. EXCEPT the pronominal adjectives τηλίκος 'of such an age, so big', ἡλίκος 'as old as, as big as', πηλίκος 'how old, how big?', ὁπηλίκος 'however big, how big'.

Most compounds with the suffix -ικο- are also oxytone, but some are recessive, e.g. ἀφύσικος 'unscientific', ὑπερσυντέλικος 'pluperfect'.

5. Nouns and Adjectives: Base Forms (§§ 158–65)

161. Adjectives in -ιμος are recessive: γνώριμος 'well known', φρόνιμος, χρήσιμος. This rule holds without exception for adjectives in which the vowel of the penultimate syllable is simply short -ι-, but note, with long -ῑ-, σῑμός 'snub-nosed', and, with -οι-, Homeric and *koiné* ἑτοῖμος. In Attic, however, the accent shifted after the fifth century to the first syllable: ἕτοιμος.

Later Attic ἕτοιμος falls under Vendryes' law: see § 317.

162. Simplex nouns in -σμος and -γμος are oxytone: δασμός 'division', λογισμός 'calculation', κελευσμός 'order', ἀλαλαγμός 'shouting', διωγμός 'pursuit'. EXCEPT κόσμος, ὄγμος 'furrow'.

163. Simplex adjectives in -τος that are neither superlatives nor ordinal numerals (on which see §§ 145–6) are oxytone: πιστός, δυνατός, κλυτός, ποιητός, etc.; note also the pronominal adjective αὐτός (with its compounds ἑαυτόν, σεαυτόν, ἐμαυτόν). The main EXCEPTIONS are:

(a) the pronominal adjectives ἕκαστος, οὗτος, τοιοῦτος, τοσοῦτος, τηλικοῦτος;

(b) the epithet of Apollo ἕκατος (shortened form of ἑκατηβόλος or ἑκηβόλος) and the obscure Homeric adjectives ἄητος and ἄϊητος.

(c) Third declension

164. Simplex nouns in -ηρ are oxytone: ἀήρ, ἀνήρ, πατήρ, αἰθήρ, ἀστήρ, γαστήρ, σωτήρ, ἰατήρ, δαήρ 'brother-in-law'. EXCEPT θυγάτηρ, μήτηρ, φράτηρ 'clansman', εἰνάτηρ 'sister-in-law', πάνθηρ 'panther'. Cf. Δημήτηρ (originally a compound; see § 225).

165. Nouns and adjectives in -ων, genitive -οντος, are paroxytone: λέων, γέρων, ἄρχων, μεδέων 'ruler'. EXCEPT ἑκών (but ἄκων from ἀ-έκων). Note the contracted Ξενοφῶν (from -φά-ων).

166. Nouns of more than one syllable in -ωρ are paroxytone: ῥήτωρ, σημάντωρ 'commander', ἀμύντωρ 'defender'. EXCEPT ἰχώρ 'ichor'.

The rule given in § 203 below also applies almost without exception, but it is placed further on for comparison with §§ 201–2.

EXERCISE 24: RULES APPLYING ALMOST WITHOUT EXCEPTION

Write the base forms given below with their correct accents:

1. στατηρ	16. θεραπων	31. διωγμος	46. θυγατηρ
2. ῥητωρ	17. τοσουτος	32. ἀνηρ	47. Ἰωνικος
3. δρακων	18. φαιδιμος	33. κριτος	48. σημαντωρ
4. αὐτος	19. τηλικος	34. δεξιτερος	49. ἀλκιμος
5. ἰχωρ	20. θεσμος	35. ἀκων	50. χρησιμος
6. τοιουτος	21. σωτηρ	36. εἰνατηρ	51. χαριεστερος
7. θασσων	22. οὑτος	37. μουσικη	52. ῥυθμικος
8. αἰθηρ	23. ἑκαστος	38. δοτηρ	53. διδακτος
9. λεων	24. φρατηρ	39. ἑκων	54. ἑτοιμος (post-fifth-
10. μειζων	25. ὀγμος	40. Ξενοφων	century Attic accent)
11. δωτωρ	26. πιστος	41. λογισμος	
12. ἀηρ	27. γερων	42. φιλτερος	
13. πανθηρ	28. ἀραγμος	43. ἀριστερος	
14. σεισμος	29. μητηρ	44. ἑκατος (epithet of Apollo)	
15. πατηρ	30. κοσμος	45. ἑτοιμος (Homeric accent)	

III. Rules with exceptions

(a) First declension

167. First-declension abstract nouns (some of them having concrete as well as abstract meanings) formed immediately from verbal roots with no addition to the root except -η-/-ᾱ-, but often

88

5. Nouns and Adjectives: Base Forms (§§ 166–9)

with a change of its vowel (esp. to -o-), are usually oxytone. Thus (with the related verb shown in parentheses): ἀκοή 'hearing' (ἀκούω), πνοή 'blowing' (πνέω), τροπή 'turning' (τρέπω), κλοπή 'theft' (κλέπτω), τροφή 'nurture' (τρέφω), πομπή 'escort' (πέμπω), φθορά 'destruction' (φθείρω), σπουδή 'haste, zeal' (σπεύδω), σπονδή 'pouring of a drink-offering' (σπένδω), συμφορά 'happening' (συμφέρω), προσβολή 'attack' (aor. προσέβαλον), ἐκδρομή 'charge' (aor. ἐξέδραμον), χαρά 'joy' (χαίρω), φυή 'stature' (φύω), σφαγή 'slaughter' (σφάζω), ἀρχή 'beginning; power' (ἄρχω), φυγή 'flight' (aor. ἔφυγον). Paroxytone EXCEPTIONS include τύχη 'fate' (aor. ἔτυχον), μάχη 'combat' (μάχομαι), αὔξη 'growth' (αὐξάνω), βλάστη 'growth' (βλαστάνω), πάθη 'suffering' (aor. ἔπαθον), λήθη 'forgetting' (λανθάνω), βλάβη 'harm' (βλάπτω). Note that the change of root vowel to -o- never occurs in the paroxytone words of this class having primarily abstract meaning.

168. First-declension nouns formed as in § 167 but having only or primarily concrete meaning are sometimes oxytone, sometimes paroxytone. Oxytone words include φορβή 'fodder' (φέρβω), δορά 'hide' (δέρω 'flay'), ὀροφή 'roof' (ἐρέφω), ἐπιστολή 'message' (ἐπιστέλλω), ἀγορά 'market-place' (ἀγείρω). Paroxytone words include στέγη 'roof, house' (στέγω), κλίνη 'couch' (κλίνω).

169. First-declension nouns in -ιᾱ (Ionic -ιη) — mostly abstracts — are usually paroxytone: βασιλείᾱ 'kingdom', σοφίᾱ, ἀνδρείᾱ, δειλίᾱ, ναυμαχίᾱ, πολιορκίᾱ, ἡλικίᾱ 'age'. EXCEPTIONS — mostly not abstracts — include παιδιά 'play', ζειά 'emmer', παρειά 'cheek', ἀνθρακιά 'hot embers', σκιά 'shadow', καλιά (Ionic καλιή) 'hut', λαλιά 'talk', δεξιά 'right hand', χροιά 'skin', σκοπιά 'lookout-place', πατριά 'descent, family', αἱμασιά 'wall of dry stones', στρατιά 'army', ἐσχατιά 'furthest part', μητρυιά 'step-mother', λοφιά 'mane', ἀνεψιά 'female cousin'.

170. Masculine first-declension nouns in -της (with Attic genitive singular -ου) that

(a) are formed with the addition of -της to the stem of a related verb, and

(b) denote the agent of the verbal action, and

(c) have a heavy penultimate syllable

are usually oxytone: θεᾱτής 'spectator' (θεάομαι), ἀθλητής 'combatant' (ἀθλέω), μηνῡτής 'informer' (μηνύω), πρεσβευτής 'ambassador' (πρεσβεύω), διορθωτής 'corrector' (διορθόω), διαλλακτής 'mediator' (διαλλάσσω), σαλπιγκτής 'trumpeter' (σαλπίζω), εὐθυντής 'judge' (εὐθύνω), δικαστής 'juror' (δικάζω), σοφιστής 'sophist' (σοφίζω), πελταστής 'targeteer' (πελτάζω), ποιητής 'maker, poet' (ποιέω). But κυβερνήτης 'steersman' (κυβερνάω), σφενδονήτης 'slinger' (σφενδονάω), ὑφάντης 'weaver' (ὑφαίνω), δυνάστης 'ruler' (δυνατέω), αἰσυμνήτης 'umpire' (αἰσυμνάω), σῡκοφάντης 'denouncer' (σῦκον φαίνω), and ἀλήτης 'wanderer' (ἀλάομαι) are paroxytone.

171. Other masculine first-declension nouns in -της (with Attic genitive singular -ου) with heavy penultimate syllable are paroxytone: στρατιώτης, πολίτης, ὁπλίτης.

172. The meaning of a word in -της with heavy penultimate syllable may be different according to whether it is oxytone or paroxytone: γεννητής 'parent' (denoting the agent of γεννάω 'father; give birth to') but γεννήτης 'clansman'; πεδητής 'fetterer' (denoting the agent of πεδάω 'fetter') but πεδήτης 'one who wears fetters'.

173. Other oxytone first-declension nouns include ὀργή, σχολή, δραχμή, ἑορτή, αὐλή, ἀκμή, τῑμή, κεφαλή, βουλή, ἡδονή, ψῡχή, ἀδελφή, αἰχμή, φωνή, ἀρετή, ὁρμή 'impulse', κραυγή 'shouting', πυρά 'funeral pyre'.

174. Other paroxytone first-declension nouns include τέχνη, χώρᾱ, ἡμέρᾱ, γῆ, ῥώμη, δίκη, ἑσπέρᾱ, νίκη, ὕλη, πύλη, ἄτη, λίμνη, σελήνη, ἀνάγκη, εἰρήνη, μνήμη.

EXERCISE 25: RULES WITH EXCEPTIONS: FIRST DECLENSION

Write the base forms given below with their correct accents:

1. μαχη	21. στρατιᾱ	41. βουλη	61. στρατιωτης
2. αναγκη	22. θεᾱτης	42. οργη	62. σφενδονητης
3. κλοπη	23. πολῑτης	43. ἡμερᾱ	63. κεφαλη
4. ληθη	24. προσβολη	44. ὑφαντης	64. πρεσβευτης
5. μηνῡτης	25. τυχη	45. ἑσπερᾱ	65. βασιλειᾱ 'kingdom'
6. ἀδελφη	26. σοφιᾱ	46. ἀτη	66. γεννητης 'parent'
7. σεληνη	27. βλαβη	47. χωρᾱ	67. γεννητης 'clansman'
8. στεγη	28. ἐπιστολη	48. νῑκη	68. πεδητης 'fetterer'
9. ῥωμη	29. αὐξη	49. φορβη	69. δικαστης
10. μνημη	30. δραχμη	50. παιδιᾱ	70. δυναστης
11. ἀρετη	31. σπουδη	51. λιμνη	71. σῡκοφαντης
12. βλαστη	32. ἡλικιᾱ	52. σοφιστης	72. πολιορκιᾱ
13. πυλη	33. ἀνειᾱ	53. φυγη	73. σχολη
14. ἀνδρειᾱ	34. πομπη	54. φωνη	74. δειλιᾱ
15. εἰρηνη	35. ἀγορᾱ	55. ποιητης	75. αἰσυμνητης
16. κλῑνη	36. ναυμαχιᾱ	56. ἀρχη	76. ὁρμη
17. δικη	37. σκοτιᾱ	57. φθορᾱ	77. κυβερνητης
18. δορᾱ	38. ὑλη	58. ψῡχη	
19. ἀθλητης	39. ὁπλῑτης	59. τεχνη	
20. παθη	40. ἀλητης	60. πεδητης 'one who wears fetters'	

(b) Second declension

175. Second-declension words built simply on a verbal root, with the root vowel replaced by -ο-, are oxytone if they are adjectives or denote the agent of the verbal action, but recessive if they are nouns denoting the action itself or some object connected with the action. Thus, φορός 'bearing, favourable' (cf. the verb φέρω), τομός 'cutting, sharp' (τέμ-νω), λοιπός 'remaining over' (λείπω), τροφός 'nurse' (τρέφω), ἀοιδός 'singer' (ἀείδω), but φόρος 'tribute' (φέρω), τόμος 'slice' (τέμ-νω), δόμος 'house' (δέμω), βρόμος 'roaring sound' (βρέμω), δρόμος 'course, race' (aor. ἔδραμον), φόνος 'murder' (aor. ἔπε-φν-ον), τρόπος 'way, manner' (τρέπω), φόβος 'fear' (φέβομαι), λόγος 'word (etc.)' (λέγω), πόνος 'work' (πένομαι), ῥοῦς from ῥόος 'stream' (ῥέω), πλοῦς from πλόος 'voyage' (πλέω), νόμος 'custom' (νέμω). The words νομός 'pasturage' (νέμω) and δορός 'leathern bag' (δέρω 'flay') are EXCEPTIONS to this pattern. The rules that follow should not be applied to words falling under the present rule.

176. Simplex adjectives in -αιος are normally properispomenon if the antepenultimate syllable is heavy: σπουδαῖος, ἀναγκαῖος, ἀρχαῖος, γενναῖος, Ἀθηναῖος, Θηβαῖος, ἀμοιβαῖος 'interchanging'. EXCEPTIONS include δείλαιος, ἠβαιός 'small', δηναιός 'long-lived, aged, after a long time'.

177. Simplex adjectives in -αιος with light antepenultimate syllable are sometimes properispomenon, sometimes recessive. E.g. ἀγελαῖος 'belonging to a herd', σχολαῖος 'leisurely', κρυφαῖος 'hidden', δρομαῖος 'swift', but δίκαιος, βέβαιος 'secure', βίαιος 'forcible'. Note ἀκμαῖος 'in prime', where the weight of the antepenultimate syllable depends on the treatment of stop plus nasal (see § 52). EXCEPTIONALLY, παλαιός 'old' is oxytone.

178. Simplex adjectives in -ειος derived from the name of an animal (and meaning 'of' or 'belonging to' the animal) are all recessive: αἴγειος, ὀονίθειος, μήλειος, ἵππειος, θήρειος, ταύρειος, βόειος, κύνειος, ὕειος, as are most other simplex adjectives in -ειος if the antepenultimate syllable is light: βασίλειος 'royal', τέλειος 'perfect, entire', βρότειος 'mortal'. EXCEPTIONS include μεγαλεῖος 'magnificent'.

179. Simplex adjectives in -ειος with heavy antepenultimate syllable are sometimes properispomenon, sometimes recessive: ἀνδρεῖος, γυναικεῖος, οἰκεῖος, but δούλειος, αὔλειος 'of the court', ὀνείδειος 'reproachful'. EXCEPTIONALLY, ἀφνειός 'wealthy' (with stop plus nasal: see § 52) is oxytone.

180. Adjectives in -ιος (in which the vowel of the penultimate syllable is simply short -ι-) are generally recessive: αἴτιος, ἄξιος, ῥάδιος, πλούσιος, ὄλβιος, ὅσιος, δημόσιος, πολέμιος, ἐλευθέριος, Καρχηδόνιος, Συρᾱκόσιος, Λακεδαιμόνιος, ἄρτιος 'suitable', ἴδιος 'private', ἄθλιος 'wretched', ἅγιος 'holy'. EXCEPTIONS include ἀντίος, ἐναντίος, δεξιός σκολιός 'crooked', πολιός 'grey'.

181. Trisyllabic nouns in -ιον (with the vowel of the penultimate syllable consisting simply of short -ι-) are generally recessive if the first syllable is light: στάδιον, σκόλιον 'song', στόμιον 'mouth, bit', ὅριον 'boundary', μόριον 'piece', ξένιον 'guest-gift', ἔριον 'wool'. The main EXCEPTION is πεδίον 'plain'.

182. Trisyllabic nouns in -ιον (with the vowel of the penultimate syllable consisting simply of short -ι-), if they have a heavy first syllable, are sometimes paroxytone, sometimes recessive. E.g. θηρίον, χωρίον, παιδίον, σχοινίον 'cord', οἰκίον 'house', χρῡσίον 'piece of gold', σῑτίον 'bread', φορτίον 'load', ἱστίον 'sail', τειχίον 'wall', ἰσχίον 'hip-joint', ἡνία (pl.) 'reins', but φρούριον 'fort', ὅρκιον 'oath', ὄργια (pl.) 'rites', γῄδιον 'little farm', λήϊον 'standing crop', παίγνιον 'plaything', δέμνιον 'bed', ποίμνιον 'flock', σίλφιον 'laserwort'. Note also the Ionic forms of ξένιον 'guest gift' and ἔριον 'wool': ξείνιον, εἴριον. Trisyllabic -ιον nouns in which the weight of the first syllable depends on the treatment of a sequence of stop plus liquid or nasal (see § 52) are mostly recessive: τρύβλιον 'cup', ἴχνιον 'footprint', ἴκρια (pl.) 'half-deck'. But βιβλίον is paroxytone.

183. Nouns in -λος and -λον are generally recessive: ὄχλος, βίβλος, δόλος, φίλος, διδάσκαλος, ἄγγελος, δοῦλος, ὅπλον, ἆθλον, φῦλον 'tribe'. EXCEPTIONS include αἰγιαλός 'sea-shore' (cf. § 221), ὀβολός 'obol', δᾱλός 'fire-brand', ὀμφαλός 'navel', βηλός 'threshold', πηλός 'mud', μυελός 'bone marrow', χηλός 'chest, coffer', χῑλός 'fodder', θαλλός 'young shoot', φαλλός 'phallus', αὐλός 'reed-pipe', καυλός 'stem', μοχλός 'bar, bolt', ναυτίλος 'sailor', τροχίλος 'Egyptian plover'.

184. Simplex nouns in -μος are generally oxytone if -μος is preceded by another consonant or by a long vowel sound: ἀρδμός 'means of watering', ὀφθαλμός 'eye', ὀλοφυρμός 'lamentation', δημός 'fat', κνημός 'shoulder of a mountain', λῑμός 'hunger', λοιμός 'plague', θῡμός 'soul', βωμός 'altar'. EXCEPTIONS with recessive accentuation include δῆμος 'people', ψάμμος 'sand', ἄμμος 'sand', μῖμος 'mime', οἶμος 'way', ὅλμος 'mortar', ὅρμος 'chain', πότμος 'destiny', ὦμος 'shoulder', κῶμος 'revel', μῶμος 'blame'. (For nouns in -θμος, -σμος, and -γμος, see §§ 147, 162.)

185. Simplex nouns in -μος are generally recessive if -μος is preceded by a short vowel sound: γάμος, θάλαμος, πόλεμος, ἄνεμος, πλόκαμος 'lock of hair', κάλαμος 'reed'. Oxytone EXCEPTIONS include ποταμός.

186. Simplex adjectives in -νος are generally oxytone: ἱκανός, δεινός, κοινός, σκοτεινός, σεμνός, καινός 'new', ἁγνός 'holy', πυκινός 'compact'. EXCEPTIONS include:

(a) adjectives in -ινος which denote the material something is made from or the material it resembles (e.g. λίθινος 'of stone', ξύλινος 'wooden'), which are all recessive;

(b) adjectives in -συνος (e.g. πίσυνος 'relying on', θάρσυνος 'bold'), which are all recessive;

(c) ἐκεῖνος, μόνος (Ionic μοῦνος), δύστηνος 'wretched', ἕνος 'old', χαῦνος 'empty, porous'.

The recessive word ξένος, with Ionic ξεῖνος, is both noun and adjective, as is βάσκανος 'slanderer, slanderous'.

187. Simplex nouns in -νος and -νον are mostly recessive: στέφανος, κίνδυνος, χρόνος, ὕπνος, τύραννος, οἶνος, θρῆνος, λύχνος 'lamp', κύκνος 'swan', ὄκνος 'hesitation', ἔπαινος 'praise' (originally a compound), κάρηνον 'head'. EXCEPTIONS include καπνός, κεραυνός, οὐρανός, Ὠκεανός, χαλινός 'bit', ῥινός 'skin', κρημνός 'bank', οἰωνός 'large bird', υἱωνός 'grandson', κολωνός 'hill', κοινωνός 'companion', παρθένος 'girl', καρκίνος 'crab', ἐχῖνος 'hedgehog' (and other animal names in -ῖνος). The following oxytone words are both nouns and adjectives: Χριστιανός (with -ιᾱνος from Latin -iānus but accented according to the normal rule for Greek adjectives in -νος); ὀρφανός.

188. Simplex adjectives in -οιος are usually properispomenon: οἶος 'alone', αἰδοῖος 'deserving respect', ἀλλοῖος 'different', παντοῖος 'manifold', ἑτεροῖος 'different', ποῖος 'of what sort?', τοῖος 'such', οἶος 'of what sort', ὁποῖος 'of what sort'. The main EXCEPTIONS are post-fifth-century Attic γέλοιος 'amusing' and ὅμοιος 'like' (but old Attic and non-Attic γελοῖος, ὁμοῖος).

Later Attic γέλοιος and ὅμοιος fall under Vendryes' law; see § 317.

189. Simplex adjectives in -ρος are generally oxytone: αἰσχρός, μακρός, τολμηρός, μῑκρός, ἰσχυρός, σφαλερός 'slippery'. Recessive EXCEPTIONS include ἐλεύθερος, ἄκρος, γλίσχρος 'sticky', ἥμερος 'tame', θοῦρος 'impetuous', λάβρος 'furious', μέρμερος 'baneful', νύκτερος 'by night', πέλωρος 'monstrous', παῦρος 'small', φλαῦρος 'paltry'; also βάρβαρος and ἕσπερος 'of evening; evening star',

A New Short Guide to the Accentuation of Ancient Greek

which are both nouns and adjectives. The terms of abuse πονηρός, μοχθηρός, and μωρός are recessive in Attic (πόνηρος, μόχθηρος, μῶρος) but oxytone in the *koiné*.

The manuscripts of Aristophanes regularly accent all forms of πονηρός and μοχθηρός on the final syllable except for the voc. sg. forms, which are accented recessively: πόνηρε, μόχθηρε (GOETTLING, pp. 304–5; for codex Ravennas 137, 4 A, which I have consulted in facsimile, the distinction holds almost consistently). If this convention reflects a genuine tradition — and it would be difficult to explain except by assuming that the copyists were ultimately following some lost statement of a grammarian —, πονηρός and μοχθηρός would have been, in Attic, among those words whose voc. sg. forms had a recessive accent not conforming to the accentuation of the rest of the paradigm (see § 128–31). The surviving grammarians' statements on the accentuation of πονηρός/πόνηρος and μοχθηρός/μόχθηρος make no mention, however, of a distinction between the voc. and the rest of the paradigm. In the light of the conflicting ancient evidence, I do not encourage a radical departure from normal editorial practice on this point.

190. Simplex nouns in -ρος and -ρον are most often recessive: ταῦρος, ἤπειρος, ὅμηρος, τάφρος, ἄργυρος, δῶρον, ἄκρον, δένδρον. EXCEPTIONS include ἑταῖρος, καιρός, νεκρός, ἰᾱτρός, ἀγρός, γαμβρός, ἑκυρός, πενθερός, θησαυρός, χορός, μηρός (pl. μῆρα and μηροί), ἀφρός 'foam', νεβρός 'fawn', νεφρός 'kidney', σταυρός 'stake, cross', τῡρός 'cheese', πῡρός 'wheat', σορός 'cinerary urn', σωρός 'heap', κηρός 'wax', πτερόν, ἱερόν, λουτρόν 'bath', ξυρόν 'razor', πλευρόν 'rib', σφυρόν 'ankle', πυρά, τά 'watch-fires'; also ἐχθρός and ἀλῑτρός 'sinful, sinner', which are both adjectives and nouns, and φρουρός 'guard', originally a compound (< προ-ορός).

191. Other oxytone adjectives of the second declension include: καλός, ἀγαθός, σοφός, ὀρθός, κακός, χαλεπός, δειλός.

192. Other oxytone nouns of the second declension include: υἱός, ὁδός, καρπός, θεός, μισθός, χρῡσός, στρατός, ἀδελφός, ἐνιαυτός, βιός 'bow', ἀσκός 'bag', πεζός 'land force' (also adjective), βοηθός 'helper' (also adjective).

96

193. Other recessive adjectives of the second declension include: μέσος, ἴσος (Ionic ἶσος), νέος, δῆλος, φαῦλος, ὅλος, ὅσος, πόσος (interrog.), τόσος, ἄλλος, ἀλλήλους.

194. Other recessive nouns of the second declension include: νοῦς, οἶκος, πλοῦτος, ἵππος, τόπος, λίθος, νῆσος, σῖτος, σκότος, ἥλιος, ἄνθρωπος, θόρυβος, θάνατος, βίος 'life', ἄρτος 'loaf', κόλπος 'bosom', λόφος 'crest', ψόφος 'noise', πόντος 'sea', γόος 'wailing', ζῷον, ἔργον, ἄριστον 'breakfast', σπήλαιον 'cave'.

195. Note also ὀλίγος, ὁπόσος; old Attic and non-Attic ἐρῆμος but post-fifth-century Attic ἔρημος; fifth-century Attic τροπαῖον 'trophy' but later τρέταιον. Note λεώς 'people' and νεώς 'temple', which follow the Attic second declension. Note also ἕως 'dawn', which follows a variant of the Attic second declension (but Ionic ἠώς, third declension; see § 125).

The forms ἔρημος and τροταιον fall under Vendryes' law; see § 317.

EXERCISE 26: RULES WITH EXCEPTIONS: SECOND DECLENSION

Write the base forms given below with their correct accents:

1. στρατος	13. μονος	25. θηριον	37. ὀλβιος
2. δουλειος	14. 'Αθηναιος	26. ταυρος	38. τελειος
3. ἐνιαυτος	15. αἰδοιος	27. δικαιος	39. θαρσυνος
4. ἐργον	16. οἰκειος	28. ἑταιρος	40. ἐλευθερος
5. ἀθλον	17. ζῳον	29. πεζος	41. βαρβαρος
6. βιβλος	18. ἀνθρωπος	30. χρονος	42. ὠμος 'shoulder'
7. χωριον	19. αἰσχρος	31. ἀξιος	43. πεδιον 'plain'
8. αὐλειος	20. ἀδελφος	32. τροπος	44. ἠπειρος
9. ἀφνειος	21. παρθενος	33. πυκινος	45. φρουριον
10. ὀλιγος	22. παιδιον	34. φυλον	46. θαλαμος
11. ἱκανος	23. ψοφος	35. δολος	47. πενθερος
12. δυστηνος	24. ὀφθαλμος	36. μακρος	48. κακος

49. ταφρος	80. φοβος	111. κυκνος	142. πυρα (neut. pl.)
50. αντιος	81. ἐλευθεριος	112. ἱερον	143. δειλαιος
51. τοπος	82. ἀρχαιος	113. ὀβολος	144. ἀνεμος
52. τειχιον	83. ἀλῑτρος	114. ἀργυρος	145. κεραυνος
53. σταδιον	84. ποταμος	115. λιθος	146. χαλεπος
54. αἰτιος	85. σχολαιος	116. καρπος	147. φιλος
55. τολμηρος	86. ἀρτιος	117. λιθινος	148. γυναικειος
56. παλαιος	87. ῥους	118. αἰγειος	149. ἀγαθος
57. δεινος	88. καπνος	119. καιρος	150. βροτειος
58. θεος	89. φλαυρος	120. θορυβος	151. ὀνειδειος
59. βοηθος	90. μῑκρος	121. πλους	152. δημος 'fat'
60. ῥᾱδιος	91. γαμος	122. ξενος	153. γενναιος
61. θῡμος	92. ὀμφαλος	123. ἑκυρος	154. δημος 'people'
62. πολεμος	93. κοινος	124. λογος	155. διδασκαλος
63. ξυλινος	94. ψαμμος	125. ποτμος	156. Χριστιᾱνος
64. ὁσιος	95. σοφος	126. δωρον	157. φορος 'tribute'
65. χρῡσος	96. ὀρθος	127. ἰσχῡρος	158. πλοκαμος
66. ὀρνῑθειος	97. ἀγγελος	128. σῑτος	159. ἀναγκαιος
67. ἀκρον	98. ὀρφανος	129. ἀθλιος	160. νεως 'temple'
68. νεκρος	99. σκολιον	130. σκοτος	161. πισυνος
69. οὐρανος	100. ἡλιος	131. βωμος	162. ἀλληλους
70. λαβρος	101. στεφανος	132. ὁποιος	163. γοος
71. θησαυρος	102. δεξιος	133. δηναιος	164. θανατος
72. πτερον	103. νησος	134. ὁρκιον	165. λεως 'people'
73. δουλος	104. αὐλος	135. ἀλλος	166. νομος 'custom'
74. ἀρτος	105. δεμνιον	136. ποσος	167. ἑως 'dawn'
75. ἀγρος	106. ὁδος	137. νους	168. νομος 'pasturage'
76. σκοτεινος	107. μεγαλειος	138. φρουρος	169. λοιπος
77. ταυρειος	108. πλουτος	139. ὁσος	170. βιος 'bow'
78. ἰδιος	109. μισθος	140. ἰᾱτρος	171. λῑμος
79. Ὠκεανος	110. ὁλος	141. ποντος	172. ἐναντιος

5. Nouns and Adjectives: Base Forms (§§ 196–8)

173. κινδυνος	187. παντοιος	201. φαυλος	213. ξενιον
174. ὀχλος	188. πολεμιος	202. δειλος	214. βιος 'life'
175. μωμος	189. οἰκος	203. ἱππος	215. λοφος
176. δηλος	190. ἀνδρειος	204. μοχλος	216. μεσος
177. ὁπλον	191. καλαμος	205. ἀριστον	217. ἀκρος
178. χορος	192. νεος	206. σεμνος	218. δενδρον
179. ἐχθρος	193. πονος	207. ἀσκος	219. κρυφαιος
180. υἱος	194. ἰσος	208. μωρος (koiné accent)	
181. γαμβρος	195. βεβαιος	209. γελοιος (non-Attic accent)	
182. καλος	196. κολπος	210. πονηρος (Attic accent)	
183. ἐκεινος	197. βιβλιον	211. ὁμοιος (later Attic accent)	
184. βασιλειος	198. σπουδαιος	212. μοχθηρος (koiné accent)	
185. πλουσιος	199. ἐρημος (post-fifth-century Attic accent)		
186. σπηλαιον	200. τροπαιον (fifth-century Attic accent)		

(c) Third declension

196. Masculine or feminine monosyllabic nouns are usually oxytone: πούς, χείρ, μήν, νύξ, ῥίς, Ζεύς, Κρής 'Cretan', Τρώς 'Trojan'. EXCEPTIONS include ναῦς, βοῦς, γραῦς, παῖς, οἶς 'sheep', Θρᾶξ 'Thracian', and all in -ῡς, as δρῦς 'oak', ῦς 'boar', μῦς 'mouse'. There are very few monosyllabic adjectives, and they are perispomenon: εἷς (but οὐδείς, μηδείς), πᾶς (but ἅπᾱς).

197. Masculine or feminine simplex nouns in -ᾱν, -ην, -ῑν or -ῑς (genitive -ῑνος) are oxytone: λιμήν, ποιμήν, Σειρήν, δελφίς or δελφίν, Σαλαμίς, αὐχήν 'neck', ἀκτίς 'ray', Doric παιάν (cf. Attic and Ionic παιών). The main EXCEPTIONS are Ἕλλην, ἄρρην.

198. Nouns and adjectives in -ης, genitive -ητος, are generally oxytone if the penultimate syllable is heavy (counting a sequence of stop plus liquid or nasal as divided between syllables; see § 52), recessive if the penultimate is light: ἐσθής 'clothing', ἀδμής

99

'unconquered', προβλής 'jutting out' but πένης 'poor man', πλάνης 'wanderer, planet'. The main EXCEPTION is Κούρητες.

199. S-stem adjectives (i.e. adjectives in -ης, genitive -ους), which are mostly compounds, are generally oxytone: σαφής, ψευδής, ἀληθής, ὑγιής, εὐτυχής, δυστυχής, εὐμενής, εὐσεβής, εὐγενής, συγγενής, ἀσθενής, ἀσφαλής, ἐπιφανής, ἐπαχθής 'burdensome', εὐπρεπής 'seemly', ἐπιεικής 'fitting', δυσχερής 'difficult'. But those in -ηρης, -ωδης, and -ωλης are paroxytone, and accented persistently in their non-contracted forms (§ 120; cf. § 124): φρενήρης 'sound of mind', εὐώδης 'sweet-smelling', ἐξώλης 'utterly destroyed', πλήρης 'full'. EXCEPTIONS with other terminations are properly recessive in their non-contracted forms (§ 120; cf. § 124) and include the following: αὐτάρκης 'self-sufficient', αὐθάδης 'self-willed', ὑπερμεγέθης 'immense', συνήθης 'living together, accustomed', κακοήθης 'ill-disposed', εὐήθης 'good-hearted, simple-minded', ἀήθης 'strange' (and other compounds of ἦθος), ἀμφήκης 'two-edged', περιμήκης 'very large', ποδώκης 'swift-footed', κατάντης 'downhill', ἀνάντης 'up-hill'. Compounds of ἔτος are oxytone in the *koiné* (διετής, τριετής...) but properly recessive in Attic (διέτης, τριέτης...).

200. Nearly all *s*-stem personal names (i.e. personal names in -ης, genitive -ους) are properly recessive: Δημοσθένης, Σωκράτης, Τισσαφέρνης. Note the contracted names in -κλῆς (from -κλέης), e.g. Ἡρακλῆς, Περικλῆς. Other than the contracted type, the only commonly encountered EXCEPTIONS are the Nereid names Νημερτής and Ἀψευδής at *Il.* 18. 46, and Εὐμενής; cf. § 222.

201. Simplex nouns in -ις or -ῑς, genitive -ιδος/-ῑδος, that form their accusatives singular in -δα only (never in -ν, at least in Attic) are generally oxytone: ἐλπίς (ἐλπίδα), ἀσπίς (ἀσπίδα), πατρίς (πατρίδα), σφραγίς 'seal' (σφραγῖδα). The main EXCEPTIONS are those nouns in -τις, genitive -τιδος, formed as feminine counterparts to paroxytone masculine ā-stems in -της. These feminines in -τις are accented on the penultimate syllable. If the penultimate syllable contains a long vowel or diphthong, the accent is circumflex in accordance with the σωτῆρα rule: πολῖτις (πολίτης), ἱκέτις (ἱκέτης).

202. Nouns in -ις, genitive -ιδος, that at least optionally form an accusative singular in -ιν are recessive (like those of § 203, which also form an accusative singular in -ιν, but unlike those of § 201) ἔρις, Ἶρις, Ἄστεμις, Κύπρις. EXCEPTIONS include νεᾶνις 'girl'.

203. (This rule applies almost without exception: see the note after § 166.) Nouns in -ις, genitive -εως, are recessive (see § 123): πόλις, μάντις, τάξις, ὕβρις, δύναμις, φρόνησις, ἀκρόπολις, μητρόπολις, Ἀμφίπολις, Σάρδεις, κρίσις 'judgement', ἔκλειψις 'abandonment', ὑπόσχεσις 'promise'. BUT note πρυλέες (possibly not a genuine i-stem in origin) 'soldiers'.

204. Simplex adjectives in -υς are oxytone: θρασύς, βραχύς, εὐρύς, ταχύς, βαθύς, πολύς, εὐθύς, ἡδύς, ὀξύς, βραδύς. The main EXCEPTIONS are θῆλυς 'female', ἥμισυς 'half'. (Note also the noun πρέσβυς 'old man'.)

205. Simplex nouns in -ων, genitive -ωνος or -ονος, are often oxytone: ἀγών, χιτών, χειμών, ἡγεμών, παιών (cf. Doric παιάν), λειμών 'meadow', χιών 'snow', αἰών 'age', εἰκών 'likeness', κανών 'rod; rule', σταγών 'drop', βουβών 'groin', ἀγκών 'elbow', λαγών 'flank', ἀηδών 'nightingale', ἀλεκτρυών 'cock', χελῑδών 'swallow', ἀλγηδών 'pain'. But there are also many recessive words, including κύων (see § 133g), κίων 'pillar', γείτων 'neighbour', τέκτων 'carpenter', ἄξων 'axle', τρίβων 'threadbare cloak', κλύδων 'wave', κώδων 'bell', πώγων 'beard', ὀπάων 'comrade', βραχίων 'arm'. Note oxytone ἀλαζών 'braggart', and recessive Λάκων 'Laconian' and οὐρανίωνες 'gods', which are adjectives as well as nouns.

101

206. Personal names and place names in -ων, genitive -ωνος or -ονος, are mostly recessive: Ἀγαμέμνων, Ἀλκμαίων, Ἀμφίων, Κίμων, Κλέων, Κόνων, Ἰάσων, Σόλων. Note also contracted Ποσειδῶν (from Ποσειδάων; but uncontracted voc. Πόσειδον: § 130d). EXCEPTIONS include Κιθαιρών, Μαραθών, Καρχηδών, Βαβυλών.

207. Note also the following: μέγας (with μεγάλη the base form of the forms with -λ-, so μεγάλοι, μεγάλαι, μεγάλα); γυνή (see § 133g); ὀδούς; αἰδώς; ἥρως; γέλως; ἔρως; ἰδρώς 'sweat'; ἰχθύς.

According to Herodian, the nouns ἰχθύς, ὀφρύς 'eyebrow', and ὀσφύς 'loins' are perispomenon (like the monosyllables in -ῦς; see § 196): see Arcadius 104. 23–4, 105. 20–2; Eust. 1859. 10–17; Hdn i. 238. 16–17. They were, however, more generally taken to be oxytone, and are normally so accented in modern texts.

EXERCISE 27: RULES WITH EXCEPTIONS: THIRD DECLENSION
Write the base forms given below with their correct accents:

1. ποδωκης	15. Ἰρις	29. ὀξυς	43. εὐπρεπης
2. ἀλεκτρυων	16. σαφης	30. Σαρδεις	44. ἐλπις
3. Δημοσθενης	17. αὐχην	31. αὐθαδης	45. φρονησις
4. Μαραθων	18. ποιμην	32. πωγων	46. Περικλης
5. Ἀγαμεμνων	19. παιαν	33. ψευδης	47. ἡγεμων
6. Κιθαιρων	20. πρυλεες	34. ἀρρην	48. ἐπιεικης
7. Βαβυλων	21. ἀδμης	35. πᾶς	49. τεκτων
8. ἀκροπολις	22. πολιτις	36. μῦς	50. κρισις
9. ὑπερμεγεθης	23. ἀληθης	37. πολυς	51. συνηθης
10. μητροπολις	24. χειμων	38. ναυς	52. εὐτυχης
11. φρενηρης	25. ὀδους	39. Λακων	53. προβλης
12. ἀσφαλης	26. δρῦς	40. βραδυς	54. πατρις
13. κακοηθης	27. ἐρις	41. πλανης	55. πληρης
14. Καρχηδων	28. αἰδως	42. ἰδρως	56. εὐσεβης

57. Σωκρατης	78. ἑις	99. θηλυς	120. δυστυχης
58. Ἡρακλης	79. οὐδεις	100. εὐηθης	121. δυσχερης
59. Κουρητες	80. Σειρην	101. Κλεων	122. βραχυς
60. ἐπαχθης	81. ταχυς	102. γυνη	123. σφρᾱγῑς
61. Ἀμφιπολις	82. γραυς	103. ἀηθης	124. ἀσθενης
62. βραχῑων	83. Τρως	104. Κρης	125. Ἰασων
63. ἐπιφανης	84. εὐρυς	105. δυναμις	126. ἀμφηκης
64. καταντης	85. ἡμισυς	106. γειτων	127. Ἀρτεμις
65. Σαλαμῑς	86. εὐμενης	107. ἐξωλης	128. ἱκετις
66. ἐκλειψις	87. ταξις	108. αἰων	129. ἀναντης
67. περιμηκης	88. κῑων	109. Κυπρις	130. συγγενης
68. εὐωδης	89. πολις	110. Ἑλλην	131. πενης
69. ὑποσχεσις	90. δασυς	111. ἀγων	132. Τισσαφερνης
70. δελφῑς	91. μην	112. εἱς	133. εὐθυς
71. γελως	92. πους	113. ὑς	134. οἱς
72. χιτων	93. παις	114. κυων	135. ἡρως
73. Ζευς	94. βους	115. Θρᾳξ	136. χιων
74. βαθυς	95. λιμην	116. ὑβρις	137. ἰχθῦς
75. ἐρως	96. χειρ	117. ὑγιης	
76. μεγας	97. ασπις	118. διετης (Attic accent)	
77. ἐσθης	98. ἡδυς	119. τριετης (*koiné* accent)	

EXERCISE 28: CUMULATIVE EXERCISE

Write the following phrases with their correct accents, remembering that an acute on a final syllable changes to a grave before another word that is not an enclitic, as long as punctuation does not intervene. (There are no enclitics in this exercise.)

1. ὀγδοον ἐτος ἐτελευτᾱ.
2. νεᾱνιᾱς ἠν φιλοτῑμοτατος.

3. πολλα γραψᾱς βιβλια ἀπεθανε.

4. καλον μειρακιῳ φιλοσοφειν.

5. μαρτυρει συγγενης εἰναι 'Αλκιβιαδῃ.

6. χειμωνα φυγοντες λιμενα εὑρηκαμεν.

7. πᾱσα ἀνθρωπου ψῡχη πληρης πολλων ἐλπιδων.

8. παντα ἀνατρεπει κυβερνητης μεθυων.

9. ἀναξ 'Οδυσσευ, καιρον ἱσθ' ἐληλυθως. (Soph., *Ajax* 1316)

10. καλον δ' ἀγαλμα πολεσιν εὐσεβης πονος. (Eur., *Supplices* 373)

11. αἰσχιστα παντων ἐργα δρωσα τυγχανεις. (Soph., *Electra* 586)

12. θαλασσα κλυζει παντα τἀνθρωπων κακα. (Eur., *Iphigenia in Tauris* 1193)

13. προνοιᾱς οὐδεν ἀνθρωποις ἐφῡ / κερδος λαβειν ἀμεινον. (Soph., *Electra* 1015–16)

14. ἀγαθους ἀνδρας ἐγκωμιαζομεν ʽἀγαθος ἀνηρ οὑτος' λεγοντες.

15. χαιρετ' 'Αττικος λεως, / ἰκταρ ἡμενᾱς Διος / παρθενου φιλᾱς φιλοι. (ἰκταρ 'close to' is recessive.) (Aesch., *Eumenides* 997–9)

16. παις μεγας μῑκρον ἐχων χιτωνα παιδα μῑκρον μεγαν ἐχοντα χιτωνα ἐξεδῡσε. (≈ Xenophon, *Cyropaedia* 1. 3. 17)

Chapter 6: Accentuation of Compounds, Proper Names, Pronouns, Numerals, and Indeclinable Words

Accentuation of compound nouns and adjectives

208. Greek has a large number of compound words. We shall use the term 'compound' to include (a) words that combine the stems of two or more smaller words (e.g. ὀνειρο-κρίτης), and (b) words in which the first element is merely a prefix (e.g. ἄ-δικος).

Some accentual problems relate to the distinction between compounds and derivatives of compounds. The latter are words containing two elements but derived by means of a suffix from a word that was itself already a compound. Thus, ἀδικίᾱ 'injustice' has been derived from ἄδικος 'unjust', itself consisting of the prefix ἀ- plus the element -δικος (cf. δίκη 'justice'). The abstract-noun-forming suffix -ίᾱ belongs semantically to the whole unit ἄδικος, not to the second part alone: the compounding is prior to the addition of the suffix. Derivatives of compounds generally follow the rules and generalities applying to simplicia with the same suffixes. Thus, ἀδικίᾱ 'injustice' is paroxytone like most abstract nouns in -ίᾱ (see § 169). Similarly, δημοκρατικός 'of democracy' is derived from δημοκρατέομαι 'have a democratic consitution' and has the usual accent for simplex adjectives in -ικος (see § 160). However, the distinction between a true compound and a derivative of a compound is often difficult to draw in practice, and even where it can be drawn it does not always determine accentuation. In the following paragraphs an attempt is made to give rules for accenting compounds (including derivatives of compounds) without requiring compounds to be distinguished from derivatives of compounds.

209. The purpose of the preceding chapter was to provide some guidance for the accentuation of simplex (non-compound) nouns

105

and adjectives. Some of the rules given there happen to apply to compounds as well as to simplicia (non-compound words), and these were distinguished from rules that cannot be taken, at least without further qualification, to apply to compounds. The purpose of the following paragraphs is to provide an introduction to the accentuation specifically of compounds; there is some repetition of information given in the preceding chapter.

210. The most common accentuation for the base form of a compound noun or adjective is recessive. (The case accents follow the rules given in chapter 4.) Thus:

(a) All feminine nouns in short -α: ἄνοια 'folly', εὔνοια 'goodwill', ἔνδεια 'lack'. (Cf. § 141.)

(b) All compound neuters in -ιον: παγκράτιον 'boxing/wrestling contest', ναυάγιον 'piece of wreckage'. (Cf. § 148.)

(c) All third-declension neuter nouns: προβούλευμα 'preliminary decree', παράδειγμα 'example'. (Cf. § 151.)

(d) All nouns in -ις, -εως: ἀκρόπολις, μητρόπολις, φιλόπολις (used as an adjective), Ἀμφίπολις, ἔκλειψις 'abandonment', ὑπόσχεσις 'promise'. (Cf. § 203.)

(e) Nearly all s-stem proper names (nominative singular in -ης, genitive in -ους): Δημοσθένης, Πολυνείκης. Note the contracted s-stem compound personal names in -κλῆς (from -κλέης): Ἡρακλῆς, Περικλῆς, Θεμιστοκλῆς. Other than the contracted type, the only commonly encountered EXCEPTIONS are the Nereid names Νημερτής and Ἀψευδής at *Il.* 18. 46, and Εὐμενής; cf. § 222.

(f) Most compound adjectives in -ιος (with the penultimate syllable consisting solely of short -ι-): ὑποχείριος 'under control', ἀναίτιος 'innocent', παράλιος 'by the sea' (cf.

παραλία (sc. γῆ or χώρα) 'coast'). EXCEPTIONS include ἐναντίος. (Cf. § 180.)

(g) Most compound nouns in the abstract-forming suffix -ία: ναυμαχία 'naval battle', ἐμπειρία 'experience', ἀπορία 'perplexity', προδοσία 'betrayal'. (Cf. § 169.)

(h) Most adjectives and proper names in -ων, genitive -ονος (properly recessive throughout the paradigm, EXCEPT those in -φρων, which are *all* paroxytone in the nominative singular masculine/feminine and accented persistently in the other cases: see §§ 118–19): ἐπιστήμων, εὐδαίμων, κακοδαίμων, ἄφρων.

(i) Other recessive compounds include: ἐπιβάτης (gen. -ου) 'marine', προδότης (gen. -ου) 'betrayer', εὔνους, ἄδικος, ἄθυμος, ἀθάνατος, ἀδύνατος, φιλόσοφος, καταγέλαστος, τριήραρχος, αἰχμάλωτος, Ἀλέξανδρος, Λύσανδρος, Φίλιππος, Πολύφημος, ἄπρακτος 'unavailing', ἀφύλακτος 'unguarded', ἀπροσδόκητος 'unexpected', ἀνέλπιστος 'unhoped-for', ἀναρίθμητος 'countless', ἀναίσχυντος 'shameless', ἔμπειρος 'experienced', ὑπήκοος 'subject', εὐώνυμος 'of good name', ἔνοικος 'inhabitant', ἐπιτήδειος 'suitable', κατάσκοπος 'scout', αὐτόνομος 'independent', στρατόπεδον, Οἰδίπους.

(j) Note that the following recessive words are compounds in origin: πολιορκία, ἔπαινος 'praise', ῥᾴθυμος 'taking things easy', Σωκράτης (gen. -ους), σώφρων, ἄκων.

211. Second-declension compounds in which the second member is of type -κτονος (i.e. is built on the same root as a related verb, with no addition to the root except for -ος, but usually with a change of root vowel to -ο-) are recessive if the meaning of the second element is passive: θηρότροφος 'fed on beasts' (cf. the related verb τρέφω), λιθόβολος 'struck with stones' (aor. ἔβαλον), τηλέπομπος 'far sent' (πέμπω).

212. If the second member of such a compound has active meaning, however, the word is generally paroxytone if the penultimate syllable is light, oxytone if the penultimate is heavy: λιθοβόλος 'throwing stones' (aor. ἔβαλον), ψῡχοπομπός 'soul-escorting' (πέμπω) (contrast λιθόβολος, τηλέπομπος of § 211). So also πατροκτόνος 'father-slaying' (κτείνω), βουκόλος 'tending cattle' (related to Latin *colō* 'take care of'), μισθοφόρος 'mercenary' (φέρω), λοχᾱγός 'leader of an armed band' (ἄγω), στρατηγός 'general' (ἄγω). EXCEPTIONS include the compounds of -οχος (ἔχω 'hold' or ὀχέω 'carry'), which are recessive when uncontracted, even when active in meaning: γαιήοχος 'earth-carrying', αἰγίοχος 'aegis-bearing', ἡνίοχος 'rein-holder, charioteer'. Compounds in -ουχος, from -ο-οχος, are properispomenon according to the rules of contraction: δᾱδοῦχος 'torch-holder', σκηπτοῦχος 'sceptre-bearing'. *Prefixed* compounds of our type are also recessive, whether active or passive: ἔφορος 'overseer, ephor' (ὁράω), σύμμαχος 'ally' (μάχομαι), διάβολος 'slanderer; Satan' (aor. ἔβαλον), πρόγονος 'ancestor' (aor. ἐγενόμην), Ἐπίγονος (aor. ἐγενόμην). Further EXCEPTIONS include πτολίπορθος 'city-sacker' (πέρθω).

213. First-declension compound nouns in which the second member is of type φορά (i.e. is built on the same root as a related verb, with no additional suffix added after the verbal root except -η/-ᾱ, but often with a change of root vowel to -ο-) are usually oxytone (cf. §§ 167–8): συμφορά 'happening' (φέρω), ἐκδρομή 'charge' (aor. ἔδραμον), προσβολή 'attack' (aor. ἔβαλον), ἐπιστολή 'message' (στέλλω).

214. Masculine first-declension nouns in -της (with Attic genitive singular -ου) that

(a) are formed with the addition of -της to the stem of a related verb, and

(b) denote the agent of the verbal action, and

(c) have a heavy penultimate syllable

are usually oxytone (cf. § 170): διορθωτής 'corrector' (διορθόω), διαλλακτής 'mediator' (διαλλάσσω), συμβουλευτής 'adviser' (συμβουλεύω). EXCEPTIONS include σῦκοφάντης 'denouncer' (σῦκον φαίνω).

215. Compound verbal adjectives in -τεος (or impersonal -τεον) are all paroxytone, like the simplicia (§ 144): συλλογιστέος, προσδιανοητέον.

216. Compound nouns in -ευς are all oxytone, like the simplicia (§ 154): ἐπιστολεύς 'secretary', συγγραφεύς 'writer'.

217. Most s-stem compound *adjectives* (nominative singular in -ης, genitive in -ους), unlike the proper names (§§ 210e, 222), are oxytone: εὐτυχής, δυστυχής, εὐσεβής, εὐγενής, ἀσεβής, ἀσθενής, ἀσφαλής, ἀληθής, ἐπιφανής, ἐπαχθής 'burdensome', εὐπρεπής 'seemly', δυσχερής 'difficult', ἀμελής 'careless'. But those in -ηρης, -ωδης, and -ωλης are paroxytone in their base forms and accented persistently in their non-contracted forms (see §§ 120, 124, 199): φρενήρης 'sound of mind', εὐώδης 'sweet-smelling', ἐξώλης 'utterly destroyed'. EXCEPTIONS with other terminations are properly recessive in their non-contracted forms (see again §§ 120, 124, 199) and include the following: αὐτάρκης 'self-sufficient', αὐθάδης 'self-willed', ὑπερμεγέθης 'immense', συνήθης 'living together, accustomed', κακοήθης 'ill-disposed' (and other compounds of ἦθος), ἀμφήκης 'two-edged', περιμήκης 'very large', ποδώκης 'swift-footed', κατάντης 'downhill', ἀνάντης 'up-hill'. Compounds of ἔτος are oxytone in the *koiné* (διετής, τριετής) but properly recessive in Attic (διέτης, τριέτης...).

218. Almost all compound adjectives in -ικος are oxytone, like the simplicia (see § 160): δημοκρατικός 'of democracy', νομοθετικός 'legislative', οἰκονομικός 'practised in managing a household'. There are occasional EXCEPTIONS, e.g. ἀφύσικος 'unscientific', ὑπερσυντέλικος 'pluperfect'.

Most compounded words in -ικος are derivatives of compounds rather than true compounds and are therefore accented like the simplicia in -ικός. The occasional exceptions are true compounds. Thus, ἀφύσικος is a compound of ἀ- and φυσικός, not a derivative in -ικος of a word already compounded: see the note to § 208.

219. Nouns and adjectives in -ξ and -ψ are normally accented on the penultimate syllable, like the simplicia (see § 156): Κύκλωψ, κώνωψ 'gnat', χέρνιψ 'water for washing the hands'. Some compounds in -ωψ, however, are oxytone — μονώψ 'one-eyed', εὐώψ 'fair-eyed' — as are compounds whose second member is a monosyllable formed from the root of a related verb, having a long vowel: ἀπορρώξ 'broken off; piece broken off' (cf. ῥήγνῡμι), βουπλήξ 'ox-goad' (cf. πλήσσω 'strike').

220. Compounds in -σμος are normally oxytone, like the simplicia (see § 162): ἀναδασμός 'partition', ἀναλογισμός 'reckoning', κατακλυσμός 'flood'. But compounds in -δεσμος, -οσμος, and -κοσμος are recessive: σύνδεσμος 'bond', δύσοσμος 'foul-smelling', εὔοσμος 'sweet-smelling', εὔκοσμος 'orderly'.

Again, most compounded words in -σμος are derivatives of compounds rather than true compounds, and are therefore accented like the simplicia in -σμος. The exceptions are true compounds. Thus, σύνδεσμος is a compound of σύν and δεσμός, not a derivative in -σμος of a word already compounded; cf. the notes to §§ 208, 218.

221. Note the accentuation of αἰγιαλός 'sea-shore', a word whose etymology is uncertain but which may well be a compound. Other non-recessive compounds include κακοῦργος and πανοῦργος.

EXERCISE 29: ACCENTUATION OF COMPOUNDS

Write the base forms given below with their correct accents:

1. δαδουχος
2. προδοτης
3. συμφορᾱ
4. οἰκονομικος
5. δυσοσμος
6. μητροπολις
7. σῡκοφαντης
8. ἀφυλακτος
9. Θεμιστοκλης
10. ἀκων
11. εὐπρεπης
12. 'Αμφιπολις
13. συνδεσμος
14. εὐνοια
15. Οἰδιπους
16. Λῡσανδρος
17. ἀναισχυντος
18. ἐφορος
19. διαβολος
20. ῥᾳθῡμος
21. ἀφρων
22. ἀπεριᾱ
23. ἐπιστολευς
24. ἐμπειρος
25. ἀδικος
26. ἀθανατος
27. αἰχμαλωτος
28. ὑποχειριος

29. αἰγιαλος
30. συγγραφευς
31. ἐμπειριᾱ
32. διορθωτης
33. τριηραρχος
34. ἐκδρομη
35. Φιλιππος
36. ἐνδεια
37. ἐκλειψις
38. Πολυφημος
39. παγκρατιον
40. ἀσθενης
41. ἀκροπολις
42. Ἡρακλης
43. σκηπτουχος
44. εὐσεβης
45. Ἐπιγονος
46. αἰγιοχος
47. πολιορκιᾱ
48. ἀδυνατος
49. ἐπιβατης
50. ναυᾱγιον
51. ἀνελπιστος
52. ἀπρᾱκτος
53. ἀνοια
54. ὑποσχεσις
55. κατασκοπος
56. παραλιᾱ

57. θηροτροφος 'fed on beasts'
58. Κυκλωψ
59. κατακλυσμος
60. ἀναριθμητος
61. δυσχερης
62. ἀναιτιος
63. συμβουλευτης
64. διαλλακτης
65. προγονος
66. συλλογιστεος
67. καταγελαστος
68. προσδιανοητεον
69. μονωψ 'one-eyed'
70. ἀπροσδοκητος
71. δημοκρατικος
72. Σωκρατης (gen. -ους)
73. ἐπιτηδειος
74. ψῡχοπομπος 'soul-escorting'
75. ἀσφαλης
76. ἐπαινος 'praise'
77. εὐκοσμος
78. δυστυχης
79. προβουλευμα (neut.)
80. Δημοσθενης (gen. -ους)
81. στρατοπεδον
82. παραδειγμα (neut.)
83. τηλεπομπος 'far sent'
84. ἀθῡμος

111

85. Ἀλέξανδρος	99. προσβολη	113. λιθοβολος 'throwing stones'
86. εὔνους	100. συμμαχος	114. βουκολος
87. προδοσιᾱ	101. ἀληθης	115. εὐδαιμων
88. ἀπορρωξ	102. γαιηοχος	116. ἀναλογισμος
89. εὐωνυμος	103. ἀμελης	117. πατροκτονος 'father-slaying'
90. εὐτυχης	104. ἐπιστημων	118. στρατηγος
91. σωφρων	105. φιλοσοφος	119. ἐνοικος
92. νομοθετικος	106. χερνιψ	120. ἡνιοχος
93. αὐτονομος	107. ἀνᾱλωτεος	
94. ὑπηκοος	108. ἀσεβης	
95. Περικλης	109. ἀναδασμος	
96. πτολιπορθος	110. φιλοπολις	
97. ναυμαχιᾱ	111. λιθοβολος 'struck with stones'	
98. ἐπιστολη	112. Πολυνεικης (gen. -ους)	

Accentuation of proper names

222. Many proper names, whether personal names or place names, have recessive accents, even if similarly-formed common nouns or adjectives are non-recessive. Thus, *s*-stem adjectives in -ης (genitive -ους) are usually oxytone (e.g. ἀμελής 'careless'), but the personal names of this formation are nearly all recessive (so Ἀριστοφάνης, Δημοσθένης, Πολυδεύκης, Πολυνείκης) or are contracted from recessive forms (Σοφοκλῆς, Περικλῆς, and other names in -κλῆς, from -κλέης).

The Nereid names Νημερτής and Ἀψευδής at *Il.* 18. 46 are oxytone (like the adjectives νημερτής and ἀψευδής), as is the name Εὐμενής. Various other *s*-stem names are listed as oxytone by late grammatical sources: see Hdn i. 82. 2–4 with Lentz' note.

223. A number of proper names that are in origin non-recessive adjectives have retracted the accent: Πύρρος 'Pyrrhus' but πυρρός 'yellowish-red'; Φαῖδρος 'Phaedrus' but φαιδρός 'bright'. On the other hand, some non-recessive words do not retract the accent when they are used as proper names: Κεφαλή, name of an Attic deme, like κεφαλή; Θεσσαλός (personal name: *Il.* 2. 679) like Θεσσαλός 'Thessalian'.

224. There are occasional instances in which a non-recessive proper name contrasts with a recessive adjective. For example, Ἀμφοτερός (personal name: *Il.* 16. 415) but ἀμφότερος; Ἀξιός (river name: e.g. *Il.* 2. 849) but ἄξιος. Such examples are, however, extremely rare. Normally, if a proper name is in origin a recessive adjective then it is recessive also as a proper name: Πλοῦτος (god of wealth: e.g. Hesiod, *Theogony* 969) like πλοῦτος; Κλυμένη (Nereid at *Il.* 18. 47) like κλυμένη (fem. of κλύμενος 'famous').

225. Frequently-occurring recessive proper names not mentioned above include the following: Ἀλέξανδρος, Δαίδαλος, Πρίαμος, Ὅμηρος, Ἡσίοδος, Κῦρος, Φίλιππος, Ἡρόδοτος, Μήδεια, Ἑλένη, Εὐριπίδης, Θουκυδίδης, Ξέρξης, Ἀρτοξέρξης, Ἀγαμέμνων, Κλέων, Ἰάσων, Ἕκτωρ, Οἰδίπους, Διόνυσος, Ἥρα, Ἀθήνη, Περσεφόνη, Κάστωρ, Δημήτηρ (properly recessive throughout the paradigm: other cases Δήμητερ, Δήμητρος, Δήμητρι), Ἀπόλλων, Ἄρτεμις, Ἄρης, Πελοπόννησος, Κόρινθος, Κύπρος, Ἑλλήσποντος, Δῆλος, Μυκήνη (or pl. Μυκῆναι; cf. Ἀθῆναι), Ἀσίᾱ, Ἀκρόπολις. Note the contracted Ποσειδῶν (from Ποσειδάων; but voc. Πόσειδον: §§ 130d, 206) and Ξενοφῶν (from Ξενοφάων).

226. By no means all proper names are recessive. The following points in particular should be noted:

(a) All names in -ευς (like other -ευς nouns: see §§ 154, 216) are oxytone: Ἀχιλλεύς, Περσεύς, Ὀδυσσεύς. Cf. Ζεύς (whose declension is irregular: see § 135).

(b) Female names in -ω are oxytone (like other feminine nouns in -ω: see § 157): Γοργώ, Σαπφώ, Ἀργώ.

Because Sappho's dialect had a consistently recessive accent (see §§ 306–7), she herself would have pronounced her name with the accent on the α, but in Attic and the *koiné* her name is oxytone.

(c) Trisyllabic personal names in -ιλος and -υλος are mostly paroxytone: Τρωΐλος, Ζωΐλος, Αἰσχύλος, Ῥωμύλος.

(d) Other non-recessive proper names include Ἑλλάς, Βαβυλών, Κιθαιρών, Καρχηδών, Μαραθών, Σαλαμίς, Δελφοί, Δαρεῖος.

EXERCISE 30: ACCENTUATION OF PROPER NAMES
Write the proper names given below with their correct accents:

1. Ζωιλος	18. Ὀδυσσευς	35. Ἀπολλων	52. Ἀριστοφανης
2. Κῦρος	19. Κιθαιρων	36. Φιλιππος	53. Πελοποννησος
3. Φαιδρος	20. Αἰσχυλος	37. Ἡροδοτος	54. Ἀγαμεμνων
4. Ἑλλας	21. Σοφοκλης	38. Ἀθηναι	55. Ἑλλησποντος
5. Ἀθηνη	22. Εὐριπιδης	39. Ἀχιλλευς	56. Δαρειος
6. Σαλαμῑς	23. Ἀκροπολις	40. Ῥωμυλος	57. Πυρρος
7. Καστωρ	24. Γοργω	41. Ἀργω	58. Δαιδαλος
8. Ἑλενη	25. Καρχηδων	42. Τρωιλος	59. Δελφοι
9. Ὁμηρος	26. Περσεφονη	43. Ἀλεξανδρος	60. Πριαμος
10. Περσευς	27. Περικλης	44. Μυκηναι	61. Μηδεια
11. Κυπρος	28. Ἡσιοδος	45. Ξερξης	62. Ζευς
12. Κορινθος	29. Θουκυδιδης	46. Δημοσθενης	63. Βαβυλων
13. Κλεων	30. Δημητηρ	47. Πολυνεικης	64. Ἀσιᾱ
14. Ἑκτωρ	31. Ἀρτοξερξης	48. Δηλος	65. Ἰασων
15. Οἰδιπους	32. Ποσειδων	49. Ξενοφων	66. Ἀρτεμις
16. Ἡρᾱ	33. Διονῡσος	50. Πολυδευκης	67. Σαπφω
17. Ἀρης	34. Μαραθων	51. Πλουτος	

6. Compounds, Proper Names, Pronouns, etc. (§§ 226–9)

Accentuation of non-enclitic pronouns

227. Some forms of pronouns are *enclitic* and will be treated in the next chapter. The following paragraphs concern non-enclitic forms of pronouns. (For the circumstances under which the non-enclitic forms of the personal pronouns are used, see § 281.)

228. The accentuation of the non-enclitic personal pronoun forms shown below can best be seen from their complete paradigms. Observe that in most forms the accentuation is the same for the pronouns of all three persons, but notice also the differences in the dative singular and dative plural:

	First person SG.	Second person SG.	Third person SG.
Nom.	ἐγώ	σύ	—
Acc.	ἐμέ	σέ	ἕ
Gen.	ἐμοῦ	σοῦ	οὗ
Dat.	ἐμοί	σοί	οἷ
	DUAL	DUAL	DUAL
Nom./Acc	νώ	σφώ	—
Gen./Dat.	νῷν	σφῷν	—
	PL.	PL.	PL.
Nom.	ἡμεῖς	ὑμεῖς	σφεῖς
Acc.	ἡμᾶς	ὑμᾶς	σφᾶς
Gen.	ἡμῶν	ὑμῶν	σφῶν
Dat.	ἡμῖν	ὑμῖν	σφίσι

The acc., gen., and dat. forms of the plural pronouns ἡμεῖς and ὑμεῖς have unemphatic variants that occur in poetry and are accented on the first syllable (ἥμας, etc.); for these see § 292.

229. The perispomenon forms have for the most part arisen from contraction, and uncontracted forms may be found in poetry: ἐμέο,

115

σέο, ἡμέων. Beside ἡμῖν and ὑμῖν there exist forms with short -ι-, which are oxytone: ἡμίν, ὑμίν.

230. When a personal pronoun is strengthened by the addition of -γε, the accent is usually unchanged: ἐμέγε, σύγε, σοῦγε (or ἐμέ γε, σύ γε, σοῦ γε). But the forms ἔγωγε and ἔμοιγε are proparoxytone in Attic.

Vendryes argued that ἔγωγε and ἔμοιγε resulted from earlier *ἐγῶγε and *ἐμοῖγε (the expected results of adding -γε to ἐγώ, ἐμοί and applying the σωτῆρα rule) by the Attic accent shift that has come to be known as Vendryes' law: a properispomenon word ending in a sequence consisting of a light syllable followed by a heavy syllable followed by a light syllable tended to become proparoxytone in Attic (see § 317, with references). Vendryes' argument is supported by the fact that Ap. Dysc. (*Pron.* 49. 9, *Adv.* 181. 30, *Synt.* 138. 9; cf. Sch. *Il.* 1. 174 (A)) specifies that ἔγωγε and ἔμοιγε are Attic forms. Although the hypothetical *ἐγῶγε and *ἐμοῖγε are not attested for any dialect, this is likely to be because in dialects other than Attic the sequences retained their original status as full words followed by enclitics (see §§ 278–89, esp. § 285; cf. § 298); West accordingly restores ἐγώ γε and ἐμοί γε in Homer (see WEST, *ILIAD* i, p. xviii).

231. The base forms of possessive pronouns are oxytone: ἐμός, σός, ἑός. But those in -τερος are recessive (compare § 159): σφέτερος, ἡμέτερος, ὑμέτερος.

232. The relative pronoun is accented like an oxytone adjective of the second (and first) declension. Thus ὅς, ἥ, οὗ, etc., like σοφός, σοφή, σοφοῦ. So also the article, apart from the forms with a rough breathing (these are written in isolation without an accent; see § 267a and more generally §§ 267–77): τόν, τήν, τό, τοῦ, τῆς, etc.

233. The pronoun ὅδε is similarly accented, with the particle -δε having no effect on the accent of the element ὅ, ἥ, etc. if a syllable with a short vowel precedes: ὅδε, τόδε, τόνδε, τάδε. Where a syllable with a long vowel or diphthong precedes, the particle -δε again has no effect on the accent if the accent on the corresponding form of the article is a circumflex: τοῦδε, ταῖσδε, etc. Where the corresponding form of the article has an acute on a long vowel or diphthong, however, Herodian prescribed properispomenon accentuation, retaining the accent on the same syllable as in the article but changing the acute to a circumflex to comply with the σωτῆρα law: ἥδε, τοῦσδε, etc. However, for the dual τώδε he prescribed paroxytone accentuation in violation of the σωτῆρα law (as if the two parts were treated for accentuation as separate elements, the second part being enclitic; cf. §§ 298–9). Most modern editors ignore Herodian here, however, printing ἥδε, τούσδε, etc., as well as τώδε.

For Herodian's rule, see Sch. *Il.* 8. 109c (A), with other sources cited by Erbse *ad loc.* For modern texts with τούσδε etc. as well as τώδε, see for example D.B. Monro and T.W. Allen's OCT edition or M.L. West's Teubner edition of the *Iliad*, e.g. *Il.* 2. 346 (τούσδε), *Il.* 8. 109 (τώδε).

234. The pronominal adjectives τοιόσδε and τοσόσδε are accented on the same principle as ὅδε (despite τοῖος and τόσος). Forms such as τοιούσδε/τοιοῦσδε present the same difficulty as forms such as τούσδε/τοῦσδε (§ 233); modern editors usually print τοιούσδε etc., but τοιοῦσδε is likely to be the authentic form.

235. The pronominal adjectives οἷος, ὁποῖος, ποῖος (interrogative), and τοῖος are properispomenon; ὅσος, πόσος (interrogative), ὁπόσος, and τόσος are paroxytone.

236. The pronoun αὐτός (with its compounds ἑαυτόν and contracted αὑτόν; σεαυτόν and contracted σαυτόν; ἐμαυτόν) is oxytone, but οὗτος, ἐκεῖνος, τοιοῦτος, τοσοῦτος, τηλικοῦτος, and δεῖνα 'so-and-so' are properispomenon.

237. The interrogative pronoun τίς accents the first syllable throughout: τίς, τίνα, τί, τίνος/τοῦ, τίνι/τῷ, τίνε, τίνοιν, τίνες, τίνας, τίνα, τίνων, τίσι. The forms τίς and τί never change their final acute to a grave (§ 76). On the indefinite τις, which is enclitic, see § 279a and more generally §§ 278–98.

EXERCISE 31: ACCENTUATION OF PRONOUNS (NON-ENCLITIC FORMS)

Write the non-enclitic forms of pronouns given below with their correct accents:

1. ταις
2. ἡμεις
3. ἡμᾱς
4. ἐμοι
5. τοιοσδε
6. σφω
7. σφᾱς
8. ἐμον
9. αὐτο
10. του (article)
11. οὑτος
12. οἱν
13. σφετερη
14. τοιν
15. ὑμων
16. τοιουτος
17. ᾱς
18. ἡμετερην
19. νῳν
20. σεαυτη
21. τῳδε
22. αἱς
23. ἐκεινω
24. δεινα
25. ὑμῑν
26. τονδε

27. αὐτοιν
28. το
29. σαις
30. της
31. ὁς
32. τοδε
33. τω
34. σῳ
35. σφισι
36. τοιουδε
37. τησδε
38. ἐμος
39. ὁδε
40. ταυταις
41. τουτῳ
42. σφῳν
43. ἐγω
44. οὑτοι
45. αὐτους
46. αὐτη
47. ὠ
48. σφων
49. ἡμῑν
50. αὐτῳ
51. τοσαισδε
52. αὐται

53. ὑμετερος
54. ἐμης
55. τοσουτος
56. ὑμᾱς
57. τους
58. ἐκεινος
59. ἐγωγε (Attic accent)
60. ὡν (gen. pl. fem.)
61. τινων (interrog.)
62. σοι (poss. pron.)
63. τοιουτους
64. τωνδε (gen. pl. fem.)
65. ἡμετερων (gen. pl. fem.)
66. δεινος (gen. sg.)
67. ὡν (gen. pl. neut.)
68. οὑ (pers. pron.)
69. ἐμου (pers. pron.)
70. ἐκεινοις
71. αὐτων (gen. pl. fem.)
72. ὑμετερον
73. ἐμοιγε (Attic accent)
74. τοσωνδε (gen. pl. masc.)
75. ὁ (rel. pron.)
76. σε
77. σου (pers. pron.)
78. τουτων (gen. pl. neut.)

79. νω	96. τουτο	109. σοι (pers. pron.)
80. ἑος	97. ἐμεγε	110. τινες (interrog.)
81. ἡμων	98. ση	111. οἱ (pers. pron.)
82. ᾧ	99. ἁ	112. ἡ (rel. pron.)
83. σφεις	100. σων	113. ἐκεινα
84. ἡν	101. τοις	114. τι (interrog.)
85. τοιονδε	102. σοις	115. σφετερον
86. ταισδε	103. τουδε	116. τουσδε (Herodian's accent)
87. τα	104. ἑ	117. ἡμετερων (gen. pl. masc.)
88. ἐμε	105. σουγε	118. ἐμαυτης
89. τᾱς	106. ταυτην	119. σφετερης
90. τηλικοιτος	107. συ	120. ταυτα 'these things'
91. ὑμεις	108. συγε	121. τις (interrog.)

92. τινα (interrog., nom. pl. neut.)
93. τηνδε (accent that most editors prefer)
94. τοιᾱνδε (accent that most editors prefer)
95. τοιᾱσδε (acc. pl. fem., accent likely to be authentic)

Accentuation of numerals

238. Cardinals are recessive — εἷς, δύο, τρεῖς, τέτταρες — EXCEPT for ἑπτά, ὀκτώ, ἐννέα, and ἑκατόν. (On the case accent of εἷς, δύο, and τρεῖς, see § 133c.) The word μύριοι is recessive in the sense 'ten thousand' but paroxytone in the sense 'countless' (μῡρίοι); μῡριάς (in δύο μῡριάδες, τρεῖς μῡριάδες) is oxytone, like other nouns in -ας, genitive -αδος (see § 152).

239. Ordinals are recessive: πρῶτος, δεύτερος, τρίτος... EXCEPT those in -στος, which are oxytone: εἰκοστός, τριᾱκοστός, τεσσαρακοστός... (but πόστος 'which in numerical order?' and ὁπόστος 'in which place in numerical order').

240. Compound cardinals and ordinals (not in -στος) including καί, when treated as a single word, are recessive: τρεισκαίδεκα,

119

ὀκτωκαιδέκατος. Compound numerals without καί, when treated as a single word, keep the accent of the second member only: δεκατρεῖς, δεκατέσσαρες. But ἕνδεκα and δώδεκα are recessive.

241. Numeral adverbs in -ακις are all paroxytone: τετράκις, πεντάκις, ἑξάκις. Similarly πολλάκις, τοσαυτάκις and other adverbs in -ακις. Note also the accentuation of ἅπαξ, δίς, τρίς.

EXERCISE 32: ACCENTUATION OF NUMERALS
Write the numerals given below with their correct accents:

1. ὀκτω
2. τριτος
3. ἐνδεκα
4. ἑπτα
5. μια
6. πεμπτος
7. ἐν
8. ἑβδομος
9. δευτερος
10. χιλιοι
11. εἱς
12. ἁπαξ
13. εἱκοσι
14. δεκα
15. δυο
16. τετταρες
17. ἑκατον
18. πρωτος
19. ἑξ
20. πεντε
21. τρεις
22. δεκατος
23. ἐνατος
24. τρια
25. δωδεκα
26. ἐννεα
27. ὀκτωκαιδεκατος
28. δωδεκακις
29. δεκατρεις
30. τριᾱκοντα
31. δυο μῡριαδες
32. τριᾱκοστος
33. ἑξηκοντα
34. δισμῡριοι
35. ἐννεακαιδεκα
36. ἑπτακοσιοι
37. ἑπτακαιδεκατος
38. πεντεκαιδεκα
39. μῡριοι 'ten thousand'
40. ἑβδομηκοστος
41. τετταρακοστος
42. τετταρακοντα
43. ἑνδεκατος
44. ἑκκαιδεκατος
45. ὀγδοηκοστος
46. μῡριοι 'countless'
47. μῡριοστος
48. τρεισκαιδεκα
49. δωδεκατος
50. ποστος (interrog.)

Accentuation of indeclinable words

(a) Adverbs and particles

242. Many adverbs are cases of nouns or adjectives used adverbially and are accented accordingly. Thus, βίᾳ, εὐθύ (also an improper preposition: see § 253), μακράν, σχολῇ, ἀνάγκῃ, τέλος, ἰδίᾳ, δημοσίᾳ, δρόμῳ, ἔργῳ. The adverb ἀμέλει 'don't trouble, of course' is an imperative of ἀμελέω. BUT ἄληθες 'really!' is

120

6. Compounds, Proper Names, Pronouns, etc. (§§ 240–6)

recessive in Attic, although the neuter singular of ἀληθής is oxytone: ἀληθές.

243. Other adverbs consist of a preposition and case-form of a noun, written as one word; these have the accent of their second element: παραχρῆμα 'straightaway', ἐπίσης 'equally', καθόλου 'on the whole', προὔργου (for πρὸ ἔργου) 'serviceable'. EXCEPTIONS include ἐκποδών 'out of the way' (not *ἐκποδῶν).

244. Adverbs in -ως are accented like the genitives plural masculine of the corresponding adjectives. So καλῶς like καλῶν (base form καλός); οὕτως like τούτων (οὗτος); ἄλλως like ἄλλων (ἄλλος); ἀξίως like ἀξίων (ἄξιος); ἡδέως like ἡδέων (ἡδύς); εὐσεβέως, contracted εὐσεβῶς, like εὐσεβέων, contracted εὐσεβῶν (εὐσεβής). But note αὕτως 'just so; in vain' (cf. αὐτῶν), and cf. ὡσαύτως 'just so'. Note also ὁμῶς 'likewise' (ὁμός) but ὅμως 'all the same, nevertheless'.

245. Adverbs in -ω are normally recessive: οὕτω, ἄφνω, ἄνω, εἴσω, ἔξω (the last three also as improper prepositions: see § 253).

246. Adverbs in -θε(ν), -θι, -σι, -σε and -οι normally follow the accent of the word from which they are derived, subject to the law of limitation and the σωτῆρα rule:

ἀγρόθεν (ἀγρός)
ἄλλοθεν, ἄλλοθι, ἄλλοσε (ἄλλος)
ἀρχῆθεν (ἀρχή)
αὐτόθεν, αὐτόθι, αὐτόσε (αὐτός)
ἐγγύθεν, ἐγγύθι (ἐγγύς)
ἐκεῖθεν, ἐκεῖθι, ἐκεῖσε (ἐκεῖ)
ἑτέρωθεν, ἑτέρωθι, ἑτέρωσε (ἕτερος)
θύρᾶθεν 'from outside', θύρᾱσι 'outside' (θύρᾱ)
οἴκοθεν, οἴκοθι, οἴκοι (οἶκος)
ὁποτέρωθε(ν), ὁποτέρωθι, ὁποτέρωσε (ὁπότερος)
ὥρᾱσι 'in season' (ὥρᾱ)

121

Notice that since the nominative plural ending -οι counts short for accentuation whereas the adverbial ending counts long (see §§ 66–8), the σωτῆρα rule requires a circumflex accent in οἶκοι (nominative plural) but an acute in οἴκοι (adverb). Adverbs in -οι that are accented on the ending have a circumflex: ἁρμοῖ 'lately' (cf. ἁρμοί 'joints'); Ἰσθμοῖ 'at the Isthmus' (cf. ἰσθμοί 'isthmuses'); Μεγαροῖ 'at Megara' (cf. Μεγαρόθεν 'from Megara'; but note Μέγαρα 'Megara').

κυκλόθε(ν) and κυκλόσε follow the original accent of κύκλος, which was *κυκλός; this accentuation is not attested in Greek but is found in the Sanskrit cognate *cakrás*. The tradition regarding the accentuation of πάντοθεν/παντόθεν varies: see Ap. Dysc., *Adv.* 192. 2–3.

247. Adverbs in -ου are perispomenon: οὐδαμοῦ, πανταχοῦ, ὑψοῦ, αὐτοῦ. EXCEPT ὅπου, καθόλου, προὔργου. (On καθόλου and προὔργου, see § 243.)

248. A number of these adverbs in -ου have cognates in -θε(ν), -θι, -σε, -οι, -η (or -ῃ) belonging to the same bases and keeping the accent on the same syllable:

ὅθεν 'from where', οἷ 'to where' (οὗ 'where')

ὅποι (ὅπου). Note, however, ὁπόθεν, ὁπόθι, ὁπόσε.

οὐδαμόθεν, οὐδαμόθι, οὐδαμόσε, οὐδαμοῖ, οὐδαμῇ (οὐδαμοῦ)

πανταχόθεν, πανταχόθι, πανταχόσε, πανταχοῖ, πανταχῇ (πανταχοῦ)

πόθεν, ποῖ (ποῦ) (all interrogatives; for the indefinites ποθέν 'from somewhere', etc., see § 279b and more generally §§ 278–98)

ὑψόθεν, ὑψόθι, ὑψόσε (ὑψοῦ)

249. The following adverbs in -δε are accented on the penultimate syllable: ὧδε 'thus', ἐνθάδε 'here', ἐνθένδε 'from here'. For the accentuation of words such as οἶκόνδε, in which -δε is added to an accusative and indicates motion towards, see § 300.

6. Compounds, Proper Names, Pronouns, etc. (§§ 246–51)

250. Most other adverbs are recessive: εὖ, αὖ, νῦν 'now', πῶς (interrog.), πότε (interrog.), τότε, ἤδη, μάλα, σφόδρα, ἔνθα, αὖθις, ἄρτι, ἅπαξ, πάλαι, πάλιν, πάνυ, λίαν, μάτην, μόλις, δεῦρο, λάθρᾳ (also an improper preposition: see § 253), ἐνταῦθα, τήμερον, ἑκάστοτε. EXCEPTIONS include πρώ, ὀψέ, ἐκεῖ, ἀεί/αἰεί, θαμά, σχεδόν, ἀντικρύ, μεταξύ (also an improper preposition: see § 253), ἐμποδών (like ἐκποδών), αὐθημερόν, αὐτίκα, παραυτίκα.

251. In addition to the adverbs mentioned above, Greek has a large number of conjunctions, connectives, and other particles. Many of these are written with an acute (or grave, according to the rule given in § 75) on the final or only syllable: οὐδέ, μηδέ, ἀλλά, ἠδέ 'and' (poetic), ἰδέ 'and' (poetic), ἐπεί, καί, ἀτάρ 'but', αὐτάρ 'but' (poetic), ἠμέν 'both' (picked up by ἠδέ 'and'; poetic), μή, ἤ (and Homeric ἠέ) 'either/or', ἤ 'than', πρίν, γάρ, μέν, δέ, μήν, δή, νή, μά, ἄν, ἐάν/ἄν/ἤν, ὡς 'thus' (except after καί or οὐδ'), πλήν (also an improper preposition: see § 253), ἐπειδή. The following are recessive: ἆρα (particle of interrogation), ἄρα (expresses inference), ὧς 'thus' (after καί or οὐδ'), γοῦν, οὔκουν 'therefore not', δήπου, δῆτα, ἔπειτα, μέντοι, ἕως 'until, while, as long as', πότερον, ὅπως, ἵνα, ὅτι, ἄτε, ὅτε, ἔτι, ἦ 'indeed' (also used to introduce a question not containing alternatives: ἦ οὐχ ὁρᾷς;). Note the accentuation of the following, each compounded from two particles, with the second keeping its accent: οὐκοῦν 'therefore', οὐκέτι, μηκέτι, ὁτιοῦν '(anything) whatsoever', ὁπότε. Note also ἡνίκα 'when'.

Apollonius Dyscolus, Herodian, and other grammarians prescribed a circumflex for ὧς 'thus' in the phrases καὶ ὧς and οὐδ' ὧς (where it means the same as ὅμως 'even so') and an acute (ὥς) in all other contexts: see LEHRS, *ARISTARCHUS*, pp. 378–81; WACKERNAGEL, *BEITRÄGE*, pp. 16–19. Modern editors do not always follow this rule.

Oxytone ἤ (or ἠέ) is used to introduce the first half of an alternative question, perispomenon ἦ to introduce the second half: ἤ δολιχὴ νοῦσος, ἦ "Αρτεμις

123

ἰοχέαιρα /...κατέπεφνεν; 'was it a long illness, or was it arrow-handed Artemis...who killed you?' (*Od.* 11. 172–3). See Ap. Dysc., *Conj.* 224. 18–225. 1; Arcadius 210. 15–21; cf. LSJ, s.v. ἤ.

252. Recall that the five disyllabic conjunctions ending in a short vowel written with an acute, οὐδέ, μηδέ, ἀλλά, ἠδέ, and ἰδέ, do not acquire an accent on the first syllable if the final vowel is elided (§ 78): ἀλλ᾽ οὖν. This is due to the fact that some of our conjunctions (the first twelve listed in § 251) are *proclitic*. Proclitics will be discussed in further detail in the next chapter, but for the purposes of writing the accent correctly on the conjunctions given above the only practical effect of proclisis is the lack of accent on elided οὐδέ, μηδέ, ἀλλά, ἠδέ, and ἰδέ.

EXERCISE 33: ACCENTUATION OF ADVERBS AND PARTICLES

Write the adverbs and particles given below with their correct accents:

1. οὐδαμοθι	15. δηπου	29. ἀντικρυ	43. θυραθεν
2. ἠ 'than'	16. ὁποθι	30. καθολου	44. αὐθις
3. αὐτοθεν	17. τημερον	31. πανταχοι	45. δη
4. μεταξυ	18. εὐθυ	32. σφοδρα	46. ἐκεισε
5. οὐδαμοι	19. αὐτως	33. ὁπου	47. ἠ 'indeed'
6. ἠδη	20. ὑψοσε	34. ὀψε	48. ἠδε
7. πανταχη	21. ἑτερωσε	35. εἰσω	49. ἑως 'until'
8. δευρο	22. εὐσεβως	36. ἑτερωθι	50. ἐπισης
9. παλιν	23. σχολη	37. ἐξω	51. ὁποτερωθεν
10. ἐγγυθι	24. ἑτερωθεν	38. προὐργου	52. ὁτι
11. μηκετι	25. ἁτε	39. ἀλλοθι	53. οἰκοι 'at home'
12. ὑψου	26. ἀει	40. ἀγροθεν	54. μην
13. οὐδαμου	27. οἰκοθεν	41. μολις	55. νη
14. οὐτω	28. θυρασι	42. ἰδιᾳ	56. οἰ 'to where'

6. Compounds, Proper Names, Pronouns, etc. (§§ 251–2)

57. δε	87. ἡνίκα	117. δημοσίᾳ	147. ἀξίως
58. ὅπως	88. ἵνα	118. μακράν	148. πρίν
59. καί	89. μάτην	119. πρω	149. ὅμως 'all the same'
60. ὡρᾶσι	90. ἀναγκη	120. αὐτου	150. μη
61. οὐδαμη	91. ἀλλα	121. ἐκει	151. παραυτικα
62. βιᾳ	92. οἰκοθι	122. πανταχου	152. οὐδαμοθεν
63. λιᾱν	93. ἐαν	123. γαρ	153. ἠμεν (conjunction)
64. ἀρχηθεν	94. μα	124. ὁποσε	154. μαλα
65. οὐδε	95. ἀμελει	125. νῦν	155. ἠ 'either/or'
66. μεν	96. ἀν	126. ἀνω	156. πανταχοθεν
67. πλην	97. αὐτικα	127. ἐμποδων	157. οὐδαμοσε
68. οὐκετι	98. ἰδε 'and'	128. ἀλλοσε	158. ὁποτερωσε
69. γουν	99. ἀταρ	129. μεντοι	159. ὁποτερωθι
70. Μεγαροι	100. τελος	130. ὁποθεν	160. παραχρημα
71. ἐκαστοτε	101. αὐτοθι	131. ὁτιουν	161. ὅμως 'likewise'
72. ὑψοθεν	102. ἐογω	132. ὁποτε	162. που (interrog.)
73. καλως	103. ὅτε	133. ἐγγυθεν	163. ποι (interrog.)
74. δρομω	104. ἁπαξ	134. ποτερον	164. αὐθημερον
75. ἐκειθι	105. εὐ	135. πανταχοθι	
76. ἐτι	106. ἐφνω	136. οὐ 'where'	
77. ἀλλοθεν	107. ἐπει	137. οὐκουν 'therefore'	
78. θαμα	108. ἐκειθεν	138. πανταχοσε	
79. ὁποι	109. μηδε	139. οὐκουν 'therefore not'	
80. ἐκποδων	110. δητα	140. ὡς 'thus' (after καί or οὐδ')	
81. ὑψοθι	111. ἐπειτα	141. ποθεν (interrog.)	
82. αὐτοσε	112. ἀρτι	142. ἀρα (particle of interrogation)	
83. ὡσαυτως	113. αὐταρ	143. ὡς 'thus' (not after καί or οὐδ')	
84. σχεδον	114. ἐπειδη	144. Ἰσθμοι 'at the Isthmus'	
85. λαθρᾱ	115. ἐνθα	145. ἀρα (expresses inference)	
86. παλαι	116. πανυ	146. ἀληθες 'really!' (Attic accent)	

(b) Prepositions

253. Most 'improper prepositions' (those incapable of forming compound verbs) are recessive: ἄχρι, μέχρι, εἴσω, ἔξω, ἄνω, ἄνευ, ἅμα, λάθρᾱ, χάριν, ὄπισθεν, ἔμπροσθεν, ἄνευθε(ν), ἕνεκα. But πλήν, χωρίς, ἐγγύς, ἰθύς, εὐθύ, ἐντός, ἐκτός, and μεταξύ are oxytone. Note also the accent of ὁμοῦ, πλησίον, ἐναντίον. The improper preposition ὡς 'to, towards' follows the same rules of accentuation as the monosyllabic prepositions proper, and will be treated together with these (§ 257).

254. Prepositions proper are either monosyllables or disyllables. Disyllabic prepositions contain either two light syllables or one light and one heavy syllable (in either order). The following rules explain where accents are written on the prepositions proper; the meaning of these written accents for pronunciation will be discussed in §§ 268, 277.

255. Disyllabic prepositions in which one of the syllables is heavy are oxytone: ἀμφί, ἀντί, διαί, ὑπαί, ὑπείρ.

256. Most disyllabic prepositions containing two light syllables have an accent that differs according to their position in a sentence. They are usually oxytone, as ἀπό, ἐπί, κατά, μετά, παρά, περί, ὑπέρ, ὑπό, ἐνί (all with the acute on the final syllable normally turned into a grave by § 75; see further §§ 268, 277), but sometimes recessive, as ἄπο, ἔπι, κάτα, μέτα, πάρα, πέρι, ὕπερ, ὕπο, ἔνι. The latter accentuation occurs when the preposition follows its case, as in ποδῶν ὕπο; this placement of the preposition is known as 'anastrophe' (cf. § 272). EXCEPTIONS: The prepositions ἀνά and διά, and the dialectal ποτί and προτί, are oxytone in all positions (i.e. written with an acute on the final syllable, or a grave by § 75). (For ἄνα = ἀνάστηθι 'get up', see § 274.)

There is an ancient grammatical tradition that the reason why ἀνά and διά are always oxytone is to avoid confusion with ἄνα, voc. sg. of ἄναξ, and with Δία, acc. of Ζεύς. This ingenious explanation is, however, fairly unlikely to be

6. Compounds, Proper Names, Pronouns, etc. (§§ 253–60)

correct. See WACKERNAGEL, *BEITRÄGE*, p. 37; WACKERNAGEL, *REVIEW OF POSTGATE*, pp. 55–6; and cf. the note to § 272.

257. Monosyllabic prepositions are written with an acute (or a grave, according to § 75): πρό, πρός, σύν (and ξύν). But those beginning with an aspirated or unaspirated vowel are normally written without an accent (see § 267a): εἰς (and ἐς), ἐκ (and ἐξ), ἐν (and εἰν), and the improper preposition ὡς 'to, towards'. The latter are, however, written with an acute accent when they occur in anastrophe, but *only before punctuation or verse-end*: αὔριον ἔς· 'for tomorrow' (*Od.* 7. 318); κακῶν ἔξ, / (*Il.* 14. 472); but τὼ δὲ καλεσσαμένω ἀγορὴν ἐς πάντας Ἀχαιούς (*Od.* 3. 137).

258. The rules for the accentuation of prepositions in anastrophe also apply when the prepositions function as verbal prefixes (preverbs) and are placed after their verbs: φυγὼν ὕπο (*Il.* 21. 57).

259. Ancient grammarians, and modern editors, disagree as to whether disyllabic prepositions and preverbs that receive an acute on the first syllable in anastrophe do so even when one or more words intervene between the word governed by the preposition/preverb and the preposition/preverb itself. Thus, at *Il.* 5. 308 D.B. Monro and T.W. Allen (OCT) print ὧσε δ' ἀπὸ ῥινὸν... 'and it *tore off* (ὧσε...ἀπό) the *skin* (ῥινόν)', whereas M.L. West (Teubner) prints ὧσε δ' ἄπο ῥινόν... (cf. WEST, *ILIAD* i, p. xix with n. 42). We shall follow in this book the practice of applying the rules for accentuation in anastrophe whether or not words intervene (so ὧσε δ' ἄπο ῥινόν...). For discussion see LEHRS, *QUAESTIONES*, pp. 75, 78–9.

260. Ancient grammarians, and modern editors, disagree also as to whether disyllabic prepositions/preverbs that receive an acute on the first syllable in anastrophe do so even when the final syllable of the preposition/preverb is elided. Thus, at *Il.* 2. 150 A. Ludwich (Teubner) prints νῆας ἐπ' ἐσσεύοντο whereas D.B. Monro and T.W. Allen (OCT) and M.L. West (Teubner) print νῆας ἐπ' ἐσσείοντο. Ancient sources agree, however, that an accent *does* appear on the first syllable of the elided preposition/preverb in anastrophe if punctuation follows, as at *Od.* 17. 246: ἄστυ κάτ'· The practice we shall follow in this book is to apply the rules for accentuation in anastrophe regardless of elision (νῆας ἔπ' ἐσσεύοντο). For modern opinions and arguments regarding the accentuation of elided disyllabic prepositions/preverbs in anastrophe, see

127

LEHRS, *QUAESTIONES*, pp. 75–8; WACKERNAGEL, *BEITRÄGE*, p. 36; WACKERNAGEL, *REVIEW OF POSTGATE*, p. 56; WEST, *ILIAD* i, p. xix with n. 42.

261. Ancient grammarians disagreed enormously about how to accent a disyllabic preposition that fell between a noun and an adjective modifying it, as in Ξάνθῳ ἐπὶ δινήεντι versus Ξάνθῳ ἔπι δινήεντι (*Il.* 5. 479), or ἐμῷ ὑπὸ δουρί versus ἐμῷ ὕπο δουρί (*Il.* 18. 92). There were three different opinions: Aristarchus thought a disyllabic preposition capable of changing its accent in anastrophe should be accented on the first syllable only when it followed the noun (Ξάνθῳ ἔπι δινήεντι but ἐμῷ ὑπὸ δουρί); Ptolemy of Ascalon and Nicias thought it should be accented on the first syllable only when it followed the adjective (Ξάνθῳ ἐπὶ δινήεντι but ἐμῷ ὕπο δουρί); and Apollonius Dyscolus and Herodian thought the first syllable of the preposition should be accented in both cases (Ξάνθῳ ἔπι δινήεντι, ἐμῷ ὕπο δουρί). Similar disagreement concerned the accentuation of a disyllabic preposition in the position between a common noun and a proper name in apposition: at *Il.* 2. 839 Aristarchus prescribed ποταμοῦ ἀπὸ Σελλήεντος, but Ptolemy of Ascalon, Nicias, Apollonius Dyscolus, and Herodian prescribed ποταμοῦ ἄπο Σελλήεντος. A disyllabic preposition between a genitive and a noun modified by it likewise presented a problem: at *Il.* 12. 462 Tyrannio prescribed λᾶος ὑπὸ ῥιπῆς 'at the on-rush of the stone' whereas Herodian prescribed λᾶος ὑπὸ ῥιπῆς. The truth probably cannot be recovered in detail, but a consistent and linguistically plausible choice favoured by some editors is to accent a disyllabic preposition capable of changing its accent on the first syllable whenever it follows the noun that is modified (whether by an adjective or a genitive), and whenever it follows either of two nouns in apposition, but not when it follows a modifier (whether adjective or genitive) and precedes its noun: Ξάνθῳ ἔπι δινήεντι, ποταμοῦ ἄπο Σελλήεντος, ἐμῷ ὑπὸ δουρί, λᾶος ὑπὸ ῥιπῆς. For discussion see LEHRS, *QUAESTIONES*, pp. 79–86; CHANDLER, pp. 257–8; VENDRYES, pp. 247–8; DEVINE AND STEPHENS, pp. 364–5; WEST, *ILIAD* i, pp. xix–xx.

262. The prepositions proper that do not change their accent in anastrophe have been mentioned in §§ 255–7 above and may now be brought together in a final list: ἀμφί, ἀντί, διαί, ὑπαί, ὑπείρ (§ 255); ἀνά, διά, ποτί, προτί (§ 256); πρό, πρός, σύν (and ξύν) (§ 257).

EXERCISE 34: ACCENTUATION OF PREPOSITIONS

Write the prepositions given below with their correct accents. Assume that the prepositions proper precede their cases (but do not change an acute on a final syllable to a grave):

1. ἐγγυς	12. ἐναντιον	23. ἀνευ	34. ἐντος	45. ἐμπροσθεν
2. παρα	13. ἑνεκα	24. μεταξυ	35. ἀνα	46. συν
3. ποτι	14. περι	25. ἀντι	36. ἀπο	47. ὑπειρ
4. πλησιον	15. ἐκτος	26. ἐξω	37. ἀνευθεν	48. ἁμα
5. ἐν	16. χαριν	27. ὑπαι	38. ἀνω	49. εὐθυ
6. ἐπι	17. δια	28. ἰθυς	39. ἐκ	
7. εἰς	18. ὑπο	29. προ	40. εἰσω	
8. κατα	19. χωρις	30. ἀμφι	41. λαθρᾳ	
9. δια	20. πλην	31. μετα	42. ὡς (preceding its case)	
10. προτι	21. ἀχρι	32. μεχρι	43. ὀπισθεν	
11. ὑπερ	22. προς	33. ὁμου	44. ἐνι	

Write the prepositions given below with their correct accents where they follow their cases (do not change an acute on a final syllable to a grave, and assume a position before punctuation or verse-end where indicated with '·'):

50. ὑπο	54. ὡς·	58. ἐς·	62. ὑπερ	66. κατα
51. ἀμφι	55. συν	59. μετα	63. ἀντι	67. ἐξ·
52. προς	56. ἀπο	60. ἐνι	64. ποτι	68. ἀνα
53. δια	57. περι	61. παρα	65. ἐπι	

(c) Interjections

263. The accents of interjections are hardly reducible to rules. Some common interjections are φεῦ, ἰού, οἴ, ὤ 'oh!' (but cf. the particle ὦ used before vocatives), αἰαῖ, παπαῖ, παπαιάξ, οἴμοι.

264. οἴμοι is in origin the accented interjection οἴ plus enclitic μοι (see § 298). This is the reason for the acute, rather than circumflex, accent on the penultimate syllable.

265. Note that the interjection ἰδού 'behold' is oxytone whereas Herodian tells us that ἴδου as the second person singular aorist imperative middle of ὁράω is recessive (though manuscripts and modern texts sometimes print the imperative as ἰδοῦ; see § 83).

EXERCISE 35: ACCENTUATION OF INTERJECTIONS
Write the interjections given below with their correct accents:

1. ἰου   3. παπαι   5. ἰδου (interjection)   7. φευ   9. αἰαι
2. ὠ 'oh!' 4. παπαιαξ 6. ὠ (voc. particle)   8. οἰμοι

EXERCISE 36: CUMULATIVE EXERCISE
Write the following phrases with their correct accents, remembering that an acute on a final syllable changes to a grave before another word that is not an enclitic, as long as punctuation does not intervene. (There are no enclitics in this exercise.)

1. Ἑκτορα δ᾽ αἰδως εἰλε. (Homer as quoted by Aristotle, *Eudemian Ethics* 1230a19)

2. σοφιᾱς ἐνδειᾳ ποιουσι ταυτα.

3. φευ, παπαι. / παπαι μαλ᾽ αὐθις. (Soph., *Philoctetes* 792–3)

4. ὀλωλας, ὠ παι, μητρος ἁρπασθεισ᾽ ἀπο. (Eur., *Hecuba* 513)

5. ἐκεινοι δε ἐξελθοντες ἐκηρυξαν πανταχου. (Gospel of St Mark, 16. 20)

6. ἐποιησε γαρ Ἀρτεμιν εἰναι θυγατερα Δημητρος. (Herodotus, 2. 156. 6)

7. ἐγω, ὠ ἀνδρες, δεομαι ὑμων στρατευεσθαι συν ἐμοι. (Xenophon, *Anabasis* 7. 3. 10)

8. καὶ γὰρ σοφιστής ἦν ἱκανὸς καὶ συγγραφεὺς καὶ λογογραφος.
(Strabo 13. 4. 3, ed. H.L. Jones (Loeb))

9. οὐκουν ('therefore') ἰᾱτρους καλεις τους ἐπιστημονας περι
τουτων; (Plato, *Minos* 316c)

10. καὶ Εὐφρων δε τους αὑτου ἐχων μισθοφορους περι δισχῑλιους
συνεστρατευετο. (Xenophon, *Hellenica* 7. 2. 11)

11. ταυτα ('these things') δε ἀδυνατοις ἐοικεν, καὶ οὑτω δη
συμβαινει ἀγαθον φυλακα ἀδυνατον γενεσθαι. (Plato, *Republic*
375c)

12. νῦν δε τουτο μεν τετολμησθω εἰπειν, ὁτι τους ἀκριβεστατους
φυλακας φιλοσοφους δει καθισταναι. (Plato, *Republic* 503b)

13. δεισαντες δε παρελαβον το χωριον μη Λακεδαιμονιων τα κατα
Πελοποννησον θορυβουμενων Ἀθηναιοι λαβωσιν· (Thucydides 5.
52. 1)

14. οἰμοι κακοδαιμων, ὡς ἀπολωλα δειλαιος, / καὶ τρισκακοδαιμων
καὶ τετρακις καὶ πεντακις / καὶ δωδεκακις καὶ μῡριακις· (ὡς 'how'
has no accent; τρισκακοδαίμων is recessive.) (Ar., *Plutus* 850–
2)

15. ἀνδρες στρατιωται, χαλεπα μεν τα παροντα, ὁποτε ἀνδρων
στρατηγων τοιουτων στερομεθα καὶ λοχᾱγων καὶ στρατιωτων.
(Xenophon, *Anabasis* 3. 2. 2)

16. λεγω δε περι παντων, οἰον μεγεθους περι, ὑγιειᾱς (N.B. nom. sg.
ends in short -*a*), ἰσχυος, καὶ των ἀλλων ἑνι λογῳ ἁπαντων.
(ἰσχύς is oxytone.) (Plato, *Phaedo* 65d)

17. οἰδα σαφως καὶ ἐγω καὶ συ, ὁτι το μεν πρωτον ηὐδοκιμει
Περικλης καὶ οὐδεμιαν αἰσχρᾱν δικην κατεψηφισαντο αὑτου
Ἀθηναιοι, ἡνικα χειρους ἡσαν. (Plato, *Gorgias* 515e)

18. πολιται γαρ δορυφορουσι μεν ἀλληλους ἀνευ μισθου ἐπι τους
δουλους, δορυφορουσι δ' ἐπι τους κακουργους, ὑπερ του μηδενα των
πολιτων βιαιῳ θανατῳ ἀποθνησκειν. (Xenophon, *Hiero* 4. 3)

19. τι (interrog.) οὐν; ἐαν ἐγω καλω ὁτιουν των ὀντων, οἰον ὁ (rel.

pron.) νῦν καλουμεν ἀνθρωπον, ἐαν ἐγω τουτο ἱππον προσαγορευω, ὁ (rel. pron.) δε νῦν ἱππον, ἀνθρωπον, ἐσται δημοσιᾳ μεν ὀνομα ἀνθρωπος τῳ αὐτῳ, ἰδιᾳ δε ἱππος; και ἰδιᾳ μεν αὐ ἀνθρωπος, δημοσιᾳ δε ἱππος; οὐτω λεγεις; (Plato, *Cratylus* 385a)

Chapter 7: Proclitics and Enclitics

266. So far, we have been dealing mainly with what may be called the natural accent of a Greek word. The natural accent is the accent a word has when quoted by itself, for example as an entry in a dictionary. This accent is often identical to the accent that the word will have in an actual sentence. We have already seen, however, that certain modifications to the accent occur under conditions that may arise when a word is surrounded by other words within the sentence. The change of an acute to a grave on a final syllable when followed, without intervening punctuation, by another non-enclitic word (§ 75) is an example of such modification. Another example is the retraction of an accent to the penultimate syllable when a word-final accented vowel is elided (§ 78). Again, the accent of most prepositions depends on whether they precede or follow their cases (§§ 256–61). We have postponed until now discussion of the special accentual behaviour of two classes of words, *proclitics* and *enclitics*. Proclitics and enclitics have no natural accents of their own (although some proclitics and some enclitics are *written* in isolation with an accent: see below) but acquire accents in certain contexts within the sentence. An enclitic in some contexts also affects the accentuation of a preceding word.

Proclitics

267. A proclitic is a small, unemphatic word closely joined in pronunciation to the following word, rather as English *a* or *an* normally has no accent of its own but belongs closely with the following accented word (*a banána, an ápple*). The proclitics are:

(a) the following words, written in isolation without an accent:

Forms of the definite article beginning with a rough breathing: ὁ, ἡ, οἱ, αἱ (but see the fourth note to § 271).

The prepositions ἐν/εἰν, εἰς/ἐς, ἐκ/ἐξ, ὡς 'to, towards', when they precede their cases.

The conjunctions εἰ 'if, whether', ὡς 'like, as, in order that'.

The negative οὐ/οὐκ/οὐχ, except when it occurs before verse-end or punctuation.

All of these are monosyllables and begin with a vowel, with either rough or smooth breathing.

(b) The following words, written in isolation with an accent:

Forms of the definite article beginning with τ-: τό, τόν, τήν, τοῦ, τῆς, etc.

All proper prepositions other than those mentioned in (a) above: ἀμφί, ἀντί, ἀνά, ἀπό, διά/διαί, ἐνί, ἐπί, κατά, μετά, παρά, περί, πρό, πρός, σύν/ξύν, ὑπέρ/ὑπείρ, ὑπό/ὑπαί.

The conjunctions ἀλλά, καί, οὐδέ, μηδέ, ἐπεί, ἤ (and Homeric ἠέ) 'either/or', ἠμέν 'both' (picked up by ἠδέ 'and'; poetic), ἠδέ 'and' (poetic), ἰδέ 'and' (poetic), ἀτάρ 'but', αὐτάρ 'but' (poetic).

The negative μή.

The interjection ἰδού 'behold'.

None of these except ἤ 'either/or' is a monosyllable beginning with a vowel (whether aspirated or unaspirated). All except the genitive and dative forms of the article are written in isolation with an acute accent on the last or only syllable.

7. Proclitics and Enclitics (§§ 267–71)

268. Because a proclitic ordinarily precedes another word in the sentence, the acute accent written on the final syllable of many proclitics is nearly always turned into a grave within the sentence, as in διὰ τοῦτο (for exceptions, see § 270). It is likely that this grave does not represent a real accent but is written merely by convention.

The origins of the convention that monosyllabic proclitics beginning with an aspirated or unaspirated vowel are written without an accent mark (except for ἤ 'either/or') are unclear, but the necessity to write a breathing on such words clearly played a rôle. It was also useful to be able to distinguish in writing the forms of the article beginning with a rough breathing from the corresponding forms of the rel. pron.: thus ἡ (article) but ἥ (relative). See VENDRYES, pp. 66–7; POSTGATE, pp. 62–3; BALLY, pp. 107–8.

269. Genitive and dative forms of the article are written with a circumflex: τοῦ, τῆς, τῷ, τῇ, τοῖν, (rare ταῖν), τῶν, τοῖς, ταῖς. It is unclear whether these circumflexes are also purely conventional, and equally unclear whether these forms of the article should properly be included in the category of 'proclitics' (see § 277). For the purposes of writing the accent it makes no practical difference, since genitive and dative forms of the article are written with a circumflex *under all circumstances*.

270. All proclitics other than those written with a circumflex (see § 269) receive an acute on the final syllable (either instead of a conventional grave or instead of no written accent) when followed by an enclitic: περί γε τούτου, εἴ περ καί τις... The position before enclitic constitutes an exception to the general rule that a proclitic in the sentence does not have an acute on the final syllable (see § 268; on enclitics, see §§ 278–300).

271. The negative οὐ has an emphatic variant οὔ, which is accented. Accented οὔ is found when the negative appears before verse-end or punctuation (a position in which it always carries a certain emphasis): πῶς γὰρ οὔ; (e.g. Plato, *Republic* 338d);

χρήσιμον ἄρα καὶ ἐν εἰρήνῃ δικαιοσύνη; χρήσιμον. καὶ γὰρ γεωργίᾱ· ἢ οὔ; ναί (Plato, *Republic* 332e-333a).

POSTGATE, p. 63, argues (as part of a more general argument against the existence of a category of 'proclitics') that οὐ was in fact always fully accented, never proclitic. His argument is based on a misunderstanding of Aristotle, *Sophistici Elenchi* 166b3–6; see WACKERNAGEL, *BEITRÄGE*, pp. 8–12; WACKERNAGEL, *REVIEW OF POSTGATE*, p. 53. One should, however, worry (with ALLEN, p. 253) about the statement at Arcadius 209. 5 = Hdn i. 504. 6–7. Schmidt in his edition of Arcadius prints the manuscript reading τοῦτο (sc. "οὐ") καὶ ἐν τῇ συνηθείᾳ ὀξύνεται 'this word is oxytone in the *koiné* too', whereas Lentz in his edition of Herodian prints a conjecture of Goettling's, τοῦτο δὲ καὶ ἐν τῇ συνεπείᾳ ὀξύνεται 'and this word is oxytone in continuous speech too'. A reference to the *koiné* is not obviously appropriate in the context. If Goettling's conjecture is accepted, however, the sentence should mean not that οὐ was always fully accented rather than proclitic but that at least under some circumstances an accented οὐ failed to change its acute to a grave within the sentence by the rule of § 75. Yet if such were the case it would be very surprising that we do not have much clearer surviving statements to this effect. I wonder, therefore, whether Herodian originally stated something to the effect that 'sometimes this word is actually pronounced with a high pitch (even though usually it is not)'.

The negative μή can also occur before verse-end or punctuation, where it cannot be proclitic; in this position it is written with an acute, not a grave, and one should assume a genuinely accented emphatic variant: τὸν δὲ δοκοῦντα μέν, ὄντα δὲ μή, δοκεῖν ἀλλὰ μὴ εἶναι φίλον (Plato, *Republic* 335a).

Likewise ἰδού must have had an accented variant occurring before punctuation: ἆ ἆ ἰδοὺ ἰδού· (so the reading of the manuscripts, followed by most editors, at Aesch., *Agamemnon* 1125). In the case of ἰδού, the correct accentuation of the fully accented variant is likely to have been ἴδου (since ἰδού is merely a proclitic variant of the imperative ἰδοῦ: see § 277); M.L. West accordingly prints ἆ ἆ ἴδου, ἴδου· (with punctuation after each occurrence of ἴδου) at Aesch., *Agamemnon* 1125. The more widespread editorial practice is, however, to write the fully accented form as ἰδού.

Manuscript tradition suggests that the article was fully accented when used as a demonstrative or anaphoric pronoun (including the forms beginning with a rough breathing, which were oxytone), as often in Homer, and some editors follow this convention. Thus, at *Il.* 1. 12 M.L. West (Teubner) prints ὃ γὰρ ἦλθε 'for he came', while D.B. Monro and T.W. Allen (OCT) print ὁ γὰρ ἦλθε. In Attic the article is used as a pronoun mainly in the phrase ὁ μέν...ὁ δέ 'the one...the other' and its variants, where manuscripts tend not to accent the forms with rough breathing. Some editors, however, print ὃ μέν...ὃ δέ. See the examples in the third paragraph of the extract from Dionysius of Halicarnassus quoted in § 8. Cf. VENDRYES, pp. 64–5.

272. The accentuation of prepositions (and preverbs) in anastrophe has been described in §§ 256–62. Prepositions that receive an acute on their first or only syllable in anastrophe (as in ποδῶν ὕπο, and, before punctuation or verse-end, αὔριον ἔς· Ἀρτέμιδι ξύν,) are not proclitic in that position but fully accented. The acute accent on the first or only syllable of the preposition is the natural accent that the preposition has in its fully accented form.

Comparison with Vedic Sanskrit helps to confirm that the accents Greek prepositions have in anastrophe are their natural accents, since several of the Greek prepositions that acquire an accent on the first syllable in anastrophe have cognates in Vedic in which the accent falls on the first syllable, i.e. agrees with the accent of the Greek preposition in anastrophe: *ápa* = ἄπο, *pári* = πέρι, *úpa* = ὕπο. The preposition ἀμφί, which is never accented *ἄμφι, has a Vedic cognate in which the accent falls on the last syllable: *abhí*. On the other hand, the Vedic preposition *pári* does not agree with the accentuation in anastrophe of its Greek cognate ὕπερ, but the Greek rule placing an acute on the first syllable in anastrophe may have been extended from e.g. ἀπό/ἄπο or περί/πέρι to ὑπέρ/ὕπερ (so Benfey and Wackernagel, cited below). The Vedic preposition *ánti* is accented on the initial syllable although Greek ἀντί does not acquire an accent on the first syllable in anastrophe, and likewise Vedic *práti* is accented on the first syllable although the (dialectal and poetic) Greek cognate προτί (equivalent to Attic πρός) is transmitted as never taking an accent on the first syllable. (There are, however, no instances of προτί in a *clear* position of anastrophe; cf. Wackernagel, cited below.) For discussion see T. Benfey, *Vedica und Linguistica* (Trübner, 1880), pp. 100–14; F. Solmsen, 'Zur Geschichte des Dativs in den indogermanischen Sprachen', *Zeitschrift für vergleichende Sprachforschung* 44 (1911), p. 165, n. 2; WACKERNAGEL,

REVIEW OF POSTGATE, pp. 54–6 (explaining the failure of ποτί, προτί, ἀνά, and διά to be transmitted with paroxytone accentuation in anastrophe on the basis of the scarcity of clear Homeric examples of these prepositions in positions where the anastrophe rule would unambiguously apply).

273. In poetry, the conjunction ὡς 'like, as' can follow the word it governs. In this position it receives an acute accent before punctuation or verse-end, otherwise a grave: Τρῶες μὲν κλαγγῇ τ' ἐνοπῇ τ' ἴσαν ὄρνῖθες ὥς / (*Il.* 3. 2); θεὸς δ' ὣς τίετο δήμῳ (e.g. *Il.* 5. 78).

So normal editorial practice. See, however, WACKERNAGEL, *BEITRÄGE*, p. 19; VENDRYES, p. 72.

274. A disyllabic preposition standing for a verb (e.g. ἔνι for ἔνεστι, ἔπι for ἔπεστι, μέτα for μέτεστι, πάρα for πάρεστι, ἄνα 'get up!' for ἀνάστηθι) is fully accented, not proclitic, and has an acute on the first syllable.

This rule applies uncontroversially even if the preposition standing for a verb is elided, as at *Il.* 1. 174: πάρ' ἐμοί γε καὶ ἄλλοι 'At my side there are other men too'.

275. When the final vowel of a disyllabic proclitic is elided, the elision does not give rise to an accent on the preceding syllable (see § 78): ἀλλ' οὖν, ἀλλ' οὐδ' ὥς.

Opinions differ as to whether this rule applies in the case of anastrophe of an elided disyllabic preposition (or preverb) that would ordinarily take an acute on the first syllable in anastrophe (i.e. νῆας ἔπ' ἐσσεύοντο versus νῆας ἐπ' ἐσσεύοντο). The practice we follow in this book is *not* to apply the rule in such cases (so νῆας ἔπ' ἐσσεύοντο): see § 260. As noted above (§ 274), the present rule does not apply in the case of a disyllabic preposition standing for a verb.

276. A proclitic before another proclitic is written as it would be written before a fully accented word: οὐ γὰρ εἶδον.

277. The rules given above describe the practices normally adopted by modern editors of Classical texts and deriving from the statements of ancient

7. Proclitics and Enclitics (§§ 272–7)

grammarians and the practice of medieval manuscripts. The ancient grammarians do not recognise a category of proclitics as such, although the specific rules of accentuation they prescribe provide hints that our words were indeed ordinarily unaccented and closely connected in pronunciation to the following word. The main arguments, and the term 'proclitic', go back to Gottfried Hermann (HERMANN, pp. 96–101). We may summarise the most salient points (many of them due to Hermann, but for further bibliography see below) as follows.

The convention that disyllabic (proper) prepositions, such as ἐπί, and the conjunctions ἀλλά, οὐδέ, μηδέ, ἠδέ, and ἰδέ, do not acquire an acute on the first syllable when elided, suggests that the accent written on the final syllable of these words was not equivalent in value to the accent written on a 'normal' oxytone word such as πολλά. Now if disyllabic (proper) prepositions were unaccented, it would be very surprising if *monosyllabic* prepositions were accented. If we assume that they too were unaccented, their status as unaccented words helps to explain the manuscript practice of writing those beginning with an aspirated or unaspirated vowel without an accent (ἐν/εἰν, ἐς/εἰς, ἐκ/ἐξ, ὡς 'to, towards'), when it is by no means normally the case for Greek to write monosyllables beginning with an aspirated or unaspirated vowel without an accent: cf. ὦ (voc. particle), εἶ (2nd sg. pres. indic. of εἰμί 'I am' or εἶμι 'I shall go'), ἄψ, etc. The same explanation should then be extended to the other monosyllables that are not enclitic (see below) and are ordinarily written without an accent: ὁ, ἡ, οἱ, αἱ (forms of the article); εἰ, ὡς 'like, as, in order that' (conjunctions); οὐ/οὐκ/οὐχ.

Counting certain forms of the article, such as ὁ and ἡ, as unaccented raises the question as to whether other forms, such as τό, were also unaccented in pronunciation, since it would be surprising (though not impossible) if precisely the forms of the article beginning with a rough breathing were unaccented and precisely those beginning with τ- were accented. A.H. Sommerstein, *The Sound Pattern of Ancient Greek* (Blackwell, 1973), pp. 136–9, demonstrates that forms of the article in general are treated like other proclitics, but not like non-proclitic monosyllables, in their patterns of occurrence at the 'third anceps' (or 'Porson') position in the iambic trimeters of tragedy. His argument helps to confirm the suspicion that forms of the article are proclitic whether or not they are written without an accent, and indeed that those written with a circumflex are proclitic just as much as those written with an acute or (usually) grave. DEVINE AND STEPHENS, p. 357, however, point out that Sommerstein's argument implies only that the various forms of the article were 'rhythmic clitics', i.e. that they were joined closely in pronunciation to the following word, and they suggest that 'rhythmic clisis' does not inevitably go together with 'accentual clisis', i.e. lack of accent. Yet DEVINE AND STEPHENS also note (pp. 357–8) that the evidence from the fragments of ancient Greek music does not suggest any difference in accentuation between the forms of the article with and without τ-. The balance of evidence supports the inclusion of forms of the article in general under the heading of proclitics, but there is, I think, room for some doubt especially about the proclitic status of those forms written with a circumflex (τοῦ, τῆς, etc.). It would be more difficult to write purely by convention a circumflex than an acute on a final syllable, since an acute on one of our suspected proclitics is in any case ordinarily turned into a grave (which even when written on a 'normal' word implies either reduced accent or lack of accent: see §§ 31, 37c with note).

The interjection ἰδού 'behold' is in origin the imperative ἰδοῦ 'look!', which Herodian tells us is recessive (cf. § 83). In the secondary function as interjection that this imperative developed, the word carries very little emphasis itself when no punctuation follows (cf. the third note to § 271) but rather confers emphasis on what follows. (The English translation 'behold', given here *faute de mieux*, really renders the stylistic level of the Greek very badly.) It is likely that the reason for the apparent change to accentuation on the last syllable for the interjection is that the word in fact lost its accent when it became an unemphatic interjection closely connected to what follows. In other words, it became proclitic and was written with the conventional accent on the final syllable given to all disyllabic proclitics.

It is impossible to tell from the written accent whether μή is proclitic, but it is often assumed that it was equivalent in its accentuation to οὐ, and therefore proclitic. (A positive argument in favour of a proclitic interpretation of μή would arise if one were to accept the view mentioned in the note to § 282 that paroxytone ἔστι, when it occurs verse- or clause-internally, is always preceded by a proclitic, since according to the *Etymologicum Magnum* (301. 3) paroxytone ἔστι is found after μή. However, I tentatively prefer an alternative account of the distribution of paroxytone ἔστι: see the note to § 282.)

It is likewise impossible to demonstrate from the normal rules of written accentuation (but see below on Lesbian) the proclitic status of the conjunctions ἀτάρ, αὐτάρ, ἐπεί, ἤ (or Homeric ἠέ), ἠμέν, and καί, but they are generally assumed to have been similar in accentual status to ἀλλά, οὐδέ, μηδέ, ἠδέ, and ἰδέ (argued to be proclitic by the failure of an accent to appear on the first syllable when the final vowel is elided).

140

7. Proclitics and Enclitics (§ 277)

In addition, Apollonius Dyscolus and Choeroboscus tell us that the Lesbians, whose dialect generally had a recessive accent for all words (see §§ 306–7), did not have a recessive accent on prepositions or conjunctions. It is likely that this exception to the general rule that words had a recessive accent in Lesbian is due to the fact that prepositions and conjunctions were simply unaccented. Since they were unaccented, their accent did not fall on the first syllable in Lesbian because there was, as it were, no real accent to fall on *any* syllable. Choeroboscus provides as examples of such prepositions and conjunctions ἀνά, κατά, διά, μετά, παρά, ἀντί, ἀμφί, περί, ἀπό, ὑπό, ὑπέρ, ἠμέν, ἠδέ, αὐτάρ, ἀτάρ, and ἀλλά (Choer., Th. 1. 311. 12–17; cf. 2. 321. 16–18; Ap. Dysc., *Pron.* 73. 7–9, *Synt.* 443. 8–10). The mention of ἠμέν, αὐτάρ, and ἀτάρ provides some specific confirmation that these are rightly included in a list of proclitics, despite the lack of proof from their accentuation outside Lesbian (see above).

There is no doubt that, syntactically, the words treated as proclitics tend to cohere closely with what follows them. Indeed, certain combinations of proclitic plus following word have become so fixed that they tend to be written as single words: thus ὡσεί, οὐκέτι, εἰσαεί. It is worth noting the parallel with *enclitics*, words with no accent of their own that cohere closely with what *precedes* and can form similarly close groups tending to be written as single words: ὅστις, καίπερ, etc. (see §§ 298–300).

Some of our 'proclitics' can occur before verse-end or punctuation, where they cannot be closely joined in pronunciation to what follows. Likewise, prepositions can occur after instead of before the word they govern (most of them only in poetry, but πέρι in anastrophe is quite acceptable in classical Attic prose), as can ὡς 'like, as' (again in poetry). In these positions our words are fully accented, not proclitic, and the written accents that appear, for example, on οὐ before punctuation, or on ἐς in anastrophe before punctuation or verse-end (§§ 271, 257) help to confirm that the writing of οὐ or ἐς in other positions without accent is not merely the result of a decision not to indicate the accent on those words but is due to a real lack of accent when (and only when) the words can cohere closely with what follows. One may again compare the behaviour of *enclitics*, some of which are capable of appearing at the *beginning* of a phrase and are fully accented, not enclitic, in that position (see §§ 280–3).

Although the evidence for accepting the existence of a category of proclitics is fairly strong, some words can clearly be counted as proclitics with more certainty than others. For some, such as καί, their possible status as proclitics makes no difference at all to the written accent, and it is precisely in these cases that there is most room for doubt. DEVINE AND STEPHENS, pp. 356–64, argue that there is no discrete group of proclitics to which a word categorically does or does not belong, but that words which primarily have grammatical function rather than full meaning (articles, negatives, etc.), particularly if short and light, tend to have a lower-pitched accent than fully-fledged words such as nouns or verbs. For DEVINE AND STEPHENS the so-called 'proclitics' are merely grammatical function words with rather strong lowering of the accent. This conclusion is plausible on cross-linguistic grounds; if it is correct, we should not be dismayed that there is only a murky divide between those words whose traditional written accentuation clearly reflects something like lack of accent and those that can confidently be taken to have been fully accented words.

For discussion of proclitic accentuation see HERMANN, pp. 96–101; CHANDLER, pp. 255–61, 263–5; WACKERNAGEL, *BEITRÄGE*, pp. 3–19; VENDRYES, pp. 63–73, 239–49 (but attributing to Wackernagel some observations that go back to Hermann); BALLY, pp. 106–9, 113–14, 115–17.

Enclitics

278. Enclitics, like proclitics, are small, unemphatic words closely joined in pronunciation to an adjacent word. In the case of enclitics, however, the adjacent word is not the word that follows but the one that precedes.

List of enclitics

279. The following words are enclitic:

(a) The indefinite τις, with all its inflected forms (τινά, τι, τινός/του, τινί/τῳ, τινέ, τινοῖν, τινές, τινάς, τινά, τινῶν, τισί). But ἄττα/ἄσσα 'some' is non-enclitic.

(b) The indefinite adverbs πω 'up to this time', πη 'somehow', που 'somewhere', ποι 'to somewhere', πως 'somehow', ποτέ 'at some time', ποθέν 'from somewhere', ποθί 'somewhere'.

(c) The non-emphasised oblique personal pronoun forms με, μου, μοι; σε, σου, σοι; ἑ, οὑ, οἱ, and the following which are not common in Attic prose: μιν, νιν, σφε/σφεάς (frequently scanned as a monosyllable)/σφας/σφᾱς, σφεά, σφεων (scanned as a monosyllable), σφι(ν), σφισί(ν), σφωέ 'the two of them', σφωΐν 'the two of them'.

But νώ (Homeric also νῶϊ), νῷν 'we two' and σφώ (Homeric also σφῶϊ), σφῷν 'you two' are always non-enclitic; on these see WACKERNAGEL, *AKZENTSTUDIEN III*, pp. 106–7.

(d) The present indicative forms of εἰμί 'I am' and φημί 'I say', except for the second persons singular εἶ and φής. Notice that the form φής, while not enclitic, is also not recessive. The Homeric second person singular forms εἰς and ἐσσί are enclitic.

(e) The particles γε, τε, νυν (but not νῦν 'now'), νυ, κε(ν), τοι, ῥα, περ.

The most generally used convention for writing enclitics in isolation is to write them without accent if monosyllabic and to write them with an acute on the second syllable if disyllabic, except that τινῶν and τινοῖν are written perispomenon. This is the convention followed in this book, although some authors write disyllabic enclitics in isolation without accent. Notice that τινῶν and τινοῖν are the only enclitics occurring in Attic/*koiné* that are neither monosyllabic nor disyllables ending in a light syllable.

280. Observe that the enclitic forms of the personal pronouns are in some instances identical, apart from accent, to the non-enclitic forms (see § 228): so non-enclitic σέ, σοῦ versus enclitic σε, σου. In other instances the enclitic and non-enclitic forms differ not only in accent but in other respects as well: so non-enclitic ἐμέ, ἐμοῦ versus enclitic με, μου.

281. The enclitic forms of the personal pronouns (§ 279c) are used everywhere except under the following circumstances, where the non-enclitic forms (§ 228) are used:

(a) At the beginning of a verse, sentence, or clause: οὔ τις ἐμέο ζῶντος καὶ ἐπὶ χθονὶ δερκομένοιο / σοὶ κοίλης παρὰ νηυσὶ βαρείας χεῖρας ἐποίσει 'While I am alive and look upon the earth, nobody is going to lay heavy hands on you by the hollow ships' (*Il.* 1. 88–9); οὗτος, σὲ τὸν τὰς αἰχμαλωτίδας χέρας / δεσμοῖς ἀπευθύνοντα προσμολεῖν καλῶ· 'Hey there, I'm calling you to come here who are binding the captives' hands behind them with bonds.' (Soph., *Ajax* 71–2).

(b) When special emphasis is placed on them, especially when there is a contrast between one person and another: οὐδὲ γὰρ οὐδ' ἐμέ φημι λελασμένον ἔμμεναι ἀλκῆς 'For I dare say that *I* haven't forgotten my strength either' (*Il.* 13. 269).

(c) Where a personal pronoun follows a preposition or precedes ἕνεκα: ἐξ ἐμοῦ, πρὸς ἐμοί, ὑπὲρ σοῦ, σοῦ ἕνεκα. But πρός με and πρὸς ἐμέ both occur.

The combination πρός σε is sometimes also cited as an exception. See, however, CHANDLER, p. 272.

(d) In most cases where a personal pronoun is conjoined with αὐτός: ἀλλὰ σοὶ αὐτῷ / μόρσιμόν ἐστι ... 'but for you yourself it is fated...' (*Il.* 19. 416–17).

(e) The third person singular personal pronouns are non-enclitic when used reflexively, even when not conjoined with αὐτός: ἦ ὀλίγον οἷ παῖδα ἐοικότα γείνατο Τυδεύς 'Well then, Tydeus did father a child not very like himself!' (*Il.* 5. 800).

282. The form ἐστί, normally enclitic, has a fully accented variant ἔστι. This fully accented variant is used at the beginning of a verse, sentence, or clause, and when the word expresses existence or possibility (i.e. when it is translatable with expressions such as 'exists', 'there is', or 'it is possible'): ἔστιν

7. Proclitics and Enclitics (§§ 281–2)

πόλις Κάνωβος 'there is a city, Kanobos' ([Aesch.], *Prometheus Bound* 846); ἀκτή τις ἀμφίκλυστος Εὐβοίας ἄκρον / Κήναιον ἔστιν 'there is a headland Kēnaion, washed on both sides by waves, a cape of Euboia' (Soph., *Trachiniae* 752–3); οὐκ ἔστιν· 'it *is not the case*' (e.g. Soph., *Antigone* 289). In all other uses, ἐστί is enclitic (for its accentuation when enclitic, see §§ 284–97): τούτων ἄρα Ζεύς ἐστιν ἀσθενέστεος; 'So Zeus is weaker than these?' ([Aesch.], *Prometheus Bound* 517); οὐ γὰρ ἐκπέλει / φρονεῖν μέγ' ὅστις δοῦλός ἐστι τῶν πέλας 'For it doesn't befit one who is a slave of those nearby to have big ideas' (Soph., *Antigone* 478–9).

According to Herodian, the accented variant is used when the word begins a phrase and after οὐκ, καί, εἰ, ἀλλά, ὡς, or τοῦτο (see Hdn i. 553. 10–16; cf. LEHRS, *QUAESTIONES*, p. 104, n. 2); the *Etymologicum Magnum* (301. 3) adds μή to this list. HERMANN (pp. 84–90) argued that in these positions the word very often expresses existence or possibility, and that the rationale behind Herodian's rule was that the accented variant occurred whenever the word expressed existence or possibility, the enclitic variant occurring in all other instances. Together with many editors, we follow here Hermann's rule, with the addition that at the beginning of a verse, sentence, or clause, ἔστι cannot be enclitic and so must have its accented variant regardless of meaning.

Wackernagel, followed by Barrett and West (cited below), argued that Herodian's rule should be understood not in terms of the meaning of the word but purely in terms of its position in a verse or clause. According to West, who states this view the most explicitly, the word is accented ἔστι when it falls in initial position in its verse or syntactic colon or when it is preceded in its verse or syntactic colon only by a proclitic.

Hermann's hypothesis on the one hand and that of Wackernagel/Barrett/West on the other provide different rationalisations of the ancient grammatical statements. Both fit rather well with the ancient evidence, and in very many cases the accentuation will be the same no matter whose rule one follows. But there is a fundamental difference of principle.

I have favoured Hermann's hypothesis because it is difficult to see why the syntactic position in which only a proclitic precedes should prompt accented ἔστι rather than enclitic ἐστί. Enclitics generally have no aversion — indeed often a particular propensity — for the second position in their clauses, the first

145

position frequently being occupied by a proclitic particle (so rightly BARRETT, *HIPPOLYTUS*, p. 426, n. 6). It would also be difficult to see the ἔστι in these positions as simply the enclitic ἐστί having undergone a rule of accent modification when preceded by a proclitic, because sequences such as οὐκ ἔστι, εἰ ἔστι, violate the *usual* rule for the accentuation of a proclitic followed by an enclitic (§ 296; so VENDRYES, p. 109).

Eustathius (880. 22–4) reports that 'the ancients' (οἱ παλαιοί) say that ἔστι is accented on the first syllable when it means ὑπάρχει 'there exists', but on the second when it is used in reply to a question. The same rule is given by Photius (*Lexicon*, ε 2030 Theodoridis; cf. Sch. *Il.* 23. 157c (T), Sch. *Il.* 23. 549 (T), and see BARRETT, *HIPPOLYTUS*, p. 426, n. 2). It is not clear what παλαιοί Eustathius is referring to, but it is entirely plausible that Herodian attempted to list combinations of words in which ἔστι was paroxytone while later grammarians saw that the underlying distinction between his enclitic ἐστί and his accented ἔστι was one of meaning; it was merely an incidental fact that certain combinations of words tended to occur when ἔστι expressed existence or possibility. For a similar sequence of events in the grammatical tradition, see LEHRS, *ARISTARCHUS*, pp. 378–81.

The demonstrative τοῦτο is not a proclitic (cf. WACKERNAGEL, *VERBALACCENT*, pp. 466–7); VENDRYES (p. 109) suggested that the accentuation τοῦτ᾽ ἔστι was the result of the elision of accented -ό from the sequence τοῦτό ἐστι. But the normal convention would accent such a sequence τοῦτ᾽ ἐστί (see § 293). Herodian's prescription that ἔστι is paroxytone after τοῦτο is thus not explicable purely in terms of the position of ἔστι, but it presents no difficulties under Hermann's view that Herodian had in mind cases where the meaning was 'this is the case', or 'this is possible'.

For discussion of the whole issue, see HERMANN, pp. 84–90; WACKERNAGEL, *VERBALACCENT*, pp. 466–7; CHANDLER, p. 267; VENDRYES, pp. 109–10; BARRETT, *HIPPOLYTUS*, pp. 425–6; WEST, *AESCHYLUS*, p. xxxi.

283. The normally enclitic forms of εἰμί and φημί sometimes begin a verse, sentence, or clause. In this position they cannot be enclitic but must be fully accented. Most editors write an acute (or grave, in accordance with § 75) on the final syllable, with the exception of the third person singular ἔστι (§ 282). This is the practice we follow here.

7. Proclitics and Enclitics (§§ 282–5)

Comparison with Sanskrit suggests that the normally enclitic forms in the sg. and the 3rd pl. at least originally appeared as follows when fully accented: 1st sg. εἰμί (which is, however, unfortunately identical to εἶμι 'I shall go'), Homeric 2nd sg. ἔσσι, 3rd sg. ἔστι, 3rd pl. εἰσί (unfortunately identical to εἶσι 'he/she/it shall go'); 1st sg. φημί, 3rd sg. φησί, 3rd pl. φασί. M.L. West prints these forms accordingly (see WEST, *ILIAD* i, p. xx); thus at *Il.* 2. 226–7 πολλαὶ δὲ γυναῖκες / εἰσὶν ἐνὶ κλισίης 'there are many women in your hut'; compare D.B. Monro and T.W. Allen's text (OCT) with πολλαὶ δὲ γυναῖκες / εἰσὶν ἐνὶ κλισίης. There is, however, almost no ancient support for any of these forms apart from ἔστι. Only φημί is attested at all, as a form prescribed by Tyrannio at *Il.* 2. 350 (Eust. 1613. 18; cf. Barrett, cited below). But there is no suggestion that Tyrannio prescribed the accentuation φημί only when the word stood at the beginning of a verse, sentence, or clause, and the reasoning Eustathius ascribes to him does not make it especially likely. It is possible that the normally enclitic forms of εἰμί and φημί, other than the 3rd sg. of εἰμί, had given up their original accented forms and generalised an accent on the second syllable from certain contexts in which they were enclitic (see §§ 288–9, 293, 297) to the position where they were non-enclitic at the beginning of a verse, sentence, or clause. (So Wackernagel and — hesitantly — Barrett, cited below.) There is probably not enough evidence to decide the question. This being so, we follow here the practice that is more in line with ancient tradition, is followed by most modern editors, and has the incidental advantage of not making the forms εἰμί and εἰσί ambiguous. For discussion see WACKERNAGEL, *VERBALACCENT*, p. 467; WACKERNAGEL, *BEITRÄGE*, p. 15, n. 1; VENDRYES, pp. 108–10; BARRETT, *HIPPOLYTUS*, p. 426, n. 5; WEST, *ILIAD* i, p. xx.

Rules for accenting full words followed by enclitics

284. The accentuation of a sequence consisting of a full word (i.e. a word that is neither enclitic nor proclitic) plus enclitic depends on the accentuation of the full word, and in some cases also on the number of syllables comprising the enclitic.

285. An oxytone full word retains the acute on its final syllable before any enclitic, i.e. it does not change its acute to a grave, and an enclitic after an oxytone word has no accent: πατήρ τις, πατήρ που, πατρί τινι, πατήρ φησιν.

147

286. A perispomenon full word retains the circumflex on its final syllable before any enclitic, and the enclitic again has no accent: πῦρ τι, φιλῶ σε, καλῶς πως, καλοῦ τινος, καλῶς ἐστιν, καλῶν τινων.

So most of our evidence, and standard editorial practice. See, however, POSTGATE, p. 70, and F. Specht, 'Zur griechischen Enklise', *Zeitschrift für vergleichende Sprachforschung* 55 (1928), pp. 184–97.

287. A proparoxytone or properispomenon full word before an enclitic retains its own accent as usual but acquires in addition an acute on its final syllable. The enclitic again has no accent: ἔλαβέ τις, ἄνθρωπός τις, ἄνθρωποί τινες, οἶκός τις, οἶκοί τινων.

288. But a properispomenon word ending in -ψ or -ξ simply retains its own accent. The enclitic, if monosyllabic, has no accent. If disyllabic, the enclitic acquires an acute (or grave, in accordance with the rule of § 75) on its last syllable, or a circumflex in the case of τινῶν or τινοῖν: κῆρυξ τις, κῆρυξ ἐστίν, λαῖλαψ ἐστίν, κλῖμαξ τινῶν.

289. A paroxytone full word simply retains its own accent before an enclitic. The enclitic, if monosyllabic, has no accent. If disyllabic, the enclitic acquires an acute (or grave, in accordance with the rule of § 75) on its final syllable, or a circumflex in the case of τινῶν or τινοῖν: λέγε τι, λέγω τι, σῴζω πως, μεγάλοι τινές, μεγάλα τινά, μεγάλοι εἰσί, παίδοιν τινοῖν.

The practice of most editors is to apply this rule with no exceptions. However, paroxytone words ending in a trochaic sequence (heavy syllable plus light syllable), such as ἔνθα or τυφθέντα, require further discussion and are treated in § 290.

290. According to Herodian, paroxytone words with trochaic ending (heavy syllable plus light syllable) are accented before enclitics in the same way as the properispomenon words of § 287, i.e. the full word acquires an acute on its final syllable in addition to its own accent, and the enclitic has no accent (see Arcadius 160. 7–14; Hdn i. 563. 2–4). Herodian's examples include ἄλλός τις,

7. Proclitics and Enclitics (§§ 286–90)

ἐστί τις (with non-enclitic ἔστι: see § 282), ἔνθά ποτε, τυφθέντά τε. It is probable that this rule applied in reality only to words in which the penultimate syllable had a liquid or nasal consonant (or possibly σ) after the short vowel, as in ἄλλός τις, ἔνθά ποτε (and possibly ἐστί τις), and that a word such as τυφθέντα should be accented in accordance with the rule of § 289 (so τυφθέντα τε, τυφθέντα τινά). Modern editors normally ignore our rule altogether, accenting combinations of ἄλλος, ἔνθα etc. plus enclitic exactly as λέγε or λέγω plus enclitic. Thus, at *Il.* 1. 237, D.B. Monro and T.W. Allen (OCT) print φύλλα τε. M.L. West (Teubner), however, observing the ancient rule in cases involving a nasal, liquid, or σ at the end of the penultimate syllable, prints φύλλά τε. At *Il.* 2. 440, on the other hand, the editors of both these editions print ὄφρα κε, discounting the ancient rule where the penultimate syllable ends in a stop consonant.

In cases such as ἄλλός τις or ἔνθά ποτε, involving a liquid or nasal after the short vowel of the penultimate syllable, it is likely that the sequence of short vowel plus liquid or nasal counted as a diphthong (with the nasal or liquid functioning as the second element, like the ι of οἶκος) and was capable of carrying either a rising or a falling accent. In a word with trochaic ending, such as ἄλλος or ἔνθα, the σωτῆρα rule requires a falling accent on this 'diphthong'. Although a circumflex is never written in such contexts, the spoken accent of these words, and their accentuation before enclitics, would have been equivalent to that of οἶκος.

It seems counter-intuitive to a speaker of a language such as English that a diphthong could consist of a vowel plus a nasal or liquid consonant, but Lithuanian has exactly such diphthongs (also capable of carrying either a rising or a falling accent). For Greek, the extant fragments of ancient Greek music show that a syllable containing a short vowel followed by a nasal or liquid consonant could be set to more than one note, as if it were a long vowel or diphthong. The same is true, albeit rather curiously, for a short vowel followed by σ in the same syllable, making it possible that Herodian's rule genuinely applied also to sequences such as ἐστί τις (see WACKERNAGEL, *ZEUGNISS*, p. 305, and West, cited below).

The extension of the rule to *all* paroxytone words with a trochaic ending is probably the result of over-generalisation in the grammatical tradition; it is unlikely that a sequence consisting of short vowel plus stop consonant within a syllable counted as a diphthong. On the other hand, West (cited below) has pointed out that in one respect Herodian's rule is not stated generally enough. At *Il.* 7. 199 Herodian prescribed the accentuation γενέσθαί τε. The word γενέσθαι does not end in a trochaic sequence, as observed by a scholiast on the

149

line (Sch. *Il.* 7. 199b (A)), but since the final diphthong counts 'short' for accentual purposes (see § 66) the arguments given above apply equally well to a word such as γενέσθαι before enclitic as to ἔστι before enclitic. In other words, for the purposes of Herodian's rule a 'trochaic sequence' ought to be taken to include a quasi-trochaic sequence ending in a diphthong that counts 'short' for accentuation.

For discussion of the whole question see WACKERNAGEL, *BEITRÄGE*, pp. 24–5, 37; WACKERNAGEL, *ZEUGNISS*, p. 305; VENDRYES, pp. 50, 59–60, 85–6; WEST, *THEOGONY*, pp. 438–40; ALLEN, pp. 242–3.

291. According to Herodian, a paroxytone word before an enclitic beginning with σφ- received an acute on its final syllable in addition to its own accent, and the enclitic had no accent: ἄρά σφιν, ἵνά σφισι (see Arcadius 161. 13–16, 166. 19–22). Again modern editors normally ignore this rule. Thus at *Il.* 6. 367 D.B. Monro and T.W. Allen (OCT) print ἔτι σφιν. M.L. West (Teubner), on the other hand, observing the rule, prints ἔτί σφιν. For discussion of the basis of this rule, see WACKERNAGEL, *BEITRÄGE*, pp. 26–7, 37; WEST, *THEOGONY*, pp. 440–2.

292. The acc., gen., and dat. forms of the plural pronouns ἡμεῖς and ὑμεῖς have unemphatic variants that occur in poetry and are accented on the first syllable (taking an acute or circumflex in accordance with the σωτῆρα law) rather than the second: ἥμεας or ἥμᾶς or ἥμας; ἥμων; ἥμῖν or ἥμιν; ὕμεας or ὕμᾶς or ὕμας; ὕμεων (scanned as two syllables) or ὕμων; ὕμῖν or ὕμιν. These have been called 'enclitic' forms since antiquity. Historically they are likely to have originated as enclitics, and in use they stand in the same relation to the emphatic forms ἡμᾶς, ὑμᾶς, etc., as e.g. the enclitic με to the accented ἐμέ, but they are effectively full words and subject to none of the rules that concern the accentuation of enclitics. Not all editors observe the first-syllable accentuation of these unemphatic forms. Thus, at *Il.* 1. 147, D.B. Monro and T.W. Allen (OCT) print ὄφρ' ἡμῖν ἑκάεργον ἱλάσσεαι, whereas M.L. West (Teubner) prints ὄφρ' ἥμιν Ἑκάεργον ἱλάσσεαι.

The accentuation of these unemphatic pronouns was prescribed by Apollonius Dyscolus and Herodian (see Sch. *Il.* 1. 147a[1] (A), a[2] (A[il])), with further references cited by Erbse *ad loc.*), and is often required in Babrius (on whom see the note to § 13) by the rule placing an accent on the penultimate syllable of a line. Thus e.g. ἄναυλα νῦν ὀρχεῖσθε. κρεῖσσον ἦν ὕμᾶς / πάλαι χορεύειν, ἡνίκ' εἰς χοροὺς ηὔλουν (Babrius 9. 9–10, ed. M.J. Luzzatto and A. La Penna (Teubner, 1986)).

7. Proclitics and Enclitics (§§ 290–3)

According to VENDRYES, p. 97, the acc. and dat. forms of ἡμεῖς and ὑμεῖς with a light final syllable (ἥμας, ἥμιν, ὕμας, ὕμιν) are accented on the first syllable not when they are unemphatic but on the contrary when they are emphatic. The oxytone forms ἡμίν and ὑμίν, on the other hand, are according to Vendryes not emphatic but unemphatic forms. (He expresses himself somewhat too succinctly, but probably intends ἡμίν and ὑμίν to be taken as actual enclitic forms and therefore as obeying the normal rules for the accentuation of disyllabic enclitics; he also assumes the existence of enclitic accusative forms ἡμάς and ὑμάς.) His view is based on the notion (for which see WACKERNAGEL, *VERBALACCENT*, pp. 453–9) that the first-syllable accent of unemphatic forms such as ἥμας is related to the fact that a Greek word with two heavy syllables could not be enclitic in the normal way. A word with one heavy and one light syllable, on the other hand, should have been capable of being a normal enclitic (like εἰμί); there was therefore no reason why e.g. ἥμιν, with one heavy and one light syllable, should have been an unemphatic or quasi-enclitic variant of ἡμίν. Vendryes' opinion is, however, contradicted by the ancient grammatical tradition; see Ap. Dysc., *Pron.* 96. 23–97. 3, 97. 28–98. 2, 100. 1–3. We must, therefore, assume that the forms of these pronouns with light final syllable followed the accentuation of the corresponding forms with heavy final syllable: last-syllable accent when emphatic (or in 'fully accented' position), first-syllable accent when unemphatic (or in 'enclitic' position).

On the whole question see WACKERNAGEL, *VERBALACCENT*, pp. 458–9; CHANDLER, pp. 276–7; VENDRYES, pp. 96–7; POSTGATE, p. 71; BARRETT, *HIPPOLYTUS*, p. 425; ALLEN, p. 243; DEVINE AND STEPHENS, p. 353; WEST, *ILIAD* i, p. xviii, with further literature.

Elided words followed by enclitics

293. The accentuation of a word whose last vowel is elided is not affected by the presence of a following enclitic. A disyllabic enclitic following an elided word has an acute (or grave, in accordance with § 75) on its last syllable: ταῦτ' ἐστὶ τἄπη μωρίας πολλῆς πλέα (Soph., *Ajax* 745); οὗτοι δ' εἰσὶ μάρτυρες.

Logically, a *monosyllabic* enclitic following an elided word should have no accent. But I am not aware of any attestation of a monosyllabic enclitic following an elided word.

151

Elided enclitics

294. When the last vowel of enclitic τινά or ποτέ is elided, the first syllable does not acquire an acute accent (see § 78).

Logically, this rule ought to extend to all disyllabic enclitics with elided final syllable. However, neither ancient grammarians nor modern editorial tradition apply the rule to disyllabic enclitics other than τινά and ποτέ. Thus, the enclitic forms of εἰμί and φημί that are capable of undergoing elision are written with an acute accent on the initial syllable when elided — although only in positions where the enclitic would, if unelided, have been written with an accent at all: ὅσσον φερτέρη εἴμ᾽, ὅτι μοι μένος ἀντιφερίζεις (*Il.* 21. 488; for ὅσσον φερτέρη εἰμί...); but οὔ φημ᾽ ἐάσειν (Soph., *Electra* 1209; for οὔ φημι ἐάσειν. Cf. § 296).

295. The effect that an enclitic has on the accent of the preceding word is never altered by the elision of the last or only vowel of the enclitic: ἄνθρωπός τ᾽ like ἄνθρωπός τε, κακόν τιν᾽ like κακόν τινα, etc.

Proclitics followed by enclitics

296. When a proclitic is followed by an enclitic, the proclitic receives an acute on its final syllable (or a circumflex, in the case of a genitive or dative form of the article) and the enclitic has no accent: εἴ γε, πρός με, περί τε, εἴ τινα.

This rule does not apply to a sequence of proclitic followed by ἔστι expressing existence or possibility, because in such a case ἔστι is fully accented, not enclitic (§ 282): οὐκ ἔστιν 'it is not the case'.

Enclitics in succession

297. When two or more enclitics follow one another in succession, each enclitic in the sequence has an acute accent on its final syllable except the last, which is unaccented. The first enclitic in the sequence has the same effect, if any, on the accentuation of the preceding word as it would if no further

7. Proclitics and Enclitics (§§ 294–9)

enclitics followed: ἢ νύ σέ που δέος ἴσχει (*Il.* 5. 812); εἴ πού τίς τινα ἴδοι (Thucydides 4. 47. 3).

This is the rule prescribed by Apollonius Dyscolus and Herodian and normally followed by modern editors. Some modern scholars have doubted its plausibility and suggested other rules. For discussion, see GOETTLING, pp. 404–6; CHANDLER, pp. 280–2; VENDRYES, pp. 87–90; POSTGATE, p. 74; BALLY, p. 115; BARRETT, *HIPPOLYTUS*, pp. 426–7; ALLEN, p. 244; WEST, *AESCHYLUS*, p. xxxii.

Fixed sequences involving enclitics

298. Some sequences of two words are used so frequently that they have coalesced into fixed units that tend to be written as single words. Each of the following sequences originated as a proclitic followed by an enclitic and obeys the normal rule for the accentuation of such sequences (§ 296): οὔτε, μήτε, οὔτις, μήτις, οὔπω, μήπω, οὔποτε, μήποτε, εἴπερ, καίπερ, καίτοι, ὥσπερ, ὥστε, εἴθε (with an enclitic element -θε that does not occur as an independent particle). Notice that several of these 'words' apparently violate the σωτῆρα law (so οὔτε, not *οὗτε). But the violation is only apparent because the σωτῆρα rule does not apply to a sequence ending in an enclitic. Notice also the accentuation of οἴμοι and μέντοι (with full word plus enclitic), and τοίνυν (with two enclitics). The pronoun ὅστις is accented in all its forms on the first element, in the same way as the corresponding forms of the relative pronoun ὅς (§ 232), with the second element treated as an enclitic and carrying no accent: ὅστις, ἥτις, ὅντινα, ἥντινα, ὅ τι, οὗτινος, ἧστινος, ᾧτινι, ᾗτινι, ὧτινε, οἷντινοιν, οἵτινες, αἵτινες, οὕστινας, ἅστινας, ἅτινα, ὧντινων, οἷστισι, αἷστισι. Note the 'alternative' forms ὅτου, ὅτῳ, ἅττα, ὅτων, ὅτοις.

299. According to Herodian's rules for the accentuation of the pronoun ὅδε, the element -δε is not treated as an enclitic but as an integral part of the word, except in the dual form τώδε. Most

153

modern editors ignore Herodian's precepts here, treating the element -δε as an enclitic for all forms in the paradigm. Thus, Herodian applies the σωτῆρα law where relevant (except in the dual τώδε), as in the accusative singular masculine τοῦσδε. Most modern editors, on the other hand, accent the first element in the same way as the corresponding form of the article, ignoring the σωτῆρα law as it does not apply to a sequence ending in an enclitic: hence τούσδε. See § 233.

300. The element -δε indicating motion towards (as in Ἐλευσῖνάδε 'to Eleusis'; combining with preceding -σ- to give -ζ- as in Ἀθήναζε from Ἀθήνασ-δε 'to Athens') is an enclitic particle added to a word in the accusative singular or plural. The accentuation of the word to which -δε is added is affected according to the normal rules for the accentuation of a word followed by a monosyllabic enclitic. Thus, Ἐλευσῖνάδε (Ἐλευσῖνα), οἰκόνδε (οἶκον), Ἀθήναζε (Ἀθήνας), Οὐλυμπόνδε (Οὐλυμπον). Notice the irregular form οἴκαδε.

In οἴκαδε it is not obvious that the -δε is added to an acc., but οἴκαδε presupposes the existence of an *old* acc. *οἶκα (either acc. sg. of an old noun *οἶξ 'house', or perhaps an old neut. plur. or 'collective'). In this sequence the -δε is no longer felt to be an enclitic. Thus the expected accentuation *οἰκάδε has been given up in favour of οἴκαδε, an accentuation appropriate to a sequence felt to be simply a single word.

EXERCISE 37: PROCLITICS AND ENCLITICS
Write the following phrases with their correct accents:

1. ἀλλ' εἰπε μοι· (Plato, *Republic* 341c)
2. ἀντι τοι εἰμ' ἱκεταο. (*Il.* 21. 75)
3. οὐδε γ' ἀν ἐπιχειρησαιμι, ἠν δ' ἐγω. (Plato, *Republic* 341b)
4. τοιαυτα σοι ταυτ' ('these things') ἐστιν, ὠ ξενε. (≈ Soph., *Oedipus at Colonus* 62)

5. πλην σου; σε γαρ δη φυλακα φημ᾽ εἰναι στρατου. (Eur., *Rhesus* 813)

6. πατρος δ᾽ εἰμ᾽ ἀγαθοιο, θεᾱ δε με γεινατο μητηρ· (θεά is oxytone, like θεός.) (*Il*. 21. 109)

7. παρ᾽ ('there are') ἐμοι γε και ἀλλοι / οἱ κε με τῑμησουσι. (*Il*. 1. 174–5)

8. οὐκουν ('therefore') ἑκαστῳ τουτων ἐστιν τι συμφερον; πανυ γε. (Plato, *Republic* 341d)

9. και δη μοι γερας αὐτος ἀφαιρησεσθαι ἀπειλεις, / ᾡ ἐπι πολλ᾽ ἐμογησα. (*Il*. 1. 161–2)

10. οὐτε γαρ ἀν με λαθοις κακουργων, οὐτε μη λαθων βιασασθαι τῳ λογῳ δυναιο. (Plato, *Republic* 341b)

11. προς ταυτα κακουργει και σῡκοφαντει, εἰ τι δυνασαι — οὐδεν σου παριεμαι — ἀλλ᾽ οὐ μη οἰος τ᾽ ἠς. (Plato, *Republic* 341b)

12. μαντι κακων, οὐ πω ποτε μοι το κρηγυον εἰπες· / αἰει τοι τα κακ᾽ ἐστι φιλα φρεσι μαντευεσθαι. (κρήγυος is recessive.) (*Il*. 1. 106–7)

13. οὐ μην εἰασαν γε αὐτον οἱ παροντες, ἀλλ᾽ ἠναγκασαν ὑπομειναι τε και παρασχειν των εἰρημενων λογον. (Plato, *Republic* 344d)

14. δια ταυτα και ἡ τεχνη ἐστιν ἡ ἰᾱτρικη νῡν εὑρημενη, ὀτι σωμα ἐστιν πονηρον και οὐκ ἐξαρκει αὐτῳ τοιουτῳ εἰναι. (Plato, *Republic* 341e)

15. τριων ὀντων οὐν ἡμῑν, ὠντινων βουλει, τιθει, καλλιοσιν ἱνα ὀνομασι χρωμεθα. το μεν χρῡσον, το δ᾽ ἀργυρον, τριτον δε το μηδετερα τουτων. (Plato, *Philebus* 43e)

EXERCISE 38: CUMULATIVE EXERCISE
Write out the following passages with correct accents:

Τερψίων· ἀταρ πως οὐκ αὐτου Μεγαροι κατελῡεν;

Εὐκλειδης· ἠπειγετο οἰκαδε· ἐπει ἐγωγ᾽ ἐδεομην και συνεβουλευον, ἀλλ᾽ οὐκ ἠθελεν. και δητα προπεμψᾱς αὐτον, ἀπιων παλιν ἀνεμνησθην και ἐθαυμασα Σωκρατους, ὡς μαντικως ἀλλα τε δη εἰπε και περι τουτου. δοκει γαρ μοι ὀλιγον προ του θανατου ἐντυχειν αὐτῳ μειρακιῳ ὀντι, και συγγενομενος τε και διαλεχθεις πανυ ἀγασθηναι αὐτου την φυσιν. και μοι ἐλθοντι ᾿Αθηναζε τους τε λογους οὑς διελεχθη αὐτῳ διηγησατο και μαλα ἀξιους ἀκοης, εἰπε τε ὁτι πασα ἀναγκη εἰη τουτον ἐλλογιμον γενεσθαι, εἰπερ εἰς ἡλικιαν ἐλθοι.

Τερ· και ἀληθη γε, ὡς ἐοικεν, εἰπεν. ἀταρ τινες ἠσαν οἱ λογοι; ἐχοις ἀν διηγησασθαι;

Εὐ· οὐ μα τον Δια, οὐκουν οὑτω γε ἀπο στοματος· ἀλλ᾿ ἐγραψαμην μεν τοτ᾿ εὐθυς οἰκαδ᾿ ἐλθων ὑπομνηματα, ὑστερον δε κατα σχολην ἀναμιμνησκομενος ἐγραφον, και ὁσακις ᾿Αθηναζε ἀφικοιμην, ἐπανηρωτων τον Σωκρατη ὁ μη ἐμεμνημην, και δευρο ἐλθων ἐπηνωρθουμην· ὡστε μοι σχεδον τι πας ὁ λογος γεγραπται.

Τερ· ἀλλ᾿ ἠδη ἠκουσα σου και προτερον, και μεντοι ἀει μελλων κελευσειν ἐπιδειξαι διατετριφα δευρο. ἀλλα τι κωλυει νυν ἡμας διελθειν; παντως ἐγωγε και ἀναπαυσασθαι δεομαι ὡς ἐξ ἀγρου ἡκων. (Plato, *Theaetetus* 142c–143a)

δεινον γε σ᾿ οὐσαν πατρος οὐ συ παις ἐφῡς
κεινου¹ λελησθαι, της δε τικτουσης μελειν.
ἁπαντα γαρ σοι τἀμα νουθετηματα
κεινης διδακτα,² κοὐδεν ἐκ σαυτης λεγεις.
ἐπει γ᾿ ἑλου συ θατερ᾿, ἠ φρονειν κακως,
ἠ των φιλων φρονουσα μη μνημην ἐχειν·
ἡτις λεγεις μεν ἀρτιως, ὡς εἰ λαβοις
σθενος, το τουτων μισος ἐκδειξειας ἀν·
ἐμου δε πατρι παντα τῑμωρουμενης
οὐτε ξυνερδεις την τε δρωσαν ἐκτρεπεις.
οὐ ταυτα προς κακοισι δειλιᾱν ἐχει;
ἐπει διδαξον, ἠ μαθ᾿ ἐξ ἐμου, τι μοι
κερδος γενοιτ᾿ ἀν τωνδε ληξᾱσῃ γοων.
οὐ ζω; κακως μεν, οἰδ᾿, ἐπαρκουντως δ᾿ ἐμοι.
λῡπω δε τουτους, ὡστε τῳ τεθνηκοτι
τῑμᾱς προσαπτειν, εἰ τις ἐστ᾿ ἐκει χαρις.
συ δ᾿ ἡμιν ἡ μισουσα μῑσεις μεν λογῳ,

7. Proclitics and Enclitics (ex. 38)

ἔργῳ δε τοις φονευσι του πατρος ξυνει.
ἐγω μεν οὐν οὐκ ἀν ποτ᾽, οὐδ᾽ εἰ μοι τα σα
μελλοι τις οἰσειν δωρ᾽, ἐφ᾽ οἰσι³ νῦν χλιδᾳς,
τουτοις ὑπεικαθοιμι· σοι δε πλουσιᾱ
τραπεζα κεισθω και περιρρειτω βιος.
ἐμοι γαρ ἐστω τοὐμε μη λῡπειν μονον
βοσκημα· της σης δ᾽ οὐκ ἐρω τῑμης λαχειν.
οὐδ᾽ ἀν συ, σωφρων γ᾽ οὐσα. νῦν δ᾽ ἐξον πατρος
παντων ἀριστου παιδα κεκλησθαι, καλου
της μητρος. οὑτω γαρ φανη πλειστοις κακη,
θανοντα πατερα και φιλους προδουσα σους. (Soph., *Electra* 341–68)

---

¹κεῖνος is properispomenon, like ἐκεῖνος. ²διδακτός is oxytone.
³οἶσι is accented like οἶς.

Appendix: Accentuation of Dialects Other than the *Koiné*

301. Most of our information on accents relates to the language spoken by the Alexandrian grammarians, the Hellenistic *koiné* based on Attic. For the philological reasons mentioned in § 24, we know that in important respects the *koiné* retains the accentual system that operated at a much earlier period of Greek and was continued in Attic, the dialect on which the *koiné* is based. Such information as we have on the accentuation of the closely-related dialect Ionic suggests that Ionic accentuation did not differ substantially from that of Attic.

302. Significant differences in the accentual rules are found in some dialects more distantly related to Attic. In particular, we know something about the accentuation of Lesbian and of Doric.

303. Our information on this subject comes mainly from statements of ancient grammarians about the accentuation of 'Aeolic' (by which Lesbian is probably meant) and of 'Doric'. In addition, some literary papyri of dialect texts are marked with dialect accents following the precepts of the grammarians.

304. We have very little evidence about the accentuation of any dialects other than those mentioned above. However, a papyrus containing a fragment of poetry by the Boeotian poetess Corinna provides some rather tantalising hints concerning the accentuation of Boeotian (§§ 310–11). There is no direct evidence for the accentuation of Thessalian, but CHADWICK, *THESSALIAN*, has drawn some conclusions based on other Thessalian linguistic characteristics (§§ 312–14). In addition, we know that certain words were accented in Attic differently from their accentuation in the *koiné* (§§ 315–17), and we have certain rather intriguing pieces of information relating specifically to the accentuation of Homer (§§ 318–19).

305. It is not clear what sources of information the Alexandrian scholars had about the accentuation of dialects other than their own. In principle, it is possible either that their information came from observation of dialect speakers of their day, or that they had access to an oral tradition relating to the pronunciation of e.g. Sappho or Alcman. In the case of Homeric accentuation, the first possibility does not, of course, arise; on this question see further §§ 318–19.

Lesbian accentuation

306. All words in Lesbian were recessive except for proclitics and enclitics, which were treated as in the *koiné*.

There were, however, some differences between Lesbian and the *koiné* concerning which words were enclitic. The verbs φᾶμι 'I say' and ἔμμι 'I am' (for *koiné* φημί and εἰμί), in particular, were non-enclitic and therefore recessive in Lesbian throughout their paradigms. See AHRENS i, pp. 17–18.

For the statements of grammarians relating to the accentuation of 'Aeolic', see AHRENS i, pp. 10–19; MEISTER i, pp. 31–8. For papyri with Aeolic accents, see E.-M. Hamm, *Grammatik zu Sappho und Alkaios* (2nd edn, Akademie-Verlag, 1958), pp. 42–4. For some further exceptions to the recessive accent rule found in the papyri with 'Aeolic' accents, and for philological discussion, see WEST, *LESBIAN*.

307. The poems of Sappho and of Alcaeus are printed in most modern editions with Lesbian accents, as prescribed by the ancient grammarians and demonstrated in some of the papyri of those authors. Thus, Lobel and Page print the first stanza of Sappho, fr. 31 (Lobel-Page) as follows:

φαίνεταί μοι κῆνος ἴσος θέοισιν
ἔμμεν᾽ ὤνηρ, ὄττις ἐνάντιός τοι
ἰσδάνει καὶ πλάσιον ἀδυ φωνεί-
σας ὐπακούει

(E. Lobel and D.L. Page (eds), *Poetarum lesbiorum fragmenta* (Clarendon Press, 1955), p. 32.)

Notice the recessive accent on the following words, which are non-recessive in an Attic or Ionic text: θέοισιν (rather than θεοῖσιν), ὤνηρ (for ἀνήρ), ἐνάντιος (for ἐναντίος), πλάσιον (for πλησίον), ἀδυ (for ἡδύ). Observe also that μοι and τοι are enclitic as usual and obey the usual rules of accentuation for enclitics (§§ 278–300). The conjunction καί, which is proclitic, is accented in the usual way, not recessively (καὶ, not *καῖ).

Doric accentuation

308. The most important pieces of information we have on Doric accentuation are the following:

(a) Some Doric words with a long accented vowel in the penultimate syllable and a short vowel in the final syllable had an acute, not a circumflex, on the penultimate, e.g. παῖδες (not παῖδες), αἴγες (not αἶγες), φώτες (not φῶτες). In other words, the σωτῆρα rule did not apply in Doric.

It is unclear quite how the choice between an acute and a circumflex on the penultimate syllable of a word of type σωτῆρα was determined in Doric. Choeroboscus (Th. 1. 386. 12–15) apparently intends a general rule that the Dorians place an acute on all words with an accented penultimate syllable containing a long vowel followed by a final syllable with a short vowel. If so, the type of accent falling on a penultimate syllable would be as easily predictable as in Attic, but would follow a different (and very simple) rule: in Doric an accent on a penultimate syllable would *always* be an acute. In the papyri with 'Doric' accents, however, we find not only words of type παῖδες, with an acute on the penultimate syllable, but also words of type φᾶρος (e.g. at *P. Paris* 71 col. ii line 27 = Alcman, fr. 1. 61 Page), with a circumflex. It is difficult to draw conclusions from the appearance of words such as φᾶρος on papyri, because it is always possible that some accents on the papyri are simply those of the *koiné*. On the other hand, the scribes of the papyri had access to a more complete grammatical tradition than we can now recover, and they may well have written φᾶρος on the basis of knowledge that we now lack.

(b) Doric nominative plural forms in *-οι* and *-αι*, including participles in *-μενοι* and *-μεναι*, had the accent on the penultimate syllable where Attic and Ionic had a recessive accent: φιλοσόφοι for φιλόσοφοι. It is likely that Doric speakers thought of final *-οι* and *-αι* as counting 'long' for accentuation in nominative plural forms (cf. §§ 66–8).

(c) Third person plural past indicative forms ending in *-ον* or *-αν* had an acute on the penultimate syllable: ἐλέγον 'they said' (Attic ἔλεγον), ἐδώκαν 'they gave' (classical Attic ἔδοσαν).

3rd pl. past indic. forms ending in *-ον* and *-αν* had ended in *-ont* and *-ant* at an early stage in the prehistory of Greek. AHRENS ii, pp. 28–9, and MISTELI, pp. 111–12, suggested that the Doric accentuation of these forms on the penultimate syllable was a relic from the time when the forms ended with a consonant cluster (cf. § 64c). Cf., however, LUCIDI, *TRISILLABISMO*, p. 80.

For statements of grammarians relating to the accentuation of 'Doric', see AHRENS ii, pp. 26–35; for papyri with Doric accents, M. Nöthiger, *Die Sprache des Stesichorus und des Ibycus* (Juris, 1971), pp. 83–6.

309. The details of Doric accentuation are not understood in great detail. Consequently, the editors of modern texts of Doric authors do not normally print Doric accents except when the text involved is preserved on a papyrus with Doric accentuation. In such cases editors often print Doric accents, taking over the accents on the papyrus and supplying further accents where necessary in accordance with the general principles that the scribe appears to have been following. Thus, lines 10–19 of Ibycus, fr. 282a (Page) are printed by Davies as follows (cf. § 19):

νῦ]ν δέ μοι οὔτε ξειναπάτ[α]ν Π[άρι]ν
..] ἐπιθύμιον οὔτε τανί[σφ]υρ[ον
ὑμ.]νῆν Κασσάνδραν
Πρι]άμοιό τε παῖδας ἄλλου[ς
Τρο]ίας θ' ὑψιπύλοιο ἁλώσι[μο]ν
ἆμ]αρ ἀνώνυμον, οὐδεπ[
ἠρ]ώων ἀρετὰν
ὑπ]ερáφανον οὕς τε κοίλα[ι
νᾶες] πολυγόμφοι ἐλεύσα[ν
Τροί]αι κακόν, ἥρωας ἐσθ[λούς·

(M. Davies (ed.), *Poetarum melicorum graecorum fragmenta* (Clarendon Press, 1991–) i, p. 242.)

Notice παῖδας (Attic παῖδας), against the σωτῆρα rule; πολυγόμφοι (cf. πολύγομφον at Aesch., *Persae* 71), with an acute on the penultimate syllable before final -οι in a nominative plural; ἐλεύσα[ν (rather than recessive *ἔλευσαν, aorist of ἐλεύθω 'bring'), with an acute on the penultimate in a third person plural aorist indicative ending in -αν. The form κοίλα[ι also gives the appearance of violating the σωτῆρα rule — but if final -αι was treated as 'long' for accentuation in a nominative plural the σωτῆρα rule would in any case be irrelevant here.

Boeotian accentuation

310. Boeotian, a dialect of the Aeolic dialect group, is closely related to Lesbian and Thessalian. Grammarians tell us very little about its accentuation; occasional words are cited as non-recessively accented in Boeotian, and these have led scholars to assume that Boeotian did not share the Lesbian generalisation of recessive accentuation.

See AHRENS i, pp. 166–8; MEISTER i, pp. 213–14 with 214, n. 1.

311. The 'Berlin papyrus' of the Boeotian poetess Corinna (for which see von Wilamowitz-Moellendorff, cited below) is partially accented. On the whole, the accents are those one would expect to find in an Attic or *koiné* text, but there are some peculiarities. It has been debated whether these provide evidence for a special Boeotian system of accentuation or whether they are due merely to differences of detail in the accentuation of individual words or the way certain suffixes are treated. For example, μώση 'muses' (nominative plural), found at i. 19, is the equivalent of Attic μοῦσαι, the diphthong -αι having become in Boeotian a long vowel written with -η. The acute on μώση is capable of at least three (not mutually exclusive) interpretations. It could be that the Boeotian nominative plural ending -η counted as 'long' for accentuation, unlike its Attic equivalent -αι; it could be that the σωτῆρα rule did not apply in Boeotian; or it could be that a scribe wrote an acute under the influence of his knowledge of the *koiné*, where a final -η never counted 'short' for accentuation.

For further information and discussion see U. von Wilamowitz-Moellendorff, 'XIV. Korinna. Nr. 284', in W. Schubart and U. von Wilamowitz-Moellendorff (eds), *Berliner Klassikertexte* 5. 2: *Lyrische und dramatische Fragmente* (Weidmann, 1907), pp. 19–55; E. Hermann, 'Die böotische Betonung', *Nachrichten von der Königlichen Gesellschaft der Wissenschaften zu Göttingen, Philologisch-historische Klasse* (1918), pp. 273–80; G. Bonfante, 'L'accento beotico', *Rivista di filologia e d'istruzione classica* N.S. 12 (1934), pp. 535–46; S. Levin, 'The Accentuation of the Boeotian Dialect, According to the Berlin Papyrus of Corinna', in H. Beister and J. Buckler (eds), *Boiotika: Vorträge vom 5. Internationalen Böotien-Kolloquium zu Ehren von Professor Dr. Siegfried Lauffer* (Editio Maris, 1989), pp. 17–22.

Thessalian accentuation

312. Our knowledge of the Thessalian accent is based almost exclusively on indirect evidence from inscriptions. These reveal that Thessalian, uniquely among Greek dialects, underwent considerable changes in vowel quality and loss of vowels. These Thessalian developments are typical of languages with a stress accent (see § 11) and have led to speculation that Thessalian, unlike the other Greek dialects, had indeed given up the pitch accent found in the other dialects and replaced it with a stress accent.

313. CHADWICK, *THESSALIAN*, argues specifically that the Thessalian stress accent normally fell on the initial syllable, since Thessalian vowel change and loss is not normally found in initial syllables, and there are one or two examples where the vowel of an initial syllable, far from being lost, has been lengthened. He suggests that unstressed syllables underwent processes of vowel change or loss while vowel lengthening took place in initial syllables under the influence of the accent.

314. If Chadwick's conclusions are correct, of the Greek dialects for which we have evidence on accentuation Thessalian is the only one that ever abandoned the law of limitation. The two dialects most closely related to Thessalian, Lesbian and Boeotian, both retained the law of limitation; a Thessalian initial-syllable accent would therefore be an innovation characterising Thessalian alone.

Attic accentuation

315. Ancient grammarians tell us that certain words had a special accentuation in Attic, different from their accentuation in the *koiné*. Words that we have mentioned in the course of this book include: the imperatives ἰδέ, λαβέ (*koiné* ἴδε, λάβε); voc. ἄδελφε (*koiné* ἀδελφέ); the terms of abuse πόνηρος, μόχθηρος, μῶρος (koiné πονηρός, μοχθηρός, μωρός); διέτης, τριέτης... (koiné διετής, τριετής...).

On πόνηρος and μόχθηρος see, however, the note to § 189.

316. It is of interest that the information we have concerning accentual differences between Attic and the *koiné* is confined to the accentuation of a small number of particular words. Since the Alexandrian grammarians had access to information regarding the accentuation of Attic as opposed to that of the *koiné*, if there were substantial differences beyond the accentuation of certain words one would expect these to have been mentioned. We may conclude that, as one might have expected given the Attic foundation of the *koiné*, Attic and the *koiné* did not differ substantially in accentuation in the Hellenistic period.

317. In some instances, we are told that a word had a special accentuation in a 'newer' form of Attic, different from the accentuation it had had in Homer or in 'old Attic'. Words of this type that we have encountered are: newer Attic ἕτοιμος (for old ἑτοῖμος); γέλοιος (old γελοῖος); ὅμοιος (old ὁμοῖος); ἔρημος (old ἐρῆμος); τρόπαιον 'trophy' (old τροπαῖον). The words just mentioned were originally properispomenon and end in a sequence consisting of a light syllable followed by a heavy syllable followed by a light syllable. Such words tended to become proparoxytone in Attic. This Attic accent shift is known after its discoverer as Vendryes' law and probably occurred as late as the fourth century BC.

VENDRYES, p. 263, and Vendryes (cited below), pp. 222–3, suggested that the retraction of the accent was a particular characteristic of later Attic but that it was also responsible for the accentuation of a good number of words in the *koiné*, such as the recessive words of § 177 and βασίλειος etc. in § 178. Of the words mentioned in large print above, the evidence from ancient grammarians suggests that all except τρόπαιον/τροπαῖον were properispomenon in the *koiné* (as in old Attic but not later Attic), but that speakers of the *koiné* agreed with the newer Attic speakers in saying τρόπαιον (so that it was the old Attic accentuation τροπαῖον that seemed peculiar to *koiné* speakers). I hope to discuss these distinctions in more detail elsewhere.

For discussion of the whole question see J. Vendryes, 'L'accent de ἔγωγε et la loi des propérispomènes en attique', *Mémoires de la société de linguistique de Paris* 13 (1905/6), pp. 218–24. On the accentuation of the Attic forms ἔγωγε and ἔμοιγε cf. § 230. For further information and bibliography, see N.E. Collinge, *The Laws of Indo-European* (Benjamins, 1985), pp. 199–202.

Homeric accentuation

318. Most of our information on accents applies, as mentioned above, to the Hellenistic *koiné* spoken by the Alexandrian grammarians. In addition, as we have seen, grammarians provide us with some information on the accentuation of other dialects for which it is conceivable that they consulted speakers. Even if their knowledge about Lesbian, Doric, or Boeotian did not derive from living speakers, it could easily derive from living traditions of pronunciation. What is rather more surprising is that in some instances the grammarians provide us with specific information about Homeric accentuation that is clearly not simply extrapolated from the accentuation of the language of their own day.

319. For example, LEHRS (*ARISTARCHUS*, pp. 257–8) observed that Homer has six nouns in -οτης: φιλότης 'love', νεότης 'youth', κακότης 'badness', ἰότης 'desire', δηϊοτής 'battle-strife', and ἀνδροτής 'manliness' (or the variant reading ἀδροτής 'vigour'). A Homeric scholiast (Sch. *Il.* 3. 20 (A[int])) informs us that Aristarchus (see § 20) was responsible for the oxytone accentuation of the archaic word δηϊοτής. It is likely, although we do not have direct evidence, that the acute on the final syllable of the likewise archaic ἀνδροτής is also due to Aristarchus.

Words in -οτης became very productive from the fifth century BC onwards, when a demand for abstract nouns arose in the philosophical schools. These -οτης words of Attic and the *koiné* were all paroxytone except that, as we are told, the Athenians said κουφοτής 'lightness' instead of κουφότης, the latter being by implication the *koiné* accentuation of the word (Arcadius 30. 4). There is no discernible reason why Aristarchus would have accented δηϊοτής (and ἀνδροτής) as he did on the basis of the living language. Extrapolating from the numerous -ότης words known to him, he would have assumed accentuation on the penultimate syllable. Lehrs' answer is that the accents on the final syllables of δηϊοτής and ἀνδροτής were ancient accents that had been handed down in a continuous tradition of pronouncing and hearing Homer.

Lehrs' conclusion is based on an accumulation of similar examples, to which others have since added more (see the references below). In several of these cases there are philological reasons for thinking that the Homeric accent prescribed by the grammarians was indeed the original accent of the word. For example, ἀνδροτής derives from prehistoric *anṛtās*, where '*ṛ*' was a rolled '*r*' sound and functioned as the vowel of the second syllable (thus, the syllables were *a*, *nṛ*, *tās*). Comparative evidence for the accentual patterns of Indo-European languages suggests that at an early stage the sound '*ṛ*' was not capable of carrying an accent. The accent thus cannot originally have fallen on the second syllable (which later became δρο) but could have fallen on the last: *anṛtás*, becoming Aristarchus' ἀνδροτής. Aristarchus' agreement with the result of a philological argument not available to him strengthens the conclusion that he had access to a tradition of pronouncing Homer in which some genuinely old accents were preserved.

Lehrs' hypothesis must remain unprovable by nature, but it is the best available explanation for certain data, such as Aristarchus' accentuation of δηϊοτής and ἀνδροτής. It is appropriate to end with Lehrs' own statement:

Mihi in his rebus versanti iterum iterumque occurrit, etiam in obsoletioribus vocabulis aliquam de accentu traditionem fuisse. Etenim etiamsi ponamus in versibus recitandis accentum voce non notatum esse, quam saepe extra versum etiam Homericorum vocabulorum proferendi occasio erat, partim coram discipulis in ludo, partim in rhapsodorum et philosophorum confabulationibus: ut facile cogitari possit multorum vocabulorum accentus quasi per manus traditos usque ad Alexandrinos pervenisse. (LEHRS, *ARISTARCHUS*, p. 258)

'As I occupy myself with these matters it strikes me again and again that even in the case of the more obsolete words there was some tradition regarding the accent. For even supposing that the accents were not marked by the voice in the recital of verses, how often was there the opportunity of pronouncing Homeric words even outside the context of the verse: in front of pupils at school, in the conversations of rhapsodes and philosophers. It can easily be imagined, therefore, that the accents of many words were passed down as it were from hand to hand, and so reached the Alexandrians.'

See LEHRS, *ARISTARCHUS*, pp. 252–9; H. Steinthal, *Geschichte der Sprachwissenschaft bei den Griechen und Römern* (2nd edn, Dümmler, 1890–1; repr. Olms 1961) ii, p. 94; WACKERNAGEL, *BEITRÄGE*, 33–8; WACKERNAGEL, *AKZENTSTUDIEN III*; J. Wackernagel (†), 'Graeca', *Philologus* N.S. 49 (1943), pp. 177, 181–2 (repr. in WACKERNAGEL, *KS* ii, pp. 876, 880–1); M.L. West, 'The Singing of Homer and the Modes of Early Greek Music', *JHS* 101 (1981), pp. 113–29, esp. p. 114; G. Nagy, *Poetry as Performance: Homer and Beyond* (CUP, 1996), pp. 125–32 (with further literature).

Answers to Exercises

EXERCISE 1: LENGTHS OF VOWELS AND WEIGHTS OF SYLLABLES

1. κλο.πή	Vowels: short — long. Syllables: light — heavy.
2. τέ.χνη	Vowels: short — long. Syllables: light — heavy.
OR τέχ.νη	Vowels: short — long. Syllables: heavy — heavy.
3. ὀ.φρύ.ϊ	Vowels: short — short — short.
	Syllables: light — light — light.
OR ὀφ.ρύ.ϊ	Vowels: short — short — short.
	Syllables: heavy — light — light.
4. ὄγ.δο.ο(ς)	Vowels: short — short — short.
	Syllables: heavy — light — light.
5. ἄ.παξ	Vowels: short — short. Syllables: light — heavy.
6. νε.βρό(ς)	Vowels: short — short. Syllables: light — light.
OR νεβ.ρό(ς)	Vowels: short — short. Syllables: heavy — light.
7. ἔγ.νω(ν)	Vowels: short — long. Syllables: heavy — heavy.
8. ἐκ.λύ.ω	Vowels: short — long — long.
	Syllables: heavy — heavy — heavy.
9. πεν.θε.ρό(ς)	Vowels: short — short — short.
	Syllables: heavy — light — light.
10. ἀ.γρό(ς)	Vowels: short — short. Syllables: light — light.
OR ἀγ.ρό(ς)	Vowels: short — short. Syllables: heavy — light.
11. μῑ.μη.τι.κό(ς)	Vowels: long — long — short — short.
	Syllables: heavy — heavy — light — light.
12. γλαυ.κό(ς)	Vowels: long — short. Syllables: heavy — light.
13. φοῖ.νιξ	Vowels: long — short. Syllables: heavy — heavy.
14. ἐκ.λέ.γω	Vowels: short — short — long.
	Syllables: heavy — light — heavy.
15. ὀ.φλισ.κά.νω	Vowels: short — short — short — long.
	Syllables: light — heavy — light — heavy.

OR ὀφ.λισ.κά.νω	Vowels: short — short — short — long.	
	Syllables: heavy — heavy — light — heavy.	
16. ἐσ.τρά.φη(ν)	Vowels: short — short — long.	
	Syllables: heavy — light — heavy.	
17. ναυ.κρα.τέ.ω	Vowels: long — short — short — long.	
	Syllables: heavy — light — light — heavy.	
OR ναυκ.ρα.τέ.ω	Vowels: long — short — short — long.	
	Syllables: heavy — light — light — heavy.	
18. ὀφ.θαλ.μό(ς)	Vowels: short — short — short.	
	Syllables: heavy — heavy — light.	
19. τάξις = τάκ.σι(ς)	Vowels: short — short. Syllables: heavy — light.	
20. ᾽Α.θη.ναί.ου	Vowels: short — long — long — long.	
	Syllables: light — heavy — heavy — heavy.	
21. πράσ.σω	Vowels: long — long. Syllables: heavy — heavy.	
22. εὑ.ρίσ.κω	Vowels: long — short — long.	
	Syllables: heavy — heavy — heavy.	
23. μιμ.νήσ.κω	Vowels: short — long — long.	
	Syllables: heavy — heavy — heavy.	
24. Κύ.πρι(ς)	Vowels: short — short. Syllables: light — light.	
OR Κύπ.ρι(ς)	Vowels: short — short. Syllables: heavy — light.	
25. λῡ.πρό(ς)	Vowels: long — short. Syllables: heavy — light.	
OR λῡπ.ρό(ς)	Vowels: long — short. Syllables: heavy — light.	
26. ἴζω = ἴσ.δω	Vowels: short — long. Syllables: heavy — heavy.	
27. αἰσ.χρῶ(ν)	Vowels: long — long. Syllables: heavy — heavy.	
28. ἐ.πι.ει.κή(ς)	Vowels: short — short — long — long.	
	Syllables: light — light — heavy — heavy.	
29. καλ.λίσ.του	Vowels: short — short — long.	
	Syllables: heavy — heavy — heavy.	
30. ᾽Αλέξανδρος = ᾽Α.λέκ.σαν.δρο(ς)		
	Vowels: short — short — short — short.	
	Syllables: light — heavy — heavy — light.	
31. λαῖ.λαψ	Vowels: long — short. Syllables: heavy — heavy.	
32. μά.χη	Vowels: short — long. Syllables: light — heavy.	
33. δεί.κνῡ.μι	Vowels: long — long — short.	
	Syllables: heavy — heavy — light.	
OR δείκ.νῡ.μι	Vowels: long — long — short.	
	Syllables: heavy — heavy — light.	
34. τοι.ού.τῳ	Vowels: long — long — long.	

Answers to Exercises (exx. 1–2)

Syllables: heavy — heavy — heavy.

35. μῑκροψῡχίᾱ = μῑ.κροπ.σῡ.χί.ᾱ

Vowels: long — short — long — short — long.
Syllables: heavy — heavy — heavy — light — heavy.

OR μῑκ.ροπ.σῡ.χί.ᾱ

Vowels: long — short — long — short — long.
Syllables: heavy — heavy — heavy — light — heavy.

36. πρᾶγ.μα   Vowels: long — short. Syllables: heavy — light.

37. ἐμ.πλέ.κω   Vowels: short — short — long.
Syllables: heavy — light — heavy.

38. λισ.σό.με.θα   Vowels: short — short — short — short.
Syllables: heavy — light — light — light.

EXERCISE 2: NAMES FOR THE POSITIONS OF THE ACCENT

1. oxytone
2. paroxytone
3. properispomenon
4. oxytone
5. oxytone
6. paroxytone
7. perispomenon

3. paroxytone
9. properispomenon
10. paroxytone
11. paroxytone
12. properispomenon
13. perispomenon
14. perispomenon

15. proparoxytone
16. properispomenon
17. paroxytone
18. proparoxytone
19. paroxytone
20. paroxytone
21. oxytone

22. paroxytone
23. paroxytone
24. proparoxytone
25. oxytone
26. oxytone
27. properispomenon
28. oxytone

29. φοῖνιξ	39. Ἅιδου
30. μιμνήσκω	40. αἰχμάλωτος
31. λιπεῖν	41. μεταβολή
32. ἄνθρωπος	42. νοῦς
33. Κύπρις	43. οἶμαι
34. νεβρός	44. παντοῖος
35. ἀρετῇ	45. ἔγνων
36. αἰσχρῶν	46. ναυκρατέω
37. Αἰσχύλος	47. Ὤιμωζον
38. Ζεῦ	48. ἀγρός
49. ἀρεταί	53. καλλίστου
50. λιγυροῦ	54. σωτῆρα
51. ἱερεῦσι	55. ἐκλέγω
52. Ἀλέξανδρος	

EXERCISE 3: RECESSIVE WORDS

(a) ἅπαξ, ἵζω, πράσσω, λαῖλαψ, ἐκλύω, μάχη, πρᾶγμα, νοῦ, σοφώτατος, ὀφλισκάνω, δείκνῡμι, εὑρίσκω, ἐμπλέκω, τέχνη, ἕτερος, φοῖνιξ, μιμνήσκω, ἄνθρωπος, Κύπρις, Ζεῦ, Ἅιδου, αἰχμάλωτος, νοῦς, οἶμαι, ἔγνων, ναυκρατέω, Ὤιμωζον, Ἀλέξανδρος, καλλίστου, ἐκλέγω.

(b)

1. λύω	8. λῡσάτω	15. λῡσαίμεθα	22. ἐλύοντο
2. λύεις	9. λελύκοι	16. λύοι	23. λυθήσομαι
3. ἐλελύκη	10. λύονται	17. λέλυμαι	
4. λύσοιντο	11. λύειν	18. ἐλύθησαν	
5. λύουσι	12. λύσοιο	19. λῡσόμενοι	
6. λέλυνται	13. λύῃ	20. λῦσαι	
7. λύηται	14. λῦε	21. λύσαι	

EXERCISE 4: CONTRACTED WORDS

1. ῥοῦς
2. αἰδῶ
3. φιλῆτε
4. φίλει
5. φιλεῖ
6. Ἑρμῆς
7. Ἑρμῶν
8. ἐτίμα
9. φιλούμεθα
10. ἐστιοῦχος
11. ζώς

EXERCISE 5: THE GRAVE ACCENT

οὗτος ἐμός τε ἑταῖρος ἦν ἐκ νέου καὶ ὑμῶν τῷ πλήθει ἑταῖρός τε καὶ συνέφυγε τὴν φυγὴν ταύτην καὶ μεθ᾽ ὑμῶν κατῆλθε. καὶ ἴστε δὴ οἷος ἦν Χαιρεφῶν, ὡς σφοδρὸς ἐφ᾽ ὅτι ὁρμήσειεν. καὶ δή ποτε καὶ εἰς Δελφοὺς ἐλθὼν ἐτόλμησε τοῦτο μαντεύσασθαι — καί, ὅπερ λέγω, μὴ θορυβεῖτε, ὦ ἄνδρες — ἤρετο γὰρ δὴ εἴ τις ἐμοῦ εἴη σοφώτερος. ἀνεῖλεν οὖν ἡ Πυθία μηδένα σοφώτερον εἶναι. καὶ τούτων πέρι ὁ ἀδελφὸς ὑμῖν αὐτοῦ οὑτοσὶ μαρτυρήσει, ἐπειδὴ ἐκεῖνος τετελεύτηκεν.

Σκέψασθε δὴ ὧν ἕνεκα ταῦτα λέγω· μέλλω γὰρ ὑμᾶς διδάξειν ὅθεν μοι ἡ διαβολὴ γέγονεν. ταῦτα γὰρ ἐγὼ ἀκούσας ἐνεθυμούμην οὑτωσί· "Τί ποτε λέγει ὁ θεός, καὶ τί ποτε αἰνίττεται; ἐγὼ γὰρ δὴ οὔτε μέγα οὔτε σμικρὸν σύνοιδα ἐμαυτῷ σοφὸς ὤν· τί οὖν ποτε λέγει φάσκων ἐμὲ σοφώτατον εἶναι; οὐ γὰρ δήπου ψεύδεταί γε· οὐ γὰρ θέμις αὐτῷ." καὶ πολὺν μὲν χρόνον ἠπόρουν τί ποτε λέγει·

EXERCISE 6: ELIDED WORDS

1. πολλὰ κάκ᾽ ἀνθρώπους ἐέοργει·
2. πατρῷον δ᾽ ἐκτίνεις τ᾽ν ἆθλον.
3. ἀγλά᾽ ἄποινα / οὐκ ἔθελον δέξασθαι.
4. ἆ δειλ᾽, ἦ μάλα δή σε κιχάνεται αἰπὺς ὄλεθρος.
5. οὐκ ἄν τις αὔτ᾽ ἔμαρψεν ἄλλος ἀντ᾽ ἐμοῦ.
6. ἀλλ᾽ εἴ τι χρήζεις ἱστορεῖν, πάρειμ᾽ ἐγώ.
7. ἤδη ποτ᾽ εἶδον ἄνδρ᾽ ἐγὼ γλώσσῃ θρασύν.
8. ἔκλαγξαν δ᾽ ἄρ᾽ ὀϊστοὶ ἐπ᾽ ὤμων χωομένοιο.
9. ὡς ἔφατ᾽, οὐδ᾽ ἀπίθησε ποδήνεμος ὠκέα Ἶρις.
10. οἳ δ᾽ Ἀσπληδόνα ναῖον ἰδ᾽ Ὀρχομενὸν Μινύειον, / τῶν ἦρχ᾽ Ἀσκάλαφος καὶ Ἰάλμενος.

EXERCISE 7: PRODELISION AND CRASIS

1. ἀνήρ
2. κἀκεῖ
3. τοῦπος (some editors τοὔπος)
4. οὕνεκα
5. θἠμέρᾳ
6. προὔργου

7. εἰ μή 'σθιε
   (some editors εἰ μὴ 'σθιε)
8. ἢ 'ξομῇ
9. τοῦψον (some editors τοὔψον)
10. τρέπεται δή 'πειτα
    (some editors τρέπεται δὴ 'πειτα)

EXERCISE 8: FINITE VERBS

1. μάχομαι
2. λύσαιμι
3. ἐζεύξατε
4. λαθοῦ
5. πυθοῦ
6. λάθε
7. βουλεύοι
8. φαθί
9. λέλοιπα
10. λύσοι
11. διδοίην
12. θοῦ
13. χρή
14. ἔλαθον
15. λίπωμεν

16. δίδωμι
17. ἐλθέ
18. φεύγω
19. λύσαις
20. παῦσον
21. λιποῦ
22. φύγε
23. γενοῦ
24. φεῦγε
25. ἔθου
26. τίθεμεν
27. εἶπον
28. ἐθέλει
29. πυνθάνῃ
30. ἔζευξας

31. δείκνυμαι
32. ἐφύλαξα
33. γέγραμμαι
34. βούλευσον
35. πυθώμεθα
36. βασιλεύοι
37. λελύκητε
38. βουλεύοιτε
39. πυνθάνομαι
40. λίπωνται
41. βούλευσαι
42. ἴδου
43. λῦσαι
44. εἶπε
45. παῦσαι

46. πυνθάνωμαι
47. ἰδέ
48. λῦσαι
49. εἰπέ
50. παῦσαι
51. λαβέ
52. βασίλευσον
53. εὑρέ
54. βασιλεύοιμι
55. λελοίπαμεν

EXERCISE 9: CONTRACTED VERBS

1. δηλοῦσι	22. τεμεῖ	43. λειφθῶσι	64. φανοῦμαι
2. δῶτε	23. κτελεῖς	44. ἐτῑμᾶσθε	65. φιλεῖ
3. τῑμᾷς	24. θῶ	45. ἱσταίμεθα	66. τιθώμεθα
4. φιλῶσι	25. φανοῖεν	46. κομιοῦμεν	67. φανούμεθα
5. στῶμεν	26. ἱῇ	47. στήσαιτε	68. φανείητε
6. τιθῶ	27. λειφθῇς	48. ἱστῶμαι	69. φανῇ
7. τιθεῖεν	28. τιθῶμεν	49. φανεῖμεν	70. φανεῖσθε
8. διδῷς	29. φιλοῦ	50. δεδώκοιμι	71. τῑμῶμαι
9. ἱῆσθε	30. διδοίη	51. ἀροῦμεν	72. τῑμῶμαι
10. ἱεῖτε	31. στήσαιτο	52. λειφθῶμεν	73. φανοῦνται
11. ἱσταῖο	32. διδῶνται	53. λυθεῖτε	74. γελῶμεν
12. τεμεῖς	33. τιθεῖτε	54. ἱσταίης	75. φίλει
13. δῶσι	34. ἀρῶ	55. δύναιντο	76. φιλῶ
14. εἶεν	35. τῑμῷο	56. φθερεῖτε	77. φιλῶ
15. λειφθῶ	36. ἱσταῖμεν	57. λυθείης	78. κεκτῷτο
16. φανοῖσθε	37. στήσαιο	58. φανείην	79. γελῶμαι
17. ἴοιτε	38. δηλῶμεν	59. κομιοῦσι	80. κεκτῆται
18. λυθῶμεν	39. λυῆ	60. κομιούμεθα	81. τεμῶ
19. ἐδηλοῦτε	40. δεικνύοιντο	61. λυθεῖμεν	
20. κομιεῖσθε	41. διδοῖεν	62. δεδώκη	
21. ἐφίλουν	42. ἱστᾶσι	63. θεῖεν	

EXERCISE 10: FINITE VERBS IN COMPOSITION

1. κατῆλθε
2. πάρεισι
3. ἀφῖξαι
4. ἀνάδος
5. ἀπόθου
6. ἀφῆκα
7. παρέσται
8. ἀπόχρῃ
9. κατάθου
10. ἀπόδοιο
11. παρένθες
12. ἄνες
13. ἀφιᾶσι
14. πρόφερε
15. ἐκθοῦ
16. περίθες
17. ἐνθοῦ
18. ἀπολίποιεν
19. προοῦ
20. ἀπόλιπε
21. ἀπόδωται
22. ἐξηῦρον
23. ἀπόθεσθε
24. ἀντιτενεῖς
25. ἀποδιδῶ
26. ἀπολυθῆτε
27. ἀφιστᾶσι
28. σύμφημι
29. ἀποκτενεῖ
30. συνέξαγε
31. κατέδησε
32. προσῆγε
33. ἀνάσχου
34. ἀπεῖργεν
35. ἀνάστησον
36. κατάλεγε
37. συνεξῆγον
38. προλέγονται
39. προΰλαβε
40. ἀπόθειντο
41. ἀπολίποιο
42. ἐντιθῶμαι
43. συνέγραψε
44. ἀπολιποῦ
45. παραβαλοῦ
46. ἀντίσχες
47. ἀπολυθεῖτε
48. ἐπιτῑμῶμεν
49. ἀποφανῶ
50. ἔξειπε
51. ἀμφιβάλω
52. ἀποφανῶ
53. ἀποφανοῖμεν
54. ἐξαγγέλλουσι
55. ἀποκτείνω
56. ἀποφήνωμαι
57. ἀφεῖτε
58. ἀφεῖτε
59. ἀμφιβαλῶ
60. ἐξεῖπε
61. ἐξαγγελοῦσι
62. συνετῑμήθη
63. ἀποφανοῦμαι
64. περιποιοῦμεν

EXERCISE 11: INFINITIVES AND PARTICIPLES

1. πεισθείς
2. λελύσθαι
3. λαβόντος
4. δεικνύς
5. μαθοῦσα
6. πεισθῆναι
7. ἀπολιπόν
8. λαβόν
9. δόμενος
10. μαθεῖν
11. λῡσάμεναι
12. ἀπολείπειν
13. λῡσομένην
14. λελυκότα
15. δόσθαι
16. φιλεῖσθαι
17. τῑμῶσαι
18. φιλοῦντος
19. ἀποδοῦναι
20. δεικνύναι
21. λελυκέναι
22. λιπόμενον
23. λιπέσθαι
24. ἀγγελῶν
25. λαβεῖν
26. δεικνῦσαν
27. τιθεῖσα
28. λύσεσθαι
29. τιθεισῶν
30. λελυμένη
31. τιθέναι
32. ἐκτιθεῖσα
33. κεκηρῡγμένος
34. παυσαμένων
35. λυθησομένῳ
36. βουλεύσᾱσαν
37. φυλασσέμεναι
38. λειφθησόμενοι
39. ἀκουέμεν

176

Answers to Exercises (exx. 10–13)

40. δεικνύμενος
41. δείκνυσθαι
42. λειπόμενος
43. παύσασθαι

44. δηλούμενον
45. φανουμένη
46. βουλεῦσαν
47. λελυκυῖα

48. παυσαμένων
49. λιπομένων
50. βουλεῦσαι

EXERCISE 12: CUMULATIVE EXERCISE

1. λάθε βιώσᾱς.
2. ἀπέθανε καθεύδων.
3. φέρ᾽ εἰπέ, ἤκουσας;
4. ἀκούσαντες ἄπιτε.
5. ἐλπίζω ἰέναι.
6. σπεύδωμεν μάχεσθαι.
7. παθὼν γελᾷς;
8. οἰμώξᾱς ἔπεσεν.
9. ἀναστάντες ἀπῆλθον.

10. μαχόμενος ἀπώλετο.
11. νῑκᾶν ἀξιοῦσιν.
12. χρὴ μαθεῖν.
13. ἐξὸν ἀποφυγεῖν προείλοντο πολεμῆσαι.
14. ἐλείφθησαν τεθνηκότες.
15. χρὴ ἀναβῆναι.
16. σπεύδων θανεῖν ἐσῴζετο.
17. ἱσταῖντο παυσάμεναι.

EXERCISE 13: BASE ACCENT AND CASE ACCENT (i)

1. σοφοῦ, σοφαῖν, σοφῶν, σοφῶν, σοφαῖς
2. δώρου, δῶρα, δώροις, δώρων
3. πλοῦν, πλοῦς, πλώ, πλοῖ
4. χώρᾱν, χῶραι, χώρᾱς, χωρῶν, χώραις
5. λεῴ, λεώς, λεών, λεῴς
6. τάλαν, τάλανος, ταλαίνῃ, τάλανας, ταλαίνᾱς, ταλάνων, ταλαινῶν
7. σκιάν, σκιᾶς, σκιᾷ, σκιαί, σκιάς, σκιῶν, σκιαῖς
8. ῥῆτορ, ῥήτορα, ῥήτορε, ῥητόροιν, ῥήτορες, ῥήτορας, ῥητόρων, ῥήτορσι
9. ἵλεων, ἵλεων, ἵλεῳ, ἵλεως, ἵλεα
10. σατράπου, σατράπην, σατράπαι, σατραπῶν, σατράπαις
11. ἑκοῦσα, ἑκούσης, ἑκουσῶν, ἑκόντα, ἑκόντων, ἑκοῦσι, ἑκούσαις, ἑκοῦσαι
12. σῡκῆν, σῡκῆς, σῡκαῖ, σῡκῶν, σῡκῇ, σῡκαῖς
13. δεκάδος, δεκάδι, δεκάδων, δεκάδες, δεκάσι
14. σωτῆρα, σωτῆρι, σωτῆρες, σωτήρων, σωτῆρσι
15. μνᾶν, μνᾶς, μνᾷ, μνᾶ, μναῖ, μνῶν, μναῖς

EXERCISE 14: BASE ACCENT AND CASE ACCENT (ii)

1. δυσῶδες, δυσώδεσι
2. κακοδαίμονες, κακοδαιμόνων, κακόδαιμον, κακοδαίμοσι, κακόδαιμον, κακοδαιμόνων
3. τειχῆρες, τειχήρεσι
4. φιλόφρονος, φιλόφρον, φιλόφρον, φιλόφρονι, φιλόφρονα, φιλόφρονες, φιλοφρόνων, φιλόφροσι
5. ἡδίονα, ἡδίω, ἡδίονος, ἥδιον, ἡδιόνων, ἡδιόνων
6. Δημόσθενες
7. πανῶλες, πανώλεσι
8. περίμηκες, περιμήκεσι
9. αὐτάρκεσι, αὔταρκες, αὔταρκες
10. αἰσχίω, αἰσχίονα, αἰσχιόνοιν, αἴσχιον, αἰσχίονες
11. δαΐφρονα, δαΐφρον, δαΐφρον, δαϊφρόνων, δαϊφρόνων
12. κατάντεσι, κάταντες
13. ἔλᾱττον, ἐλάττοσι, ἐλάττονι, ἐλάττονας, ἐλάττους, ἐλαττόνων
14. εὔδαιμον, εὔδαιμον, εὐδαίμονος, εὐδαίμονι, εὐδαιμόνων, εὐδαίμοσι
15. ποδῆρες, ποδήρεσι

EXERCISE 15: BASE ACCENT AND CASE ACCENT (iii)

1. χρῡσοῦ, χρῡσῆς, χρῡσώ, χρῡσαῖς, χρῡσαῖ, χρῡσᾶς
2. διπλοῦν, διπλοῦ, διπλῷ, διπλῆν, διπλῆ, διπλώ, διπλᾶ, διπλοῖν, διπλᾶ, διπλαῖν, διπλοῖ, διπλαῖς
3. ἔκπλοις, ἔκπλου, ἐκπλώ, ἔκπλοι, ἔκπλῳ, ἔκπλους, ἔκπλουν, ἔκπλων
4. χαλκῆ, χαλκαῖς, χαλκώ, χαλκοῦν, χαλκᾶς, χαλκᾶ, χαλκᾶ, χαλκοῦ, χαλκῆν, χαλκοῖ, χαλκαῖ
5. δύσνουν, δύσνου, δύσνῳ, δυσνώ, δύσνοιν, δύσνοι, δύσνων, δύσνοις, δύσνους
6. περίπλουν, περίπλου, περίπλῳ, περίπλοι, περίπλων
7. εἴσπλων, εἴσπλοι, εἴσπλῳ, εἰσπλώ, εἴσπλους, εἴσπλουν, εἴσπλοιν, εἴσπλου, εἴσπλοις
8. νοῦ, νοῖ, νῷ, νῶν, νώ, νοῦν, νοῦς, νοῦ, νοῖς
9. ἀργυροῖ, ἀργυρώ, ἀργυρᾶ, ἀργυρᾶ, ἀργυρᾶ, ἀργυρᾶ, ἀργυροῦν, ἀργυρῶν, ἀργυρῶν
10. Πειρίθουν, Πειρίθου, Πειρίθῳ

EXERCISE 16: BASE ACCENT AND CASE ACCENT (iv)

1. παίδευσιν, παιδεύσεως, παιδεύσει
2. ἐγχέλεσι, ἔγχελυν, ἐγχέλεων, ἐγχέλει, ἐγχέλεις, ἐγχέλεως
3. ἀκροπόλεις, ἀκροπόλεων, ἀκροπόλεσι, ἀκροπόλεως, ἀκρόπολιν
4. πρέσβυ, πρέσβεως, πρέσβεσι, πρέσβεων, πρέσβεις
5. ἄστεων, ἄστεως, ἄστη, ἄστει, ἄστεσι
6. δυνάμει, δύναμιν, δυνάμεως, δυνάμεσι, δυνάμεις, δυνάμεων
7. κτίσει, κτίσεις, κτίσεως, κτίσεσι, κτίσεων
8. πελέκεως, πελέκεις, πέλεκυν, πελέκεων, πελέκεσι, πελέκει
9. μητροπόλεως, μητροπόλεις, μητροπόλεων, μητροπόλει, μητροπόλεσι, μητρόπολιν
10. μετάθεσιν, μεταθέσεως, μεταθέσει, μεταθέσεις, μεταθέσεων, μεταθέσεσι
11. πήχεων, πήχει, πήχεις, πήχει, πῆχυν, πήχεις, πήχεσι, πηχέοιν, πήχεως

EXERCISE 17: BASE ACCENT AND CASE ACCENT (v)

1. ἀμαθοῦς, ἀμαθῆ, ἀμαθεῖς, ἀμαθέσι, ἀμαθές
2. αἰδοῦς, αἰδῶ, αἰδοῖ
3. Δημοσθένους, Δημοσθένη, Δημόσθενες, Δημοσθένει
4. περιμήκη, περιμήκει, περίμηκες, περιμήκεσι, περιμήκη
5. αὐτάρκεις, αὐταρκῶν, αὔταρκες, αὐτάρκεσι, αὐτάρκη
6. εὐώδη, εὐῶδες, εὐώδως, εὐώδει, εὐώδεσι, εὐώδη, εὐώδεις, εὐωδῶν
7. τείχη, τείχους, τείχει, τειχῶν, τείχεσι
8. καταντῶν, κατάντεσι, κατάντεις, κατάντη, κάταντες, κατάντους
9. ἀληθοῦς, ἀληθέσι, ἀληθῶν, ἀληθές, ἀληθεῖ
10. ποδήρη, ποδήρη, ποδηρῶν, ποδῆρες, ποδήρεσι
11. πάθους, πάθη, παθῶν, πάθει, πάθεσι
12. ἠοῦς, ἠῶ, ἠοῖ
13. θεοειδές, θεοειδές, θεοειδεῖ, θεοειδεῖς, θεοειδέσι, θεοειδῶν
14. ξίφος, ξίφει, ξίφη, ξίφους, ξίφει, ξιφῶν, ξιφοῖν, ξίφεσι
15. τειχήρη, τειχήρει, τειχηροῖν, τειχήρεις, τειχήρους, τειχῆρες, τειχήρεσι, τειχηρῶν
16. εὐσεβῆ, εὐσεβέσι, εὐσεβεῖς, εὐσεβεῖ, εὐσεβοῦς, εὐσεβῶν
17. πανώλους, πανώλεις, πανωλῶν, πανῶλες, πανώλεσι

EXERCISE 18: BASE ACCENT AND CASE ACCENT (vi)

1. ἱερέᾱς, ἱερεῦσι, ἱερέᾱ, ἱερέως, ἱερεῦ, ἱερέων, ἱερεῖ, ἱερεῖς
2. Καλυψώ, Καλυψοῦς, Καλυψοῖ, Καλυψοῖ
3. ἠχοῖ, ἠχώ, ἠχοῦς, ἠχοῖ
4. ἱππεῖ, ἱππεῦ, ἱππέᾱ, ἱππέων, ἱππέᾱς, ἱππῆς, ἱππέως, ἱππεῦσι
5. Ἀργώ, Ἀργοῦς, Ἀργοῖ, Ἀργοῖ
6. γραμματεῦ, γραμματέως, γραμματεῦσι, γραμματέᾱ, γραμματέᾱς, γραμματέων
7. Λητοῦς, Λητοῖ, Λητοῖ, Λητώ
8. φειδοῦς, φειδοῖ, φειδώ
9. γονεῦσι, γονέᾱ, γονεῖς, γονέων, γονεῖ, γονεῦ, γονέᾱς, γονέως
10. πειθώ, πειθοῖ, πειθοῖ, πειθοῦς
11. Ἀχιλλέως, Ἀχιλλεῖ, Ἀχιλλεῦ, Ἀχιλλέᾱ
12. Ἐρατοῖ, Ἐρατώ, Ἐρατοῖ, Ἐρατοῦς
13. χαλκεῦ, χαλκεῖς, χαλκεῖ, χαλκέᾱς, χαλκέως, χαλκεῦσι, χαλκέων, χαλκέᾱ
14. Σαπφοῖ, Σαπφώ, Σαπφοῦς, Σαπφοῖ
15. φονεῖς, φονέᾱ, φονεῦσι, φονέων, φονεῦ, φονέᾱς, φονεῖ, φονέως, φονεῦσι

EXERCISE 19: THE VOCATIVE

1. σῶτερ	23. Δημόσθενες
2. μιαρέ	24. Ἀστύαγες
3. βουλή	25. Πόσειδον
4. υἱέ	26. βασιλεῦ
5. καλέ	27. Ἄπολλον
6. ἄνερ	28. θύγατερ
7. ἱερεῦ	29. στρατιῶτα
8. Λητοῖ	30. εὔδαιμον
9. φίλε	31. κακόδαιμον
10. πάτερ	32. Δήμητερ
11. μῆτερ	33. νεᾱνίσκε
12. αἰδώς	34. Διόγενες
13. ἠχοῖ	35. φκενῆρες
14. Πηλεῦ	36. εὔπατερ
15. αὔταρκες	37. πρέσβυ
16. παρθένε	38. ἄδελφε
17. δαῖμον	39. αὐτοκράτορ
18. βουκόλε	40. δέσποτα
19. δαΐφρον	41. Σώκρατες
20. παιδίον	42. Λυκόφρον
21. δᾶερ	43. Ἡράκλεις
22. Ἐρατοῖ	44. Λακεδαῖμον
45. γονεῦ	47. ταλαῖφρον
46. γύναι	48. γραμματεῦ

EXERCISE 20: NOUNS AND ADJECTIVES WITH MOBILE ACCENT

1. παισί, παίδων, παιδός, παῖδα, παιδί, παῖδε, παῖδας, παῖδες, παῖ, παίδοιν
2. ἕνα, ἕν, ἑνός, ἑνί, μία, μίαν, μιᾶς, μιᾷ
3. ἄνερ, ἄνδρα, ἀνδρός, ἀνδρί, ἄνδρε, ἀνδροῖν, ἄνδρες, ἄνδρας, ἀνδρῶν, ἀνδράσι, ἄνδρεσσι
4. φρένα, φρενός, φρένες, φρενῶν, φρεσί
5. μῆτερ, μητέρα, μητρός, μητρί, μητέροιν, μητέρας, μητέρων, μητράσι

6. πάντα, πᾶν, παντός, πᾶσαν, πάσης, παντί, πάσῃ, πάντες, πάντας, πάντων, πᾶσι, πάντα, πᾶσαι, πάσᾱς, πᾱσῶν, πάσαις

7. γύναι, γυναῖκα, γυναικός, γυναικί, γυναῖκες, γυναῖκας, γυναικῶν, γυναιξί

8. Τρωός, Τρῶα, Τρωΐ, Τρῶες, Τρῶας, Τρωσί, Τρώων

9. θύγατερ, θυγατέρα, θυγατρός, θυγατρί, θυγατέρε, θυγατέρες, θυγατέρων, θυγατράσι

10. ὠτός, ὦτε, ὠτί, ὦτα, ὤτων, ὤτοιν, ὠσί

11. τρία, τριῶν, τρισί

12. μηδένα, μηδεμίαν, μηδενός, μηδένων, μηδέν, μηδενί, μηδεμιᾷ, μηδεμιᾶς, μηδεμία, μηδένας, μηδένες, μηδέσι

13. πάτερ, πατέρα, πατρός, πατρί, πατέρες, πατέρας, πατέρων, πατράσι

14. γόνατος, γούνατος, γουνός, γούνατα, γοῦνα, γουνάτων, γούνων, γούνασι, γούνεσσι

EXERCISE 21: ναῦς, γραῦς, βοῦς, οἶς, Ζεύς

1. Ζεῦ	11. γραῦν	21. νεώς	31. οἶε	41. οἶς
2. νεοῖν	12. Δία	22. γρᾱΐ	32. γραυσί	42. γραῦς
3. βοοῖν	13. νηΐ	23. νῆες	33. βόε	43. ναῦς
4. νῆε	14. ναυσί	24. οἶν	34. γρᾱός	44. οἶς
5. βοῶν	15. γραῦ	25. οἴϊ	35. Ζεύς	45. βοῦς
6. Διΐ	16. οἰῶν	26. Διός	36. βόες	46. γρᾱοῖν
7. οἶες	17. οἰσί	27. γρᾶε	37. ναῦ	47. βοῦς
8. βοός	18. γρᾱῶν	28. νεῶν	38. βουσί	48. βοΐ
9. οἶ	19. ναῦν	29. οἰοῖν	39. γρᾶες	49. γραῦς
10. βοῦν	20. οἰός	30. βοῦ	40. ναῦς	

EXERCISE 22: CUMULATIVE EXERCISE

1. σῑγᾶν κελεύω.

2. αἰδοῦς μετέχειν δύναιο.

3. πλήρης εἴην δυνάμεως.

4. παθήματα μαθήματα.

5. βοῦς ἔχουσι καλλίστους.

6. κελεύομεν αὐτοὺς διδόναι δίκην.

7. αὐτοὶ πεπεισμένοι ἄλλους ἔπειθον.

8. διαβολῇ χρώμενοι ἄνδρας ἀνέπειθον.

9. ἥττους λόγους κρείττους ποιοῦσιν.

10. βούλῃ ἀκοῦσαι Γοργίου;

11. θύγατερ, θεοὺς χρὴ δεσπότᾱς καλεῖν.
12. ἀπολογοῦ Καλυψοῖ, βασιλέως κατηγοροῦντος.
13. ταῦτα δρᾱσᾱσ᾽ ἥλιον προσβλέπεις, ἔργα τλᾶσα δυσσεβῆ;
14. οὐδὲν βέλτῑον, Ἡράκλεις, ἀγαθῶν πολῑτῶν.
15. διέκπλοι νεῶν ἄμεινον πλεουσῶν ἔργα ἦσαν.
16. τῑμαῖς ἡρωικαῖς ἐτίμησαν αὐτὸν τετελευτηκότα, νεὼν οἰκοδομοῦντες.
17. φίλη δέσποινα, χρῡσῆς κόμης ἀνάδημα δέξαι.
18. πάντων τούτων διδασκάλους εἶναι δεῖ κοινούς, ἀρνυμένους μισθόν.
19. κακῶν γυναικῶν ἔργα ποιεῖ Λῡσιστράτην ἄθῡμον περιπατεῖν.
20. γύναι γεραιά, βασιλίδος πιστὴ τροφέ, Φαίδρᾱς ὁρῶμεν πολλὰς δυστήνους τύχᾱς.

EXERCISE 23: RULES APPLYING WITHOUT EXCEPTION

1. βασιλεύς	19. σταθμός	37. λαμπάς
2. μέλι	20. γένος	38. ἁβροσύνη
3. σῶμα	21. ἔσχατος	39. τριάς
4. νεᾱνίσκος	22. φοῖνιξ	40. πεντηκοστός
5. ἀλώπηξ	23. νοητέον	41. δικαιοσύνη
6. χαρίεις	24. ποιητέος	42. φειδώ
7. τάχιστος	25. σιδηροῦς	43. παλλάδιον
8. χαλκοῦς	26. χάρις	44. σατράπης
9. φίλτατος	27. ἀργύριον	45. σάλπιγξ
10. ὄγδοος	28. ἀλήθεια	46. δεκάς
11. θέμις	29. ἰχθυόεις	47. ὀβελίσκος
12. μέλιττα	30. Βορέᾱς	48. κλεπτοσύνη
13. χαλκεύς	31. κεραμεύς	49. Ὀλύμπια
14. ῥυθμός	32. πέμπτος	50. βασίλεια
15. θάλαττα	33. νεᾱνίᾱς	51. τριᾱκοσιοστός
16. πρῶτος	34. ἀργυροῦς	52. Ἑλλάς
17. ἀριθμός	35. ὕδωρ	53. σοφώτατος
18. ἥδιστος	36. παιδίσκος	54. πειθώ

55. Ὀλυμπιάς
56. μεταπύργιον

EXERCISE 24: RULES APPLYING ALMOST WITHOUT EXCEPTION

1. στατήρ	16. θεράπων	31. διωγμός	46. θυγάτηρ
2. ῥήτωρ	17. τοσοῦτος	32. ἀνήρ	47. Ἰωνικός
3. δράκων	18. φαίδιμος	33. κριτός	48. σημάντωρ
4. αὐτός	19. τηλίκος	34. δεξιτερός	49. ἄλκιμος
5. ἰχώρ	20. θεσμός	35. ἄκων	50. χρήσιμος
6. τοιοῦτος	21. σωτήρ	36. εἰνάτηρ	51. χαριέστερος
7. θάσσων	22. οὗτος	37. μουσική	52. ῥυθμικός
8. αἰθήρ	23. ἕκαστος	38. δοτήρ	53. διδακτός
9. λέων	24. φράτηρ	39. ἑκών	54. ἕτοιμος
10. μείζων	25. ὄγμος	40. Ξενοφῶν	
11. δώτωρ	26. πιστός	41. λογισμός	
12. ἀήρ	27. γέρων	42. φίλτερος	
13. πάνθηρ	28. ἀραγμός	43. ἀριστερός	
14. σεισμός	29. μήτηρ	44. ἕκατος	
15. πατήρ	30. κόσμος	45. ἑτοῖμος	

EXERCISE 25: RULES WITH EXCEPTIONS: FIRST DECLENSION

1. μάχη
2. ἀνάγκη
3. κλοπή
4. λήθη
5. μηνῦτής
6. ἀδελφή
7. σελήνη
8. στέγη
9. ῥώμη
10. μνήμη
11. ἀρετή
12. βλάστη
13. πύλη
14. ἀνδρείᾱ
15. εἰρήνη
16. κλίνη
17. δίκη
18. δορά
19. ἀθλητής
20. πάθη

21. στρατιά
22. θεᾱτής
23. πολῑτης
24. προσβολή
25. τύχη
26. σοφίᾱ
27. βλαβη
28. ἐπιστολή
29. αὔξη
30. δραχμή
31. σπουδή
32. ἡλικίᾱ
33. ἀνευιά
34. πομπή
35. ἀγορά
36. ναιμαχίᾱ
37. σκοτιά
38. ὕλη
39. ὁπλῑτης
40. ἀλήτης

41. βουλή
42. ὀργή
43. ἡμέρᾱ
44. ὑφάντης
45. ἑσπέρᾱ
46. ἄτη
47. χώρᾱ
48. νίκη
49. φορβή
50. παιδιά
51. λίμνη
52. σοφιστής
53. φυγή
54. φωνή
55. ποιητής
56. ἀρχή
57. φθορά
58. ψῡχή
59. τέχνη
60. πεδήτης

61. στρατιώτης
62. σφενδονήτης
63. κεφαλή
64. πρεσβευτής
65. βασιλείᾱ
66. γεννητής
67. γεννήτης
68. πεδητής
69. δικαστής
70. δυνάστης
71. σῡκοφάντης
72. πολιορκίᾱ
73. σχολή
74. δειλίᾱ
75. αἰσυμνήτης
76. ὁρμή
77. κυβερνήτης

185

EXERCISE 26: RULES WITH EXCEPTIONS: SECOND DECLENSION

1. στρατός	13. μόνος	25. θηρίον	37. ὄλβιος
2. δούλειος	14. ᾿Αθηναῖος	26. ταῦρος	38. τέλειος
3. ἐνιαυτός	15. αἰδοῖος	27. δίκαιος	39. θάρσυνος
4. ἔργον	16. οἰκεῖος	28. ἑταῖρος	40. ἐλεύθερος
5. ἆθλον	17. ζῷον	29. πεζός	41. βάρβαρος
6. βίβλος	18. ἄνθρωπος	30. χρόνος	42. ὦμος
7. χωρίον	19. αἰσχρός	31. ἄξιος	43. πεδίον
8. αὔλειος	20. ἀδελφός	32. τρόπος	44. ἤπειρος
9. ἀφνειός	21. παρθένος	33. πυκινός	45. φρούριον
10. ὀλίγος	22. παιδίον	34. φῦλον	46. θάλαμος
11. ἱκανός	23. ψόφος	35. δόλος	47. πενθερός
12. δύστηνος	24. ὀφθαλμός	36. μακρός	48. κακός

186

49. τάφρος
50. ἀντίος
51. τόπος
52. τειχίον
53. στάδιον
54. αἴτιος
55. τολμηρός
56. παλαιός
57. δεινός
58. θεός
59. βοηθός
60. ῥᾴδιος
61. θῡμός
62. πόλεμος
63. ξύλινος
64. ὅσιος
65. χρῡσός
66. ὀρνίθειος
67. ἄκρον
68. νεκρός
69. οὐρανός
70. λάβρος
71. θησαυρός
72. πτερόν
73. δοῦλος
74. ἄρτος
75. ἀγρός
76. σκοτεινός
77. ταύρειος
78. ἴδιος
79. Ὠκεανός

80. φόβος
81. ἐλευθέριος
82. ἀρχαῖος
83. ἀλῑτρός
84. ποταμός
85. σχολαῖος
86. ἄρτιος
87. ῥοῦς
88. κατηός
89. φλαῦρος
90. μῑκρός
91. γάμος
92. ὀμφαλός
93. κοινός
94. ψάμμος
95. σοφός
96. ὀρθός
97. ἄγγελος
98. ὀρφανός
99. σκολιόν
100. ἥλιος
101. στέφανος
102. δεξιός
103. νῆσος
104. αὐλός
105. δέμνιον
106. ὀδός
107. μεγαλεῖος
108. πλοῦτος
109. μισθός
110. ὅλος

111. κύκνος
112. ἱερόν
113. ὀβολός
114. ἄργυρος
115. λίθος
116. καρπός
117. λίθινος
118. αἴγειος
119. καιρός
120. θόρυβος
121. πλοῦς
122. ξένος
123. ἑκυρός
124. λόγος
125. πότμος
126. δῶρον
127. ἰσχῡρός
128. σῖτος
129. ἄθλιος
130. σκότος
131. βωμός
132. ὁποῖος
133. δηναιός
134. ὅρκιον
135. ἄλλος
136. πόσος
137. νοῦς
138. φρουρός
139. ὅσος
140. ἱᾱτρός
141. πόντος

142. πυρά
143. δείλαιος
144. ἄνεμος
145. κεραυνός
146. χαλεπός
147. φίλος
148. γυναικεῖος
149. ἀγαθός
150. βρότειος
151. ὀνείδειος
152. δημός
153. γενναῖος
154. δῆμος
155. διδάσκαλος
156. Χριστιᾱνός
157. φόρος
158. πλόκαμος
159. ἀναγκαῖος
160. νεώς
161. πίσυνος
162. ἀλλήλους
163. γόος
164. θάνατος
165. λεώς
166. νόμος
167. ἕως
168. νομός
169. λοιπός
170. βίος
171. λῑμός
172. ἐναντίος

173. κίνδυνος
174. ὄχλος
175. μῶμος
176. δῆλος
177. ὅπλον
178. χορός
179. ἐχθρός
180. υἱός
181. γαμβρός
182. καλός
183. ἐκεῖνος
184. βασίλειος
185. πλούσιος
186. σπήλαιον

187. παντοῖος
188. πολέμιος
189. οἶκος
190. ἀνδρεῖος
191. κάλαμος
192. νέος
193. πόνος
194. ἴσος
195. βέβαιος
196. κόλπος
197. βιβλίον
198. σπουδαῖος
199. ἔρημος
200. τροπαῖον

201. φαῦλος
202. δειλός
203. ἵππος
204. μοχλός
205. ἄριστον
206. σεμνός
207. ἀσκός
208. μωρός
209. γελοῖος
210. πόνηρος
211. ὅμοιος
212. μοχθηρός

213. ξένιον
214. βίος
215. λόφος
216. μέσος
217. ἄκρος
218. δένδρον
219. κρυφαῖος

EXERCISE 27: RULES WITH EXCEPTIONS: THIRD DECLENSION

1. ποδώκης
2. ἀλεκτρυών
3. Δημοσθένης
4. Μαραθών
5. Ἀγαμέμνων
6. Κιθαιρών
7. Βαβυλών
8. ἀκρόπολις
9. ὑπερμεγέθης
10. μητρόπολις
11. φρενήρης
12. ἀσφαλής
13. κακοήθης
14. Καρχηδών

15. Ἶρις
16. σαφής
17. αὐχήν
18. ποιμήν
19. παιάν
20. πρυλέες
21. ἀδμής
22. πολῖτις
23. ἀληθής
24. χειμών
25. ὀδούς
26. δρῦς
27. ἔρις
28. αἰδώς

29. ὀξύς
30. Σάρδεις
31. αὐθάδης
32. πώγων
33. ψευδής
34. ἄρρην
35. πᾶς
36. μῦς
37. πολύς
38. ναῦς
39. Λάκων
40. βραδύς
41. πλάνης
42. ἰδρώς

43. εὐπρεπής
44. ἐλπίς
45. φρόνησις
46. Περικλῆς
47. ἡγεμών
48. ἐπιεικής
49. τέκτων
50. κρίσις
51. συνήθης
52. εὐτυχής
53. προβλής
54. πατρίς
55. πλήρης
56. εὐσεβής

188

57. Σωκράτης	78. ῥίς	99. θῆλυς	120. δυστυχής
58. Ἡρακλῆς	79. οὐδείς	100. εὐήθης	121. δυσχερής
59. Κούρητες	80. Σειρήν	101. Κλέων	122. βραχύς
60. ἐπαχθής	81. ταχύς	102. γυνή	123. σφρāγίς
61. Ἀμφίπολις	82. γελαῦς	103. ἀήθης	124. ἀσθενής
62. βραχίων	83. Τρώς	104. Κρής	125. Ἰάσων
63. ἐπιφανής	84. εὐρύς	105. δύναμις	126. ἀμφήκης
64. κατάντης	85. ἥμισυς	106. γείτων	127. Ἄρτεμις
65. Σαλαμίς	86. εὐμενής	107. ἐξώλης	128. ἱκέτις
66. ἔκλειψις	87. τάξις	108. αἰών	129. ἀνάντης
67. περιμήκης	88. κύων	109. Κύπρις	130. συγγενής
68. εὐώδης	89. πόλις	110. Ἕλλην	131. πένης
69. ὑπόσχεσις	90. θρασύς	111. ἀγών	132. Τισσαφέρνης
70. δελφίς	91. μήν	112. εἷς	133. εὐθύς
71. γέλως	92. πούς	113. ὗς	134. οἷς
72. χιτών	93. παῖς	114. κύων	135. ἥρως
73. Ζεύς	94. βοῦς	115. Θρᾷξ	136. χιών
74. βαθύς	95. λιμήν	116. ὕβρις	137. ἰχθύς (ἰχθῦς according
75. ἔρως	96. χείρ	117. ὑγιής	to Herodian)
76. μέγας	97. ἀσπίς	118. διέτης	
77. ἐσθής	98. ἡδύς	119. τριετής	

EXERCISE 28: CUMULATIVE EXERCISE

1. ὄγδοον ἔτος ἐτελεύτā.
2. νεᾱνίᾱς ἦν φιλοτῑμότᾱτος.
3. πολλὰ γράψᾱς βιβλία ἀπέθανε.
4. καλὸν μειρακίῳ φιλοσοφεῖν.
5. μαρτυρεῖ συγγενὴς εἶναι Ἀλκιβιάδῃ.
6. χειμῶνα φυγόντες λιμένα εὑρήκαμεν.
7. πᾶσα ἀνθρώπου ψῡχὴ πλήρης πολλῶν ἐλπίδων.
8. πάντα ἀνατρέπει κυβερνήτης μεθύων.
9. ἄναξ Ὀδυσσεῦ, καιρὸν ἴσθ᾽ ἐληλυθώς.
10. καλὸν δ᾽ ἄγαλμα πόλεσιν εὐσεβὴς πόνος.
11. αἴσχιστα πάντων ἔργα δρῶσα τυγχάνεις.
12. θάλασσα κλύζει πάντα τἀνθρώπων κακά.
13. προνοίᾱς οὐδὲν ἀνθρώποις ἔφῡ / κέρδος λαβεῖν ἄμεινον.
14. ἀγαθοὺς ἄνδρας ἐγκωμιάζομεν ‘ἀγαθὸς ἀνὴρ οὗτος᾽ λέγοντες.

15. χαίρετ' Ἀττικὸς λεώς, / ἵκταρ ἡμένᾱς Διός / παρθένου φίλᾱς φίλοι. (Some editors print Διὸς despite verse-end.)

16. παῖς μέγας μῑκρὸν ἔχων χιτῶνα παῖδα μῑκρὸν μέγαν ἔχοντα χιτῶνα ἐξέδῡσε.

EXERCISE 29: ACCENTUATION OF COMPOUNDS

1. δᾱδοῦχος	29. αἰγιαλός	57. θηρότροφος
2. προδότης	30. συγγραφεύς	58. Κύκλωψ
3. συμφορά	31. ἐμπειρίᾱ	59. κατακλυσμός
4. οἰκονομικός	32. διορθωτής	60. ἀναρίθμητος
5. δύσοσμος	33. τριήραρχος	61. δυσχερής
6. μητρόπολις	34. ἐκδρομή	62. ἀναίτιος
7. σῡκοφάντης	35. Φίλιππος	63. συμβουλευτής
8. ἀφύλακτος	36. ἔνδεια	64. διαλλακτής
9. Θεμιστοκλῆς	37. ἔκλειψις	65. πρόγονος
10. ἄκων	38. Πολύφημος	66. συλλογιστέος
11. εὐπρεπής	39. παγκράτιον	67. καταγέλαστος
12. Ἀμφίπολις	40. ἀσθενής	68. προσδιανοητέον
13. σύνδεσμος	41. ἀκρόπολις	69. μονώψ
14. εὔνοια	42. Ἡρακλῆς	70. ἀπροσδόκητος
15. Οἰδίπους	43. σκηπτοῦχος	71. δημοκρατικός
16. Λύσανδρος	44. εὐσεβής	72. Σωκράτης
17. ἀναίσχυντος	45. Ἐπίγονος	73. ἐπιτήδειος
18. ἔφορος	46. αἰγίοχος	74. ψῡχοπομπός
19. διάβολος	47. πολιορκίᾱ	75. ἀσφαλής
20. ῥᾴθῡμος	48. ἀδύνατος	76. ἔπαινος
21. ἄφρων	49. ἐπιβάτης	77. εὔκοσμος
22. ἀπορίᾱ	50. ναυάγιον	78. δυστυχής
23. ἐπιστολεύς	51. ἀνέλπιστος	79. προβούλευμα
24. ἔμπειρος	52. ἄπρᾱκτος	80. Δημοσθένης
25. ἄδικος	53. ἄνοια	81. στρατόπεδον
26. ἀθάνατος	54. ὑπόσχεσις	82. παράδειγμα
27. αἰχμάλωτος	55. κατάσκοπος	83. τηλέπομπος
28. ὑποχείριος	56. παραλίᾱ	84. ἄθῡμος

85. Ἀλέξανδρος	99. προσβολή	113. λιθοβόλος
86. εὔνους	100. σύμμαχος	114. βουκόλος
87. προδοσίᾱ	101. ἀληθής	115. εὐδαίμων
88. ἀπορρώξ	102. γαιήοχος	116. ἀναλογισμός
89. εὐώνυμος	103. ἀμελής	117. πατροκτόνος
90. εὐτυχής	104. ἐπιστήμων	118. στρατηγός
91. σώφρων	105. φιλόσοφος	119. ἔνοικος
92. νομοθετικός	106. χέρνιψ	120. ἡνίοχος
93. αὐτόνομος	107. ἀνᾱλωτέος	
94. ὑπήκοος	108. ἀσεβής	
95. Περικλῆς	109. ἀναδασμός	
96. πτολίπορθος	110. φιλόπολις	
97. ναυμαχίᾱ	111. λιθόβολος	
98. ἐπιστολή	112. Πολυνείκης	

EXERCISE 30: ACCENTUATION OF PROPER NAMES

1. Ζωΐλος	18. Ὀδυσσεύς	35. Ἀπόλλων	52. Ἀριστοφάνης
2. Κῦρος	19. Κιθαιρών	36. Φίλιππος	53. Πελοπόννησος
3. Φαῖδρος	20. Αἰσχύλος	37. Ἡρόδοτος	54. Ἀγαμέμνων
4. Ἑλλάς	21. Σοφοκλῆς	38. Ἀθῆναι	55. Ἑλλήσποντος
5. Ἀθήνη	22. Εὐριπίδης	39. Ἀχιλλεύς	56. Δαρεῖος
6. Σαλαμίς	23. Ἀκρόπολις	40. Ῥωμύλος	57. Πύρρος
7. Κάστωρ	24. Γοργώ	41. Ἀργώ	58. Δαίδαλος
8. Ἑλένη	25. Καρχηδών	42. Τρωΐλος	59. Δελφοί
9. Ὅμηρος	26. Περσεφόνη	43. Ἀλέξανδρος	60. Πρίαμος
10. Περσεύς	27. Περικλῆς	44. Μυκῆναι	61. Μήδεια
11. Κύπρος	28. Ἡσίοδος	45. Ξέρξης	62. Ζεύς
12. Κόρινθος	29. Θουκυδίδης	46. Δημοσθένης	63. Βαβυλών
13. Κλέων	30. Δημήτηρ	47. Πολυνείκης	64. Ἀσίᾱ
14. Ἕκτωρ	31. Ἀρτοξέρξης	48. Δῆλος	65. Ἰάσων
15. Οἰδίπους	32. Ποσειδῶν	49. Ξενοφῶν	66. Ἄρτεμις
16. Ἥρᾱ	33. Διόνῡσος	50. Πολυδεύκης	67. Σαπφώ
17. Ἄρης	34. Μαραθών	51. Πλοῦτος	

EXERCISE 31: ACCENTUATION OF PRONOUNS (NON-ENCLITIC FORMS)

1. ταῖς
2. ἡμεῖς
3. ἡμᾶς
4. ἐμοί
5. τοιόσδε
6. σφώ
7. σφᾶς
8. ἐμόν
9. αὐτό
10. τοῦ
11. οὗτος
12. οἷν
13. σφετέρῃ
14. τοῖν
15. ὑμῶν
16. τοιοῦτος
17. ἅς
18. ἡμετέρην
19. νῷν
20. σεαυτῇ
21. τῷδε
22. αἷς
23. ἐκείνω
24. δεῖνα
25. ὑμῖν
26. τόνδε

27. αὐτοῖν
28. τό
29. σαῖς
30. τῆς
31. ὅς
32. τόδε
33. τώ
34. σῷ
35. σφίσι
36. τοιοῦδε
37. τῆσδε
38. ἐμός
39. ὅδε
40. ταύταις
41. τούτῳ
42. σφῶν
43. ἐγώ
44. οὗτοι
45. αὐτούς
46. αὕτη
47. ὤ
48. σφῶν
49. ἡμῖν
50. αὐτῷ
51. τοσαῖσδε
52. αὗται

53. ὑμέτερος
54. ἐμῆς
55. τοσοῦτος
56. ὑμᾶς
57. τούς
58. ἐκεῖνος
59. ἔγωγε
60. ὦν
61. τίνων
62. σοί
63. τοιούτους
64. τῶνδε
65. ἡμετέρων
66. δεῖνος
67. ὦν
68. οὗ
69. ἐμοῦ
70. ἐκείνοις
71. αὐτῶν
72. ὑμέτερον
73. ἔμοιγε
74. τοσῶνδε
75. ὅ
76. σέ
77. σοῦ
78. τούτων

Answers to Exercises (exx. 31–2)

79. νώ
80. ἑός
81. ἡμῶν
82. ᾧ
83. σφεῖς
84. ἥν
85. τοιόνδε
86. ταῖσδε
87. τά
88. ἐμέ
89. τάς
90. τηλικοῦτος
91. ὑμεῖς
92. τίνα
93. τήνδε
94. τοιάνδε
95. τοιᾶσδε

96. τοῦτο
97. ἐμέγε
98. σή
99. ἅ
100. σῶν
101. ⁻οῖς
102. σοῖς
103. ⁻οῦδε
104. ἕ
105. σοῦγε
106. ⁻αύτην
107. σύ
108. σύγε

109. σοί
110. τίνες
111. οἷ
112. ἥ
113. ἐκεῖνα
114. τί
115. σφέτερον
116. τοῦσδε
117. ἡμετέρων
118. ἐμαυτῆς
119. σφετέρης
120. ταῦτα
121. τίς

EXERCISE 32: ACCENTUATION OF NUMERALS

1. ὀκτώ
2. τρίτος
3. ἕνδεκα
4. ἑπτά
5. μία
6. πέμπτος
7. ἕν
8. ἕβδομος
9. δεύτερος
10. χίλιοι
11. εἷς
12. ἅπαξ
13. εἴκοσι
14. δέκα
15. δύο
16. τέτταρες
17. ἑκατόν
18. πρῶτος
19. ἕξ
20. πέντε
21. τρεῖς
22. δέκατος
23. ἔνατος
24. τρία
25. δώδεκα
26. ἐννέα
27. ὀκτωκαιδέκατος
28. δωδεκάκις
29. δεκατρεῖς
30. τριάκοντα
31. δύο μυριάδες
32. τριᾱκοστός
33. ἑξήκοντα
34. δισμύριοι
35. ἐννεακαίδεκα
36. ἑπτακόσιοι
37. ἑπτακαιδέκατος
38. πεντεκαίδεκα
39. μύριοι
40. ἑβδομηκοστός
41. τετταρακοστός
42. τετταράκοντα
43. ἑνδέκατος
44. ἑκκαιδέκατος
45. ὀγδοηκοστός
46. μύριοι
47. μυριοστός
48. τρεισκαίδεκα
49. δωδέκατος
50. πόστος

EXERCISE 33: ACCENTUATION OF ADVERBS AND PARTICLES

1. οὐδαμόθι	15. δήπου	29. ἀντικρύ	43. θύραθεν
2. ἤ	16. ὁπόθι	30. καθόλου	44. αὖθις
3. αὐτόθεν	17. τήμερον	31. πανταχοῖ	45. δή
4. μεταξύ	18. εὐθύ	32. σφόδρα	46. ἐκεῖσε
5. οὐδαμοῖ	19. αὕτως	33. ὅπου	47. ἦ
6. ἤδη	20. ὑψόσε	34. ὀψέ	48. ἠδέ
7. πανταχῆ	21. ἑτέρωσε	35. εἴσω	49. ἕως
8. δεῦρο	22. εὐσεβῶς	36. ἑτέρωθι	50. ἐπίσης
9. πάλιν	23. σχολῇ	37. ἔξω	51. ὁποτέρωθεν
10. ἐγγύθι	24. ἑτέρωθεν	38. προὔργου	52. ὅτι
11. μηκέτι	25. ἅτε	39. ἄλλοθι	53. οἴκοι
12. ὑψοῦ	26. ἀεί	40. ἀγρόθεν	54. μήν
13. οὐδαμοῦ	27. οἴκοθεν	41. μόλις	55. νή
14. οὕτω	28. θύρασι	42. ἰδίᾳ	56. οἷ

57. δέ	87. ἤϊκα	117. δημοσίᾳ	147. ἀξίως
58. ὅπως	88. ἵνα	118. μακράν	148. πρίν
59. καί	89. μάτην	119. πρώ	149. ὅμως
60. ὥρᾱσι	90. ἀνάγκη	120. αὐτοῦ	150. μή
61. οὐδαμῇ	91. ἀλλά	121. ἐκεῖ	151. παραυτίκα
62. βίᾳ	92. οἴκοθι	122. πανταχοῦ	152. οὐδαμόθεν
63. λίᾱν	93. ἑῷ	123. γάρ	153. ἠμέν
64. ἀρχῆθεν	94. μα	124. ὁπόσε	154. μάλα
65. οὐδέ	95. ἀμέλει	125. νῦν	155. ἤ
66. μέν	96. ἆι	126. ἄνω	156. πανταχόθεν
67. πλήν	97. αὐτίκα	127. ἐμποδών	157. οὐδαμόσε
68. οὐκέτι	98. ἴδε	128. ἄλλοσε	158. ὁποτέρωσε
69. γοῦν	99. ἀτάρ	129. μέντοι	159. ὁποτέρωθι
70. Μεγαροῖ	100. τέλος	130. ὁπόθεν	160. παραχρῆμα
71. ἑκάστοτε	101. αὐτόθι	131. ὁτιοῦν	161. ὁμῶς
72. ὑψόθεν	102. ἐγγω	132. ὁπότε	162. ποῦ
73. καλῶς	103. ἔτε	133. ἐγγύθεν	163. ποῖ
74. δρόμῳ	104. ἅπαξ	134. πότερον	164. αὐθημερόν
75. ἐκεῖθι	105. εὖ	135. πανταχόθι	
76. ἔτι	106. ἄφνω	136. οὗ	
77. ἄλλοθεν	107. ἐπεί	137. οὐκοῦν	
78. θαμά	108. ἐκεῖθεν	138. πανταχόσε	
79. ὅποι	109. μηδέ	139. οὔκουν	
80. ἐκποδών	110. δῆτα	140. ὡς	
81. ὑψόθι	111. ἔπειτα	141. πόθεν	
82. αὐτόσε	112. ἄρτι	142. ἆρα	
83. ὡσαύτως	113. αὐτάρ	143. ὥς	
84. σχεδόν	114. ἐπειδή	144. Ἰσθμοῖ	
85. λάθρᾳ	115. ἔνθα	145. ἄρα	
86. πάλαι	116. πάνυ	146. ἄληθες	

EXERCISE 34: ACCENTUATION OF PREPOSITIONS

1. ἐγγύς	12. ἐναντίον	23. ἄνευ	34. ἐντός	45. ἔμπροσθεν
2. παρά	13. ἕνεκα	24. μεταξύ	35. ἀνά	46. σύν
3. ποτί	14. περί	25. ἀντί	36. ἀπό	47. ὑπείρ
4. πλησίον	15. ἐκτός	26. ἔξω	37. ἄνευθεν	48. ἅμα
5. ἐν	16. χάριν	27. ὑπαί	38. ἄνω	49. εὐθύ
6. ἐπί	17. διαί	28. ἰθύς	39. ἐκ	
7. εἰς	18. ὑπό	29. πρό	40. εἴσω	
8. κατά	19. χωρίς	30. ἀμφί	41. λάθρᾳ	
9. διά	20. πλήν	31. μετά	42. ὡς	
10. προτί	21. ἄχρι	32. μέχρι	43. ὄπισθεν	
11. ὑπέρ	22. πρός	33. ὁμοῦ	44. ἐνί	

50. ὕπο	54. ὥς·	58. ἔς·	62. ὕπερ	66. κάτα
51. ἀμφί	55. σύν	59. μέτα	63. ἀντί	67. ἔξ·
52. πρός	56. ἄπο	60. ἔνι	64. ποτί	68. ἀνά
53. διά	57. πέρι	61. πάρα	65. ἔπι	

EXERCISE 35: ACCENTUATION OF INTERJECTIONS

1. ἰού	3. παπαῖ	5. ἰδού	7. φεῦ	9. αἰαῖ
2. ὤ	4. παπαιάξ	6. ὦ	8. οἴμοι	

EXERCISE 36: CUMULATIVE EXERCISE

1. Ἕκτορα δ᾽ αἰδὼς εἷλε.
2. σοφίας ἐνδείᾳ ποιοῦσι ταῦτα.
3. φεῦ, παπαῖ. / παπαῖ μάλ᾽ αὖθις.
4. ὄλωλας, ὦ παῖ, μητρὸς ἁρπασθεῖσ᾽ ἄπο.
5. ἐκεῖνοι δὲ ἐξελθόντες ἐκήρυξαν πανταχοῦ.
6. ἐποίησε γὰρ Ἄρτεμιν εἶναι θυγατέρα Δήμητρος.
7. ἐγώ, ὦ ἄνδρες, δέομαι ὑμῶν στρατεύεσθαι σὺν ἐμοί.
8. καὶ γὰρ σοφιστὴς ἦν ἱκανὸς καὶ συγγραφεὺς καὶ λογογράφος.
9. οὐκοῦν ἰατροὺς καλεῖς τοὺς ἐπιστήμονας περὶ τούτων;
10. καὶ Εὔφρων δὲ τοὺς αὑτοῦ ἔχων μισθοφόρους περὶ δισχιλίους συνεστρατεύετο.
11. ταῦτα δὲ ἀδυνάτοις ἔοικεν, καὶ οὕτω δὴ συμβαίνει ἀγαθὸν φύλακα ἀδύνατον γενέσθαι.

12. νῦν δὲ τοῦτο μὲν τετολμήσθω εἰπεῖν, ὅτι τοὺς ἀκριβεστάτους φύλακας φιλοσόφους δεῖ καθιστάναι.

13. δείσαντες δὲ παρέλαβον τὸ χωρίον μὴ Λακεδαιμονίων τὰ κατὰ Πελοπόννησον θορυβουμένων Ἀθηναῖοι λάβωσιν·

14. οἴμοι κακοδαίμων, ὡς ἀπόλωλα δείλαιος, / καὶ τρισκακοδαίμων καὶ τετράκις καὶ πεντάκις / καὶ δωδεκάκις καὶ μυριάκις·

15. ἄνδρες στρατιῶται, χαλεπὰ μὲν τὰ παρόντα, ὁπότε ἀνδρῶν στρατηγῶν τοιούτων στερόμεθα καὶ λοχαγῶν καὶ στρατιωτῶν.

16. λέγω δὲ περὶ πάντων, οἷον μεγέθους πέρι, ὑγιείας, ἰσχύος, καὶ τῶν ἄλλων ἑνὶ λόγῳ ἁπάντων.

17. οἶδα σαφῶς καὶ ἐγώ καὶ σύ, ὅτι τὸ μὲν πρῶτον ηὐδοκίμει Περικλῆς καὶ οὐδεμίαν αἰσχρὰν δίκην κατεψηφίσαντο αὐτοῦ Ἀθηναῖοι, ἡνίκα χείρους ἦσαν.

18. πολῖται γὰρ δορυφοροῦσι μὲν ἀλλήλους ἄνευ μισθοῦ ἐπὶ τοὺς δούλους, δορυφοροῦσι δ᾿ ἐπὶ τοὺς κακούργους, ὑπὲρ τοῦ μηδένα τῶν πολιτῶν βιαίῳ θανάτῳ ἀποθνήσκειν.

19. τί οὖν; ἐὰν ἐγὼ καλῶ ὁτιοῦν τῶν ὄντων, οἷον ὃ νῦν καλοῦμεν ἄνθρωπον, ἐὰν ἐγὼ τοῦτο ἵππον προσαγορεύω, ὃ δὲ νῦν ἵππον, ἄνθρωπον, ἔσται δημοσίᾳ μὲν ὄνομα ἄνθρωπος τῷ αὐτῷ, ἰδίᾳ δὲ ἵππος; καὶ ἰδίᾳ μὲν αὖ ἄνθρωπος, δημοσίᾳ δὲ ἵππος; οὕτω λέγεις;

EXERCISE 37: PROCLITICS AND ENCLITICS

1. ἀλλ᾿ εἰπέ μοι·

2. ἀντί τοί εἰμ᾿ ἱκέταο.

3. οὐδέ γ᾿ ἂν ἐπιχειρήσαιμι, ἦν δ᾿ ἐγώ.

4. τοιαῦτά σοι ταῦτ᾿ ἐστίν, ὦ ξένε.

5. πλὴν σοῦ; σὲ γὰρ δὴ φύλακά φημ᾿ εἶναι στρατοῦ.

6. πατρὸς δ᾿ εἴμ᾿ ἀγαθοῖο, θεὰ δέ με γείνατο μήτηρ·

7. πάρ᾿ ἐμοί γε καὶ ἄλλοι / οἵ κέ με τιμήσουσι.

8. οὐκοῦν ἑκάστῳ τούτων ἔστιν τι συμφέρον; πάνυ γε.

9. καὶ δή μοι γέρας αὐτὸς ἀφαιρήσεσθαι ἀπειλεῖς, / ᾧ ἔπι πόλλ᾿ ἐμόγησα.

10. οὔτε γὰρ ἄν με λάθοις κακουργῶν, οὔτε μὴ λαθὼν βιάσασθαι τῷ λόγῳ δύναιο.

11. πρὸς ταῦτα κακούργει καὶ σύκοφάντει, εἴ τι δύνασαι — οὐδέν σου παρίεμαι — ἀλλ᾿ οὐ μὴ οἷός τ᾿ ᾖς.

12. μάντι κακῶν, οὔ πώ ποτέ μοι τὸ κρήγυον εἶπες· / αἰεί τοι τὰ κάκ᾿ ἐστὶ φίλα φρεσὶ μαντεύεσθαι.

13. οὐ μὴν εἴασάν γε αὐτὸν οἱ παρόντες, ἀλλ᾿ ἠνάγκασαν ὑπομεῖναί τε καὶ παρασχεῖν τῶν εἰρημένων λόγον.

14. διὰ ταῦτα καὶ ἡ τέχνη ἐστὶν ἡ ἰᾱτρικὴ νῦν εὑρημένη, ὅτι σῶμά ἐστιν πόνηρον καὶ οὐκ ἐξαρκεῖ αὐτῷ τοιούτῳ εἶναι. (For πόνηρον some editors print the koiné form πονηρόν: see also the note to § 189.)

15. τριῶν ὄντων οὖν ἡμῖν, ὧντινων βούλει, τίθει, καλλίοσιν ἵνα ὀνόμασι χρώμεθα, τὸ μὲν χρῡσόν, τὸ δ᾽ ἄργυρον, τρίτον δὲ τὸ μηδέτερα τούτων.

EXERCISE 38: CUMULATIVE EXERCISE

Τερψίων· ἀτὰρ πῶς οὐκ αὐτοῦ Μεγαροῖ κατέλῡεν;

Εὐκλείδης· ἠπείγετο οἴκαδε· ἐπεὶ ἔγωγ᾽ ἐδεόμην καὶ συνεβούλευον, ἀλλ᾽ οὐκ ἤθελεν. καὶ δῆτα προπέμψᾱς αὐτόν, ἀπιὼν πάλιν ἀνεμνήσθην καὶ ἐθαύμασα Σωκράτους, ὡς μαντικῶς ἄλλα τε (or ἄλλά τε: see § 290) δὴ εἶπε καὶ περὶ τούτου. δοκεῖ γάρ μοι ὀλίγον πρὸ τοῦ θανάτου ἐντυχεῖν αὐτῷ μειρακίῳ ὄντι, καὶ συγγενόμενός τε καὶ διαλεχθεὶς πάνυ ἀγασθῆναι αὐτοῦ τὴν φύσιν. καί μοι ἐλθόντι Ἀθήναζε τούς τε λόγους οὓς διελέχθη αὐτῷ διηγήσατο καὶ μάλα ἀξίους ἀκοῆς, εἶπέ τε ὅτι πᾶσα ἀνάγκη εἴη τοῦτον ἐλλόγιμον γενέσθαι, εἴπερ εἰς ἡλικίᾱν ἔλθοι.

Τερ· καὶ ἀληθῆ γε, ὡς ἔοικεν, εἶπεν. ἀτὰρ τίνες ἦσαν οἱ λόγοι; ἔχοις ἂν διηγήσασθαι;

Εὐ· οὐ μὰ τὸν Δία, οὔκουν οὕτω γε ἀπὸ στόματος· ἀλλ᾽ ἐγραψάμην μὲν τότ᾽ εὐθὺς οἴκαδ᾽ ἐλθὼν ὑπομνήματα, ὕστερον δὲ κατὰ σχολὴν ἀναμιμνησκόμενος ἔγραφον, καὶ ὁσάκις Ἀθήναζε ἀφικοίμην, ἐπανηρώτων τὸν Σωκράτη ὃ μὴ ἐμεμνήμην, καὶ δεῦρο ἐλθὼν ἐπηνωρθούμην· ὥστε μοι σχεδόν τι πᾶς ὁ λόγος γέγραπται.

Τερ· ἀλλ᾽ ἤδη ἤκουσά σου καὶ πρότερον, καὶ μέντοι ἀεὶ μέλλων κελεύσειν ἐπιδεῖξαι διατέτριφα δεῦρο. ἀλλὰ τί κωλύει νῦν ἡμᾶς διελθεῖν; πάντως ἔγωγε καὶ ἀναπαύσασθαι δέομαι ὡς ἐξ ἀγροῦ ἥκων.

δεινόν γέ σ᾽ οὖσαν πατρὸς οὗ σὺ παῖς ἔφῡς
κείνου λελῆσθαι, τῆς δὲ τικτούσης μέλειν.
ἅπαντα γάρ σοι τἀμὰ νουθετήματα
κείνης διδακτά, κοὐδὲν ἐκ σαυτῆς λέγεις.
ἐπεί γ᾽ ἑλοῦ σὺ θάτερ᾽, ἢ φρονεῖν κακῶς,
ἢ τῶν φίλων φρονοῦσα μὴ μνήμην ἔχειν·
ἥτις λέγεις μὲν ἀρτίως, ὡς εἰ λάβοις
σθένος, τὸ τούτων μῖσος ἐκδείξειας ἄν·

ἐμοῦ δὲ πατρὶ πάντα τιμωρουμένης
οὔτε ξυνέρδεις τήν τε δρῶσαν ἐκτρέπεις.
οὐ ταῦτα πρὸς κακοῖσι δειλίαν ἔχει;
ἐπεὶ δίδαξον, ἢ μάθ᾽ ἐξ ἐμοῦ, τί μοι
κέρδος γένοιτ᾽ ἂν τῶνδε ληξάσῃ γόων.
οὐ ζῶ; κακῶς μέν, οἶδ᾽, ἐπαρκούντως δ᾽ ἐμοί.
λυπῶ δὲ τούτους, ὥστε τῷ τεθνηκότι
τιμὰς προσάπτειν, εἴ τις ἔστ᾽ ἐκεῖ χάρις.
σὺ δ᾽ ἡμὶν ἡ μῖσοῦσα μῖσεῖς μὲν λόγῳ,
ἔργῳ δὲ τοῖς φονεῦσι τοῦ πατρὸς ξύνει.
ἐγὼ μὲν οὖν οὐκ ἄν ποτ᾽, οὐδ᾽ εἴ μοι τὰ σά (some editors σὰ despite
μέλλοι τις οἴσειν δῶρ᾽, ἐφ᾽ οἷσι νῦν χλιδᾷς,   verse-end)
τούτοις ὑπεικάθοιμι· σοὶ δὲ πλουσία
τράπεζα κείσθω καὶ περιρρείτω βίος.
ἐμοὶ γὰρ ἔστω τοὐμὲ μὴ λυπεῖν μόνον
βόσκημα· τῆς σῆς δ᾽ οὐκ ἐρῶ τῖμῆς λαχεῖν.
οὐδ᾽ ἂν σύ, σώφρων γ᾽ οὖσα. νῦν δ᾽ ἐξὸν πατρός (some editors πατρὸς
πάντων ἀρίστου παῖδα κεκλῆσθαι, καλοῦ   despite verse-end)
τῆς μητρός. οὕτω γὰρ φανῇ πλείστοις κακή,
θανόντα πατέρα καὶ φίλους προδοῦσα σούς.

Index

All references are to paragraph numbers. The abbreviation 'n' is used where an entry refers exclusively to a note in small print. Nouns, adjectives, and adverbs not listed separately in section (c) (Greek words and terminations) may be found by following the references under an appropriate termination. Thus, for δικαιοσύνη see '-σύνη, nouns in'; for καλῶς, see '-ως, adverbs in'.

Index (Greek)

205

A New Short Guide to the Accentuation of Ancient Greek

Index (Greek)

-ις/-ῑς (gen. -ιδος/-ῑδος), nouns in: 201–2
-ίς (gen. -ῖνος), nouns in: 197
-ις (gen. -ιτος), nouns in: 155
-ίσκος, nouns in: 149
ἴσος/ῖσος: 193
ἵστημι
  ἑστᾶσι, ἱστᾶσι: 88c, 95; inf. and part. forms: 98–101, 103, 117; subj. and opt. forms: 88d–e, 95
-ιστος, superlatives in: 146
ἰχθύς/ἰχθῦς : 207
ἰχώρ: 166
-ίων, comparatives in: 118, 159
καθόλου: 243, 247
καί: 251, 267b, 268, 270, 276–7, 282n, 296
  in numerals: 240
καίπερ: 277, 298
καίτοι: 298
κακοήθης: 120, 124, 130e, 199, 217
  gen. pl.: 124n
κακός: 191
κακότης: 319
κακοῦργος: 221
καλιά/καλιή: 169
καλός: 191
καρπός: 192
Καρχηδών: 206, 226d
Κάστωρ: 166, 225

κατά/κάτα: 78, 256, 258–61, 267b, 268, 270, 272, 275–7, 296
καταγέλαστος: 210i
κατάσκοπος: 210i
κε/κεν: 77e, 279e, 284–90, 295–7
κεφαλή: 173, 223
Κεφαλή: 223
κῆρυξ: 65n, 156, 288
Κιθαιρών: 206, 226d
Κλέων: 206, 225
-κλῆς, names in: 130e, 200, 210e, 222
κλίνη: 168
κλοπή: 167
Κλυμένη: 224
κόλπος: 194
κομίζω, fut. κομιῶ: 88b, 95, 102–3
Κόρινθος: 225
κόσμος: 162
Κούρητες: 198
κουφοτής/κουφότης: 319
κραυγή: 173
κρέμαμαι, subj. and opt. forms: 88d–e
Κρής: 133a, 196
κριτής: 110, 158
κτάομαι, perf. subj. and opt. mid.: 88f, 95
κτείνω, fut. κτενῶ: 88b, 95, 102–3
κύκλος, κυκλόθε(ν), κυκλόσε: 246n
Κύκλωψ: 219
Κύπρος: 225
Κῦρος: 225

κύων: 133g, 205
  κύνεσσι: 134
κώνωψ: 219
λαγῶς/λαγώς: 113n
λάθρᾳ: 250, 253
λαμβάνω
  λαβέ/λάβε: 84, 315; λαβοῦ: 83, 94; inf. and part. forms: 98–101, 103, 117
λείπω
  λιποῦ: 83, 94; inf. and part. forms: 98–101, 103, 117
λεώς 'people': 113, 195
λήθη: 167
λίαν: 250
λιγύς, fem. λίγεια/λιγεῖα: 106n
λιθόβολος 'struck with stones': vs λιθοβόλος 'throwing stones': 211–12
λίθος: 194
λιμήν: 197
λίμνη: 174
λόγος: 175
λοιπός: 175
-λος/-λον, nouns in: 183
λόφος: 194
λοχαγός: 212
Λύσανδρος: 210i
λύω
  λυθῶ, λυθείην: 88d–e, 95; inf. and part. forms: 98–101, 103, 117
λῷστος: 146
μά: 251

209

Index (Greek)

Σειρήν: 197
σελήνη: 174
σημάντωρ: 166
-σι, adverbs in: 246
-σι (dat. pl. ending): 42ꟼ,
  109–10, 133
σῑμός: 161
σῖτος: 194
σκεδάννῡμι, fut. σκεδῶ:
  88b, 95, 102–3
σκιά: 169
σκότος: 194
-σμος, nouns in: 162, 220
  (+ some adjectives)
σός: 231
σοφός: 110, 191
σπήλαιον: 194
σπονδή: 167
σπουδή: 167
στέγη: 168
-στος, ordinals etc. in:
  145, 239
στρατηγός: 212
στρατόπεδον: 210i
στρατός: 192
σύ
  enclitic σε, σου, σοι:
    77c, 279c, 280–1,
    284–90, 295–7; non-
    enclitic forms: 228–30,
    280–1
σύγε: 230
σῡκῆ (< σῡκέᾱ): 111
σύμμαχος: 212
σύμπᾱς: 133cn
συμφορά: 167, 213
σύν/ξύν: 257, 262, 267b,
  268, 270, 272, 276–7,
  296

σύνδεσμος: 220
-σύνη, nouns in: 142
συνήθης: 120, 124, 199,
  217
  gen. pl.: 124n
-συνος, adjectives in:
  186b
σφαγή: 167
σφε: 279c, 280–1, 284–
  91, 295–7
σφεῖς
  enclitic forms: 279c,
    280–1, 284–91, 296–7;
    non-enclitic forms:
    280–1
σφέτερος: 231
σφόδρα: 250
σφώ, σφῷν 'you two':
  228, 279cn
σχεδόν: 250
σχολή: 173
σχολῇ (adv.): 242
Σωκράτης: 120, 124,
  130e, 200, 210e, j, 222
σωτήρ: 105, 164
  voc. sg.: 130d
σώφρων: 210j (cf. 210h)
ταμίᾱς, 114, 143
-τατος, superlatives in:
  146
τε: 77e, 279e, 284–90,
  295–7
τέλειος: 178, 317n
τέλος (adv.): 242
τέμνω
  τεμῶ (fut.): 88b, 95,
    102–3; inf. and part.
    forms: 98–103, 117

-τεος/-τεον, verbal
  adjectives in: 144, 215
-τερος, comparatives etc.
  and poss. pronouns in:
  159, 231
  δεύτερος: 145, 239
  τεσσαρακοστός: 145, 239
  τέταρτος: 145, 239
  τέτταρες: 238
  τέχνη: 174
  τηλέπομπος: 211
  τηλίκος: 160
  τηλικοῦτος: 163, 236
  τήμερον: 250
-της, masc. 1st-decl.
  nouns in: 158, 170–2,
  214
-της (gen. -τητος), nouns
  in: 319
τίθημι
  θές, θοῦ, compounds of:
    92–3; inf. and part.
    forms: 98–101, 103
    117; subj. and opt.
    forms: 88d–e, 95–6
τῑμάω, pres. and imperf.
  forms: 88a, 95, 102–3
τῑμή: 173
-τις (gen. -τιδος), nouns
  in: 201
τις, τι (indef.): 77a, 279a,
  284–90, 296–7
  τινά: 78, 294–5
τίς, τί (interrog.): 76, 237
τοι (particle): 77e, 279e,
  284–90, 296–7
τοίνυν: 298
τοῖος: 188, 235
τοιόσδε: 234

213